20 Legends
Sheffield Wednesday

20 Legends
Sheffield Wednesday

Tom Whitworth
Chris Olewicz

VERTICAL EDITIONS
www.verticaleditions.com

First published in the United Kingdom in 2012 by Vertical Editions, Unit 4a,
Snaygill Industrial Estate, Skipton, North Yorkshire BD23 2QR

www.verticaleditions.com

ISBN 978-1-904091-65-3

A CIP catalogue record for this book is available from the British Library

Cover design by HBA, York

Printed and bound by MPG, Bodmin

Contents

Tom Whitworth's work has appeared in *When Saturday Comes*, *FC Business* and *The Football Supporter* magazines. He lives in Manchester – an Owl in exile.

Chris Olewicz is a history graduate from Sheffield. His earliest memory of watching Wednesday was a dour draw with Southampton – he's been hooked ever since.

This is their first book.

Acknowledgements

We are grateful to a number of people for their assistance during this project.

Lee Bullen, David Hirst, Jimmy Mullen, Ron Springett, and his daughter Terry, Howard Wilkinson and Nigel Worthington generously shared their memories of their time at Wednesday. Don Megson, again and again, was willing to reveal candidly the highlights of his long career. And, whoever said you should never meet your heroes is very wrong, because hearing Roland Nilsson recount his story was a treasured experience that helped sustain us through the more trying moments of the process. Colin Dobson, Martin Hodge, Lawrie Madden and Peter Shreeves were also kind enough to share their recollections.

John Foot provided us his views on the Italian game and its specific links to the club – namely, Paolo Di Canio and Des Walker. John Bain spoke of Don Megson's spell in America, and Tim Bredbury of Lee Bullen's years' in Hong Kong.

Dave Leonard and Andy Lyons slogged through earlier drafts of the manuscript – their time and honest words of advice were greatly appreciated during the editing process. James Caruth gave substance to, clarified or helpfully dismissed many of the thoughts and themes we covered. Alan Biggs' input helped further shape the book in to something people might actually want to read. Terry Henfleet provided unending inspiration. And, even if they didn't know what we were up to, our family and friends provided us the support we needed to get us across the line.

At Vertical we thank Karl Waddicor for giving us the chance to write the book in the first place, for having the confidence in us to deliver and always being at the end of the telephone to offer guidance and reassurance.

Finally we thank James Titterton (jamestitterton.co.uk), whose advice throughout, along with his design of the diagrams and graph is massively appreciated, Steve Ellis and Louis Clay with the photos and everyone else who helped us along the way.

'Would you like some fruit?'

– Roland Nilsson
Malmo, Sweden, 2010

Introduction

In the modern era Sheffield Wednesday have juggled long periods of ignominy with fleeting moments of glory. One of the most successful teams in England during the early 20th century – four First Division titles and three FA Cups – the post-war years brought more mixed outcomes for the club. As football transformed into the game we know today, Wednesday fought to attain, and maintain a position among the best in the country. Struggling more often than they triumphed, they savoured the occasional promotion and cup run, and endured the numerous relegations, setbacks and scandals: incidents which have defined the club.

The efforts of an ever changing roster of players and managers are central to its history. Dependent on the fortunes of the side during a specific individual's time in S6, we recall their contributions with different shades of memory. Some spent their entire careers with us, working towards that place in the first team. A small number were the big signings, designed to propel the club to a higher level. A few were here today and gone the next, but whose splendour took our breath away. And others, while perhaps not the most gifted, managed to endear themselves through a staggering level of effort and commitment. In *20 Legends: Sheffield Wednesday* we tell some of their stories.

The portraits in this volume, of those whose contributions have left a lasting impression, do not reveal a comprehensive history of the club. Rather, they provide snapshots – some naturally more unforgettable than others – of the more memorable experiences from the 1950s to the (almost) present day. Our choices are ranked in no order of personal preference or perceived contribution; certainly there will be players who people believe should have been included but who are not; and players who are but people think should not be. But therein lays the subjectivity of the football fan.

In producing these pages we have consulted an ocean of material both written and visual. We did not sit idle in our research but actively sought the stories of these players and managers. Our search took us to a few homes and pubs in Sheffield, a bar in Scotland, a kit room in Rotherham, a Euston restaurant and the underneath's of the Malmo FF stadium in southern Sweden. Many words of correspondence were exchanged, and many hours were spent on the telephone or with our heads in a book, magazine or newspaper report.

We also recall memories of our own, picked up through the standard education of most fans and supplemented by our own (fiercely debated) views. The rest, we gain through 'Legislated Nostalgia', the idea from Douglas Coupland of the implantation of memories on to those who do not actually possess them: a collective history belonging to the fans passed on with care from one generation to the next. Or as J.P.W. Mallalieu more simply expresses, 'my most vivid memories are of events which happened years ago . . . perhaps even before I was born . . . But I was there.' So were we.

Up Sheffield. Up the Owls!

Tom Whitworth and Chris Olewicz
Manchester and Sheffield, July 2012

1

David Hirst

1986-1997
358 appearances, 128 goals

For Sheffield Wednesday, David Hirst was a striker of ferocious energy and great goal scoring capacity: fast, strong and commanding in the air, with, said one former team mate, 'a sledgehammer of a left foot'. He played in an era that is lovingly recalled by Wednesday supporters, the early 1990s, a period that brought promotion from the Second Division through an exciting and effective brand of play and a first major trophy since 1935. This, along with European adventures and four trips to Wembley in a single season.

Doubtless the side of that era was the best seen at Hillsborough in decades. And at its centre was the swashbuckling Hirst, a forward in his prime and without pretension, the hero of the fans. Though injuries sadly limited his appearances in the blue and white of Wednesday, and in the white of England, he rightly is remembered as one of the club's greatest – the 128 goals of various styles and variations in 11 years proof of his fine contribution.

In his first season in charge in 1983-84, manager Howard Wilkinson guided the club to promotion from the Second Division. Once in the First he took them as high as fifth place. With limited funds for players, his top purchase had been Garry Thompson for a then club record £450,000. The £250,000 spent on Hirst appeared a significant outlay, even for someone who had shown great promise for his home town club, Barnsley. The Reds had given him a two-year apprenticeship, his progress had been rapid and it wasn't too long before Wilkinson took notice. Arriving at Hillsborough in 1986, Hirst was nurtured and

15

gradually, albeit under the guide of a different manager, developed into a brilliant Wednesday man.

For much of his first season Hirst competed with Carl Shutt for a place alongside Lee Chapman and Brian Marwood in the forward positions. His debut came away to Charlton Athletic on the first day of 1986-87. With 25 minutes to go, the 18 year old left the bench, 'wound up like a mouse, running around like a schoolboy, getting booked for a tackle.' The week after at home to Everton he scored with his second touch of the ball. 'But I didn't play again for five months after that. I was a youngster who needed to learn more about the game, and more about myself.'

He worked hard in training, taking advice from others to help him improve. 'You have to listen to other people,' says Hirst, 'people who know more than you. You have to take it all in. And I did.' At one stage, manager Peter Eustace, an ex-Wednesday player let him stay over at his house before match days. 'We'd have a meal, go to bed early then get to the ground on time the next day. I don't know if he didn't trust me, or maybe he thought that the hotel wasn't the right environment.'

When Wilkinson decamped to Leeds United in 1988, Eustace succeeded him following a successful spell as caretaker. In contrast to his predecessor, his time in charge was brief and unsuccessful. In three months Wednesday won just once in 16 league matches and he was sacked not long after the New Year. 'That was unfortunate,' says Hirst. 'The regime under him hadn't really changed. We just didn't win games, we had a bad run.'

Eustace's replacement, Ron Atkinson, was a manager whose talents Hirst quickly came to admire, and who helped him take his nascent career to the next level. Atkinson had built his reputation with West Bromwich Albion, won two FA Cups with Manchester United and, after a brief spell in charge of Atletico Madrid, arrived at Hillsborough in early 1989. He was tasked with improving the fortunes of the relegation-threatened club. 'It was very daunting when Ron arrived,' says Hirst. 'He was a man who'd dealt with some of the best players in the world. But he was a breath of fresh air. At the time I was going through a sticky patch, I wasn't scoring very much. But Ron took me into the office and said, "You don't worry, just keep on doing what you're doing and the goals will come." I still felt the pressure, but it was good to know that someone else believed in you.'

The goals eventually came, and with increasing regularity. A handful of important strikes in the 1988-89 run-in succeeded in keeping Wednesday in the First. The following year, paired with Dalian Atkinson, the strong and swift striker bought from Ipswich Town, he got a packet more. Between them Hirst and Atkinson notched all but 11 of the club's 35 league goals that year. 'We played really well and scored on a regular basis. Dalian was a phenomenal player, but he was only there for a season so unfortunately we didn't have time to carry that on.'

While that partnership brought a number of goals, the team struggled, perched in the bottom half all through 1989-90. After losing five of their last six fixtures, Wednesday dropped on goal difference to the Second Division. The board demanded immediate promotion, as did the manager and the supporters. Backed by the club's hierarchy, Atkinson was able to keep the squad together for the next campaign. Apart from the £1.75 million sale of Dalian Atkinson to Real Sociedad, the team comprised largely of the same individuals who had taken the club down. In Atkinson's place was Paul Williams, brought in from Charlton to partner Hirst. 'Paul was a great foil,' says Hirst, 'he worked hard, running down the channels, and gave all he got; "You do all the running and I'll score the goals", I'd say, "then I'll mention you on Match of the Day."'

Thanks in part to the excellent service he enjoyed from all areas of the field, Hirst scored 29 times that year. Ammunition came from Nigel Worthington and Phil King on the left, John Sheridan and Carlton Palmer in the middle, Roland Nilsson advancing from the right, and Williams or Trevor Francis beside him. Wednesday played glorious football in 1990-91 down in the Second, a fluent symphony of inter-passing from the whole team. While well supported, Hirst could pull off the spectacular himself, receiving the ball into feet, turning to shoot powerfully from distance and score. In the first game at Hillsborough that season he got four against Hull City. For his third, the ball was collected from far back, the defence left in his wind before a missile shot was sent past the goalkeeper. So fast, so strong, such a fine finisher.

That season Wednesday managed to reach the final of the

League Cup. After despatching Chelsea in the two-legged semi (Hirst contributing one of the five goals), they met Manchester United at Wembley. As underdogs that day the Owls battled hard, played uncharacteristically direct and, through John Sheridan's outside-of-the-area strike, won 1-0. Hirst played a key part in the upset, running tirelessly to cause nuisance to Steve Bruce and Gary Pallister in the United defence. 'After John's goal the team felt that after we'd got through all the rounds they've now got to score more than we have to win now,' he remembers. 'They had a couple of opportunities but didn't take them.' It was Wednesday's first trophy for over 56 years.

Despite that success, however, Wednesday were by no means perfect that year. A frustrating run of draws around Christmas threatened their promotion place – a draw against Wolves on Boxing Day seeing them slip from the automatic places for the first time since the opening day. 'People still come up to me and say what a great side we had,' explains Hirst. 'But we didn't. We had a great team spirit, players helping each other out. It wasn't about individuals but about getting together to do a job. We weren't world beaters but we had a spirit that was.' Happily in the final months of the season, thanks to that spirit and spurred on by the League Cup victory, they were able to hold on to third place, and were promoted with one game to spare after a 3-1 win over Bristol City.

***

'This is a good club with a good atmosphere and good people to work with', said Ron Atkinson in November 1990. Yet, weeks after that season ended, he left for Aston Villa. Having earlier pledged his future to Wednesday, he couldn't resist the call to manage the club he had supported growing up. 'I had', he said, 'previously considered Villa to be my ultimate destiny as a manager.' As the Owls seemed set to build on the momentum begun in 1990-91, his departure came as a massive blow. For abandoning them the fans, heartbroken, called him Judas.

Atkinson's replacement was Trevor Francis, promoted from player to player-manager. He had been signed as an impact forward and had performed well in the promotion season, contributing added vitality to the attack, scoring or making goals in close games. Though in his late 30s, he had retained the calm attacking intelligence that had made him a star for Birmingham, Nottingham Forest and Sampdoria. His previous managerial experience amounted to an uncomfortable period at Queens Park Rangers, but he was ready for Wednesday and what would be a tough return to the First. Francis acknowledged that the team he inherited was capable of playing with great style and, crucially, that it could deliver results.

His first match in charge in 1991-92 was at home to Aston Villa. It saw the immediate return of Atkinson to Hillsborough. And as Wednesday raced to a two goal lead they appeared in control. Hirst's excellent, swerving top corner strike from the edge of the penalty area for 1-0; Danny Wilson, set up by Hirst's good work for 2-0. But thanks to the defensive frailties of the hosts, Villa managed a comeback. First Chris Woods flapped Gordon Cowans' corner into the path of Cyril Regis who dived low to head past a crowd of motionless Wednesday players. Then, an incisive through ball from Regis to Paul Mortimer split the defence, leaving Mortimer clean through on goal. Woods parried his weak shot into the path of Dalian Atkinson who, too fast for the desperately tracking back Wednesday players, finished for 2-2. For their third a long through ball found Atkinson alone on the left of midfield, he ran on, squared it to Steve Staunton who, alone in the area, had time to place his shot for 3-2. It was an eye-opening beginning to the season, demonstrating how such disorganised and amateur defending, even far up the field, would be more regularly punished in the First than it had in the Second.

Fortunately those problems were eventually remedied and Wednesday settled into a pattern of play more purposeful and even more effective than during Atkinson's time in charge. Players were given clearer, more specific roles to cope with the improved standard of opposition – for instance, Carlton Palmer becoming less involved in the team's forward advances than he had previously. He played a more retracted role which served to better protect the back-four, leaving John Sheridan, Palmer's regular midfield sidekick, to pull the attacking strings.

As the season drew on results improved dramatically and Wednesday found their way in to the title race. Hirst's four goals in October helped pick up nine points and, after the 6-1 home defeat early in the New Year to Leeds had been put behind them, they managed to keep the pressure on the league's two frontrunners Leeds and Manchester United. 'You're going to get blips in a season,' says Hirst, referring to the Leeds defeat and the 7-1 loss to Arsenal. 'But eventually people were coming to Hillsborough thinking they were going to get beat.' Wednesday suffered only three home defeats that year finishing seven points behind the eventual winners Leeds. Going into the last two games, the Owls had still been in with a chance of taking the championship and in all it had been a great season, the club's best finish since 1961, earning them a place in Europe the following year.

Such was Hirst's form around the time – 20 goals in 37 appearances in 1991-92 alone – he became the subject of several unsuccessful approaches from Alex Ferguson and Manchester United. In the summer of '92 United had been interested in Southampton's Alan Shearer, but as Ferguson later admitted, 'I was even keener on Hirst.' On that occasion neither Hirst nor Shearer made the move to Old Trafford, instead it was Frenchman Eric Cantona, but the United manager remained interested. A few months later a second approach came when United, suffering the loss of Dion Dublin to injury and left with *only* Cantona, Mark Hughes and Brian McClair as their main strikers, tried again with a £3.5 million bid. But as Hirst recalls, 'I'd just signed a four year contract and Wednesday wouldn't allow me to go. We had a good side, but I would have gone there. I've still got the bag packed just in case.'

Prior to United's interest, in early indication of his progress, Hirst had received several call-ups to the England squad. He played twice on a tour of Australasia in 1991, scoring against New Zealand in Wellington – 'a near post tap in,' he recalls, 'the pinnacle of my career. Now I can say I've played for my country and scored a goal.' He later started alongside Shearer against France. As Gary Lineker's international career neared its end the Hirst-Shearer partnership was billed as the future of English football. But it wouldn't work out quite like that.

That night at Wembley the two were supported by Nottingham Forest's Nigel Clough, acting as a deeper lying forward. For most of the first half, though, the ball was sent long, leaving the trio to chase lost causes against a tight French defence. Hirst worked hard to chase these balls, but it was Shearer who took the plaudits when, just before the break, he scored the first of England's two goals. At half-time Hirst was substituted for Lineker. The Wednesday striker 'did not look the part', according to *The Guardian*, even though in those 45 minutes poor supply had prevented him from making any impact, depriving him of showing his true capabilities. After that, still considered one of the best strikers in England, he was called up to a few more squads but sadly injury problems barred any further appearances.

For early 1992-93, the only major additions Wednesday made to their squad were Chris Waddle, the superstar signing from Olympique Marseille and, significantly for Hirst, Mark Bright. Bright arrived from Crystal Palace for £850,000, Paul Williams going the opposite way. As good as Williams was, especially when working in tandem with Hirst, he did not provide the outlet Francis required. The new signings honed a mostly settled Wednesday side, helping bring a season of near-cup glory, reaching as they did, the finals of both the FA and League Cups. The achievement demanded four gruelling visits to Wembley.

By February '93 Wednesday were progressing well in each competition. Having eliminated Hartlepool, Leicester (7-1, Hirst got one), QPR and Ipswich in the League Cup, a semi-final against Blackburn Rovers was to come. Meanwhile, in the FA Cup, narrow victories over Cambridge, Sunderland and Southend set-up a quarter-final with Derby County at the Baseball Ground. That saw a thrilling 3-3 draw in which Paul Warhurst, a defender converted to striker, scored twice. A week later they replayed in Sheffield, Warhurst again the scorer with the solitary goal which meant a semi against bitterest city rivals Sheffield United.

In the League Cup, after defeating Blackburn 6-3 on aggregate in the semi, Wednesday faced George Graham's Arsenal at Wembley. It was a poor game, the Gunners employing a fast and close-pressing style which led to John Sheridan in midfield receiving the ball less far less than he was used to. Man-marked out of the game by Steve Morrow, it meant supply to Waddle out on the wing was cut, thereby limiting the frequency the Wednesday forward line of Bright and Warhurst saw the ball.

Some chances still came, Warhurst hit the post, the American John Harkes even gave Wednesday the lead, striking a cleared ball past

David Seaman, but it would be Arsenal's day. The Londoners equalised through a fine Paul Merson volley. Then, having hardly created a thing themselves, they went ahead through Morrow's header, the ball reaching him after Carlton Palmer failed to deal properly with a cross.

Despite that disappointment, Wednesday still had another chance of glory in the capital. Following the defeat of Derby in the quarter finals, the draw for the semis of the FA Cup paired them with Sheffield United. Originally the tie was scheduled to take place at Leeds' Elland Road, but such was demand for tickets that the Football Association, following much harassment, agreed to switch the game. For one day, then, London, or at least one corner of it, was Sheffield as 75,000 supporters emptied the city and filled the old stadium. In bright sunshine Wednesday triumphed 2-1 thanks to an unbelievable Chris Waddle free kick and a Mark Bright header in extra-time. It was one of 20 for Bright that season, helping fill the gap in the scoring charts left by an increasingly injured Hirst.

A few weeks later, on a similarly dazzling day, the Wednesday and Arsenal players emerged from the Wembley tunnel for a second time that year. Although the Hirst and Bright partnership had not been seen together as often as it might have that season, they were together from the start of that season's biggest game.

Both sides began cautiously. As in the League Cup final, Arsenal again worked to cut out the effect of Sheridan and Waddle. Their guarded approach was deemed boring by many, yet as George Graham said, 'My philosophy has always been to work out the opposition strengths, and then nullify them.' It would work, Arsenal taking a second trophy that year. This time, though, it took a replay to win it.

The first final finished 1-1. Ian Wright gave Arsenal the lead in the first half, beating Warhurst to the ball as Andy Linighan flicked on a header. But Wednesday responded well. As Waddle managed to roam (to some extent at least) and Sheridan similarly probed, chances arrived. Bright had a goal marked offside before Hirst got the equaliser. Sheridan to Bright. Bright to Harkes. A header across goal and Hirst, unmarked, to finish. 'I've got a picture of that goal,' he says. 'I can't remember what I was thinking, but it was probably ecstasy.'

The following Thursday (a few international matches held the previous night meant the Wednesday had been unavailable) the two teams, now so familiar with each other, met for the fifth time that season. As the rain poured on the 62,000 crowd, they looked on at a spectacle that at least was some improvement on the previous Saturday's attempt. Ultimately, though, for Wednesday, backed wonderfully by those who could make it to Wembley for the fourth time that year, it would end in similarly grim fashion to April's final.

In the replay, with both teams fatigued from over 60 games each that season, the play opened up, space and time becoming more available as the game drew on. And despite the constant hindering tactics of Arsenal, Waddle was more dangerous, switching flanks to trouble Nigel Winterburn on one side, then Lee Dixon on the other. His cross in the first half may have helped put Wednesday ahead had Harkes connected, but it was Arsenal's Wright who, as he had in the first game, opened the scoring. Alan Smith's flick through allowed him to slip between Palmer and Warhurst for 1-0.

In the second half Wednesday improved. Short, lofted but effective balls were played as they tensely sought the equaliser. With 20 minutes left their determined efforts were rewarded. Harkes' cross found Waddle who struck towards goal. A deflection off Dixon went by David Seaman and it was 1-1. Bright then hit the post, while Hirst had a few further opportunities to get the winner. The score remained unmoved, however, and again extra time was required. A few more chances came, Smith for Arsenal, saved by Woods, Bright again for Wednesday. Then Andy Linighan . . .

Earlier that night the Arsenal centre-half had had his nose broken by the elbow of Bright. The forward was booked but may well have been dismissed for what appeared an unfair challenge. With sad irony, for Bright and the Wednesday fans, it was Linighan who scored the winner. As a corner flew over in the final pulses of extra time, he dashed in from the edge of the penalty area, rose to beat the elbower Bright, and headed firmly towards goal. The wet ball slipped through the grasp of Woods, behind and into the net. 2-1 to Arsenal – double cup winners. 'That season had promised everything', wrote Daniel Gordon in *A Quarter of Wednesday*. For Hirst, for Waddle and Sheridan (both in tears on the pitch), for the rest of the team and the supporters of the club, 'It had delivered nothing.'

In the subsequent analysis of that night it was argued both sides had come to know each other too well for a dominant winner to emerge (even though Arsenal won both finals, each game was very close). Indeed, as Hirst believes, 'if we'd played any other team we would have won at least one of the two cups. Having got to two finals it was unfortunate that they were both against the same team.' It has also been said that going in to the final Francis' team had 'lost the habit of winning', due to their busy end-of-season schedule (five League games in eleven days, the Wednesday line-up rotated to preserve fitness for the final). But Arsenal had faced the same punishing schedule and hadn't lost their 'habit'. As Hirst more reasonably reflects, then, 'it just wasn't to be.'

The come down after that eventful season was considerable. Wednesday went through significant squad upheaval and stagnated somewhat. Gradually Francis dismantled the team, John Harkes, Nigel Pearson, Nigel Worthington, Phil King, and Carlton Palmer would all eventually leave. Those brought in as replacements were not up to the standard of their predecessors'. Sadly for Hirst, an unending series of injuries meant his talents were often denied to the club, and his country. Beginning with a broken ankle sustained at the start of 1992-93, his troubles lingered on in some form until retirement. His big frame and bigger misfortune led to trouble after trouble, 'torn thighs, repaired Achilles tendons and broken ankles . . . bad luck.' Because of this he made less than 30 appearances over the following two seasons.

The appointment of David Pleat as manager proved even more fateful for Hirst's career. In Pleat's first season, while on a break from his injury problems, Hirst finished joint top scorer for the club, one of those goals his 100th in a Wednesday shirt. But he and the new manager never really got on and it wouldn't be too long before he was moved along. 'I never understood Pleat,' says Hirst. 'We never saw eye to eye.' And that was that.

In 1997, by which point Waddle and Sheridan had left Hillsborough having experienced similar issues with Pleat, Hirst was sold to Southampton for £2 million. The new start on the south coast seemed to revive his career. In his first season he played in most games and finished the Saints' top scorer. However, injuries soon resurfaced, restricting him to only a few more appearances. 'I smashed my knee and never really got back,' he says.

Hirst retired in 2000. And though injuries punctuated his playing time at Wednesday, he will be remembered as one of the finest ever players to have appeared for the club. 'Growing up, all I wanted to be was a footballer,' he says. 'To be at the top of the game. I was what these days you'd call an old fashioned centre forward – put my head where you'd put your foot. Some said that I worked hard, others that I didn't work hard enough, but I always I gave it my best. I played in the top flight, and internationally. And I know how fortunate I was that football was my living.'

2

Don Megson

1959-1970
442 appearances

In 1960-61 Wednesday achieved their strongest league finish since before the war, second place in the First Division to Bill Nicholson's double-winning Tottenham side. They ran their rivals close all season, the eight point gap which eventually separated them only developing in the final moments of the campaign after a loss at White Hart Lane. Spurs steamrolled their way to the title with an expensively assembled squad – they had spent around £250,000 on a series of high-profile transfers, the specific aim of which being to bring the title to north London. By contrast, the Wednesday team had been put together for only £17,000. And with a combination of home grown players and carefully selected minor fee transfers, they compensated for their comparative lack of fluency with great strength, dedication and superb organisation. Many believed the group had a promising future.

Following his arrival in 1958, the Wednesday manager Harry Catterick had made only two major changes to the side he had inherited from his predecessor Eric Taylor. The first was Bobby Craig, a new forward brought in from the Scottish club Third Lanark to replace the ageing stalwart Redfern Froggatt. The second was the promotion of Don Megson from the reserves when regular right-back Peter Johnson had picked up an injury. Finally, after a frustrating six-and-a-half year wait, the 23-year-old Megson had pushed his way into the first team. It was the beginning of a great decade-long run.

From Sale, Cheshire, Megson had begun his career with non-

League Mossley Town, playing alongside his brother Cyril. In 1952 he was spotted by a Wednesday scout and signed amateur forms as an outside-left forward, becoming a regular for their Hatchard and Yorkshire League teams. At 17 he began playing in the reserves alongside Froggatt and Jack Shaw. It was an exciting time to be with the club. After playing for the A team on Saturday mornings Megson and his team-mates would rush to Hillsborough to catch sight of the seniors in action. Wednesday at that time was all about Derek Dooley, the young striker who had burst onto the scene with a record scoring feat which propelled the club to promotion in 1951-52.

While his young defensive contemporaries Peter Swan, Tony Kay and Tom McAnearney gradually found their way into first team, Megson remained on the periphery as he commuted to Sheffield for games while fulfilling a joiner's apprenticeship at home. With so many good defenders at the club, opportunities for advancement were rare. It didn't help either that manager-secretary Eric Taylor did not often attend training, relying instead on the reports of his coaches to inform team selection. 'Eric would never have seen me playing much,' says Megson, 'I don't think he went to the training ground, or ever put on a tracksuit on in his life.' Of course, all players suffered from this particular reality, but Megson nonetheless felt frustrated. With the prospect of National Service to come it seemed possible his nascent football career might end before it began.

Two years later though, after completing his service, his luck changed. Catterick, who in the intervening period had taken over from Taylor as manager, took an interest. 'I'd only been out of the army about a month,' Megson recalls, 'and Harry offered me a professional contract.' Megson continued to play in the reserves, albeit in the knowledge that he now at least was in the manager's thoughts.

In November 1959 he finally got his chance. That day, home to Burnley, Wednesday's normal left-back Norman Curtis was moved to the right to fill in for Peter Johnson, Megson taking his place on the left. The brief from Catterick was straightforward. 'If it stands above two feet and it's got a different coloured shirt on, tackle it as hard as you can.' It was a difficult start to his professional career. 'Early on I remember covering Peter Swan on the far post,' he says. 'I'd expected him to deal with a cross but suddenly the ball burst through a gap, hit me on the chest and bounced down for Jimmy Robson to score.' Fortunately Wednesday equalised through Keith Ellis and the debutant's error was quickly forgotten. Indeed, when Johnson returned from injury it was Curtis and not Megson who made way. In a short while he managed to make the position his own and stayed there for the remainder of the season.

That season brought the excitement of an FA Cup run, Wednesday progressing to the semi-finals after knocking out Sheffield United in a quarter-final at Bramall Lane. United dominated the game that day. 'We were only in it for about 15 minutes in the second half,' says Megson. 'But in that time Derek Wilkinson scored twice and we won 2-0.' Over 61,000 were there to see it. In the semi at Maine Road they faced Blackburn Rovers but lost 2-1. Rovers' Derek Dougan scored a brace with John Fantham netting the consolation for the Owls. Alan Finney thought he had equalised but the referee changed his mind and disallowed the goal. 'We were so close to Wembley,' recalls Megson. 'It was a big disappointment.'

During the summer of 1960 Catterick revamped his staff, bringing in the coaches Tom Eggleston and Maurice Lindley. For the team to improve its overall effectiveness and move on to the next step Eggleston and the manager worked out a new training schedule for the pre-season. It focused more on balls skills and it was hoped that the play of the team, which already was fit, would improve.

To motivate and improve his players the manager began talking to them individually, offering encouragement while instructing them on exactly how he wanted them to play against specific opponents. In Megson's case his motivational techniques took another form. 'Harry was very determined for success, for himself and his players,' says Megson. 'I was once dropped from the side so I went to see him in his office. He looked up at me and said, "You are the best left-back at this club, now get out and prove it." That was it. The next week I was back in the side.'

At Tottenham, who were to be Wednesday's rivals that season, preparation was similarly intense. Their manager Bill Nicholson had his players working hard on ball skills, too, with special attention paid to tactical exercises and dead ball situations. These would prove a speciality of their play that year. Spurs excelled in every position, 'probed and prodded,' disorienting their opponents with diagonal running as they waited 'patiently for the right opportunity to open up a defence'. A hard outfit to match.

As the 1960-61 season got underway the preparation and efforts of both sides quickly paid off. Wednesday won three of their first four, part of a 12 match unbeaten run that comprised a succession of hard-fought narrow victories, while Tottenham went on a similarly impressive unbeaten run. For Megson, while fulfilling his primary defensive duties sternly and effectively (he was one of the toughest full-backs in the league), he also offered considerable attacking impetus to the team. Catterick required him to send long balls up from the back to the strong target man Keith Ellis. 'I wasn't encouraged to go further than the half way line,' he says, 'so I would go up the line and sail it in for Keith to head.' A significant number of these balls would turn to goals, either directly for Ellis (who got 19 that year), or for others from his knock-downs.

By the time they visited Hillsborough in November Tottenham were still unbeaten. They had already amassed over 50 goals and dropped just one point, dazzling supporters with their fluid play and unstoppable scoring. Wonderfully, though, in a match 'scalding with intensity', Wednesday emerged 2-1 victors.

Without their first-choice goalkeeper Ron Springett (out through injury, his place taken by Ron McLaren), Wednesday went in to the game at a significant disadvantage. Yet, for all the talent of the Tottenham forwards John White, Bobby Smith, and Terry Dyson, they managed to repel every early attack, consistently pressing and blocking a side which in previous matches had used the ball with such ease. After Alan Finney and Billy Griffin swapped wings to each find greater success against the Spurs full-backs, Wednesday took the lead not long before half-time. A calm back pass by Tom McAnearney to Peter Johnson was driven high up the field to Bobby Craig who, running forward and into the box, precisely pulled the ball back to Griffin who placed his shot home.

Tottenham managed to recover three minutes later through a Maurice Norman header but it was the Owls who came out stronger in the second half. And with 20 minutes left, after surviving several moments of pressure, they regained the lead. A high lobbed cross from Megson into the penalty area met the head of Ellis. The resulting mix-up in the box saw the ball land at the feet of John Fantham who hit home the winner in front of the Kop. Tottenham, so vaunted by the media, surged forward in the remaining minutes but were unable to get past Wednesday's barrier. Suddenly, a team which up to then had appeared invincible looked vulnerable.

By the time of the return fixture in April Wednesday were on a 19-game unbeaten run. They played fine football on the way and cut the lead at the top from nine points to three. Unfortunately they went into the crunch game without a manager, reeling from the sudden resignation of Catterick after the home draw with Leicester the previous week. Already unhappy over being refused permission to talk with Nottingham Forest about taking over as their manager at the end of the season, he had become increasingly disillusioned over the numerous broken promises made to him by the club over player recruitment. 'Harry wanted to sign a centre forward called Joe Baker from Hibernian who was available for a reasonable fee,' says Megson. 'But he couldn't persuade [club secretary] Eric Taylor and the board to give him the money. Taylor held the purse strings and refused to make fees available that Harry wanted. He wasn't allowed to make the signings he felt he needed to take Wednesday forward.'

With only four games of the season remaining, a win at White Hart Lane was essential if Wednesday were to close the gap and have any chance of taking the title. In 30 minutes they were ahead, Megson again at the centre of the action. John Fantham fell suspiciously from a supposed Norman tackle to win a free-kick. Megson struck the wall with his bullet left foot before smashing the rebound past Brown in the Tottenham goal. It was his first league goal for the club. 'I always ran to celebrate with the scorer,' he says, 'so it was a great feeling to have everyone run to you instead.'

Moments later, Wednesday might have gone further ahead, Ellis heading against the post just before half time. But that woke Tottenham up. A minute later, unleashing an overwhelming display of technical and attacking superiority, they equalised. Dyson, a foot smaller than Megson, outjumped him, headed to Bobby Smith who rounded Swan before hitting the ball past Springett. A minute later it was 2-1, Danny Blanchflowers' free-kick eventually finding Les Allen who volleyed home. The title surrendered in a white flurry. 'But Tottenham did have the better players,' admits Megson.

Vic Buckingham was Harry Catterick's replacement, a complete contrast in personality and management style to his predecessor. While Catterick was a strait-laced authoritarian, Buckingham was flamboyant – theatrical in the dressing room, a handkerchief sticking from his pocket, a hat on his head and a golf club in his hand. Buckingham was versed in continental techniques, having managed Ajax to the Dutch Championship, and he brought a different style of play to Wednesday. 'Rather than playing flat out at all times he wanted us to vary the pace at which we played,' remembers Megson. 'He used to say, "We will be going slowly, then quickly, then we'll knock it out wide, then Colin Dobson will go du du du du du du du." Which was his way of saying he wanted to see some skill before the final pass.'

Under the new manager the full-backs were now expected to play the ball out from the back when they regained possession – kicking it long only when there was no other option. It was a difficult change for the players. Extra training sessions were put on but they only succeeded in tiring the players before the matches. Megson himself wasn't sure of the approach. 'As a full-back I would go up the line and sail it in. I'm convinced that there was more of a tension for the defender of seeing a ball going into the box and not knowing what would happen to the ball than there was it coming in along on the floor. But that was what Vic wanted.'

In Buckingham's three seasons most of those he brought in were direct replacements for those who were moved on. Bobby Craig left for Blackburn, Keith Ellis to Scunthorpe and Billy Griffin to Bury. Incoming were the ex-England international Eddie Holliday from Middlesbrough, Peter Eustace, an elegant midfielder who was promoted from the reserves, and David Layne, an exciting young centre-forward signed for around £20,000 from Bradford City. He was the type of forward Catterick had himself wanted. 'David was quite a classy player and gave us more options with the short ball,' says Megson. 'Where Keith Ellis might have only been able to head the ball when receiving a cross, David had the ability to bring the ball under control and create more incisive opportunities for others.' Despite this, Wednesday seemed to struggle under the new manager, finishing sixth in each of his three seasons in charge. Buckingham left the club in 1964.

His replacement, Alan Brown, was a sterner and more disciplined character, perhaps what the club required following the eccentricity of Buckingham. One of his first acts was to make Megson his captain. After a poor first half during a friendly loss to Danish side Aarhus FG in 1964 Brown and the then captain Tommy McAnearney became involved in a vicious disagreement over the team's performance. Brown stripped the Scot of the armband, picked up the match ball and threw it to Megson, telling him to lead the side out in the second half. He would remain captain for the remainder of his Wednesday career. 'He made me into more than a captain though,' explains Megson. 'He told me that if I wanted to change anything on the field, I could do it. If a player didn't seem like he wanted the ball, Brown would let me switch the play to other areas. But he only let me do it if I could tell him why when I came off.'

The highlight of Brown's period at the club was the 1966 FA Cup final against Everton, now led by Harry Catterick. That day, having being 2-0 in front, Wednesday famously gave away three quick goals to lose 3-2. But although they had gained a strong lead, Megson believes the collapse was not entirely a surprise, 'People ask me what happened after the second goal, why we lost it. But when you get in front you naturally keep it more controlled. You're playing a different animal to the one that started the game, when you're dead level and want to attack, you're more vulnerable to conceding.' Despite the loss captain Megson proudly led his team on a lap of the stadium, acknowledging the travelling thousands from Sheffield in the crowd. It proved a high water mark for a team that was in decline.

By 1969-70, Megson's final season at the club, the team were struggling at the bottom of the First Division. His season was interrupted by a training ground injury which limited him to just seven appearances. 'The writing was on the wall when the chairman came up to me and asked if I wanted to go on tour to New Zealand with a Football League representative side, rather than go to Italy with the Wednesday squad. I was suffering from injuries, but they cleared up and I played 11 games on that tour.'

It wasn't the first time he had played for that League side. In 1960 he had travelled to play an Italian league team. 'That game was a kick up', he recalls. 'Denis Law went over and kicked John Charles, then everyone was kicking everyone else. It went badly and after the game our coach was pelted with stones from some angry home fans.'

Despite his recognition for the League team, however, a full England call up had never arrived for Megson. 'When the left-back position came up I got picked for the shadow squad, but I accepted that the best left-back in the country was Ray Wilson. I wasn't equipped to keep him out.

'The New Zealand tour in '69 was my swansong. But I didn't get back in the team much after that and we got relegated.' After 18 years of service and almost 450 appearances, Megson left Wednesday later that year. He had been close to accepting an offer from Southend United to become their player-manager, having taken his coaching qualifications a few years before. But Eric Taylor had his own ideas. 'Taylor saw me the very first day I came into Hillsborough in 1952,' says Megson. 'When it was my turn to leave he brought me into the office and told me that Bert Tan [general manager of Bristol Rovers] had a job for me. Eric was big friends with Bert and told me that he would put me on a good footing to becoming a good manager. So I went there instead of Southend.'

Megson spent one season as Rovers' player-coach before retiring because of injury. In 1972 he replaced Bill Dodgin as manager. His brief was to get the club out of the Third Division where they had languished for 15 years. He started well. In his third game in charge, Bristol won the Watney Cup, a shortlived competition that consisted of eight teams, two from each division, who had scored the most goals the season before but were not promoted or involved in Europe. Rovers beat Burnley and Wolves before beating Sheffield United in the final. That season Rovers also won a League Cup replay against his childhood team Manchester United at Old Trafford, 2-1.

The following year Megson led Rovers on a long unbeaten run which by the end of the season took them up to the Second Division. He had a talented group of players, his ex-Wednesday team mates Alan Warboys and Colin Dobson among them, and the big-scoring striker Bruce Bannister,. yet money was scarce. The following year Megson found it difficult to improve. 'I remember telling the club we needed to strengthen the side,' he says, 'but they said, "Mr Manager, we don't have the money. In fact, we have to sell." At that stage I badly needed a change. I was in a survival situation which lasted two-and-a-half years. After a while it was a case of who was going to motivate the motivator?'

33

After Rovers' Graeme Day was loaned to the Portland Timbers of the North American Soccer League in 1975, Bristol, as part of the arrangement, travelled to Oregon to play a friendly. In America Megson impressed the Timbers' President Keith Williams and six months later he was offered the manager's job. He accepted, becoming the first manager of a Football League club to leave a post to go to manage in the NASL. He spent three years there. 'I loved it,' he says, 'but in comparison to the New York Cosmos [the expensively assembled superstar outfit which had hosted Pele, and for whom Franz Beckenbauer was then playing] we were a team built on cheap players and imports from England, so we couldn't really compete.'

Megson returned to England in 1980. 'Overall Portland was a bad move for me career wise,' he says. He found himself out of work, competing against a host of new, younger managers. Following a short period at Bournemouth, he was only given one further interview for a manager's job – Chesterfield – but lost out to Paul Hart. Still, he enjoyed his time in the NASL and is philosophical of how his life as a manager turned out. 'I always regarded myself as a footballer and management is no substitute for playing. At Wednesday I worked for five managers and the most pleasing thing is that I played almost 40 games in almost every season I was there. That's not a bad way of proving to myself that I pleased them all.'

3

Kevin Pressman

1985-2004
478 appearances

The first game of the 1996-97 season was a special moment for goalkeeper Kevin Pressman; the first time he would own the Wednesday number one shirt. After enduring years of frustration, long spells spent on the sidelines thanks to injury and challenges from other players, he was now recognised as the undisputed first choice at the club. 'I looked at the opening day's match programme and said to myself, "Now I know I've finally made it."'

In 17 mixed years Pressman battled for a first team place. After nearly 500 appearances, he rightly deserves consideration as one of Hillsborough's most loyal and consistent servants. Surprisingly agile for his size, a reactive shot stopper with a hard kick, he was a reliable and consistent performer for the club. While in later years injury and loss of managerial support began to count against him – periods of good form matched by similarly long periods on the bench – at his height he was among the best keepers in the country.

***

'He [manager Howard Wilkinson] told me in the bath after training on the Friday morning,' recalled Pressman of his debut. Away to Southampton, September 1987. To that point Wednesday's season had been poor. Struggling at the bottom of the table, they had lost 3-0 at home to Coventry the previous Monday. At the time Martin Hodge was Wilkinson's first choice, but he was injured for the trip to the Dell so Pressman was given his chance. 'It was quick compared with what I'd known,' he said, 'but if I was busy, I felt I had a good game . . . my confidence got an early boost when I made a good save from a free kick and then got up to block the rebound.' The match finished 1-1. Only the team's second point gained that season.

Hodge returned not long after, but a change in that position was looming. For three years he had been outstanding in the Wednesday goal, an exceptionally hard worker who always kept a critical eye on the performances of his fellow players, providing encouragement and harsh words where necessary. But after poor performances against Everton in the FA Cup (a 5-0 defeat in a replay) and Manchester United at Old Trafford (a 4-1 loss in the league in March) Hodge was loaned, then sold to Leicester City. 'It was my decision to leave though,' he says. 'Howard Wilkinson wanted me to stay but I needed a change and I thought the time was right to do so.'

Hodge's initial replacement, signed in the summer of '88, was Chris Turner, returning to the club after a decade spent with Manchester United and Sunderland. Like Pressman, Turner had been a bright young stopper when in 1976 he made his first team debut aged 17. Now he was back at the club, older and wiser. For the next three seasons the two competed for that one first team spot, each demonstrating their own talents. Pressman was brave, not scared of making dives for the ball or of running far out into his box to catch crosses. Turner, on the other hand, who was smaller, was more cautious, sticking to his line to rely more on his shot-stopping ability.

In their first season together, Turner played in most of the games (32 to Pressman's 10), as Wednesday avoided relegation by only a few points. The next season, however, the youngster managed to win and hold on to the senior man's place. He even gained an England U-21 cap against Denmark. Unfortunately, though, a collision with Manchester City's David Oldfield at Hillsborough at Christmas resulted in a cruciate injury that would force him out of the rest of the season. While Pressman returned as first choice for the beginning of 1990-91, he tore a thigh muscle against Wolves on Boxing Day and missed the League Cup final success over Manchester United the following April. If not for that tear he would probably have played that day. As a goalkeeper he relied heavily on his capability of strongly and confidently commanding his penalty area, but the threat of injury, following those two major setbacks, took an increasing psychological toll. 'The danger of physical contact was at the back of my mind for a long time,' he said of his inner turmoil.

Ahead of 1991-92 the new Wednesday manager Trevor Francis broke the club's transfer record when he made the surprise signing of England's number one Chris Woods, £1.2 million from Glasgow Rangers. Having served as Peter Shilton's understudy at Nottingham Forest, and then England, Woods arrived in Sheffield with vast subsequent experience and over 20 international caps. He was a player of class, but at 31 was expensive, and considering that in Pressman and Turner the club already had two fine performers, the new man arguably was not needed. Many believed the money could have been better spent on a new strike partner for David Hirst, for instance. After Woods arrived Turner was moved on to Leyton Orient, a swap deal involving the promising forward Chris Bart Williams. Pressman warmed the bench.

It was not until early 1993-94 that he got another good chance in the first team. After Woods suffered a groin injury at an England training camp in Holland in late '93, Pressman was recalled to face Wimbledon. He had a quiet match and was disappointingly beaten by a last minute equaliser from Vinny Jones. Still, after that he performed well enough to displace Woods for the rest of the season. 'The experience of spending so long in the wilderness made me appreciate the subsequent upturn in my fortunes,' Pressman said of his long waited for return. Such was his form he again got noticed by the England set-up, called up to the B international squad for matches against Northern Ireland (held at Hillsborough) and the Republic of Ireland. He spent the next two years as the Owls' undisputed number one – when he took to the field against Aston Villa in the late summer of '96, his reputation had never been higher.

It wasn't always that straightforward, however. Resurfacing injury problems had threatened his earlier comeback, and it is testament to his subsequent professionalism that they didn't unduly hinder the remainder of his career. A double hernia in 1994-95 was particularly bothersome. 'I don't like to use excuses,' he said, 'and at the time I didn't think I was affected by them, but both needed operations'. After receiving treatment for the injury Pressman realised how important it was to keep on top of his general fitness. 'A hernia affects the sharp stuff, the reaction saves, it makes you that split-second late because you get to know what type of movement hurts you and you shy away from it. You are battling against your own mind . . . [I] learned a lesson – don't carry injuries, get them sorted out. If you are not 100 per cent in the Premiership, you get punished.' After that, he was rarely injured again.

At the end of 1994-95 Trevor Francis was sacked, replaced by David Pleat, who made his own changes to the playing squad. Incoming were Marc Degryse, a highly regarded Belgian forward from Anderlecht for £1.6 million, Mark Pembridge, a £900,000 left-sided midfielder from Derby, and later the former Liverpool man Steve Nicol. Departing was Bart-Williams, sold to Nottingham Forest for £2.5 million.

Though Wednesday fared poorly in Pleat's first season, only narrowly avoiding relegation, they improved significantly the year after, winning their first four games and for a brief while led the Premier League. That run began with a 2-1 home victory against Aston Villa, the young striker Richie Humphreys opening the scoring on his debut with a fantastic hard volley from Pembridge's flick on. Further wins came against Leeds, Newcastle and Leicester, Humphreys the star of that latter game with a run and sublime chip over Kasey Keller. For once it meant Wednesday were able to look down on the other teams in the league rather than up. While that early challenge faded quickly, they at least managed to finish seventh.

Through this time Pressman continued to give consistent performances. He was well tipped to win a full international cap and overall optimism had returned to Hillsborough, to the fans and to the team. 'When everything is going well, everyone wants a part of it. When it's not, you get little niggles and you think: "Ooh, I'm a bit stiff today." That "feel-good" factor means people are not frightened of making a mistake. When you are down at the bottom and you make a mistake, it could be three points lost and relegation. At the top, if you make a mistake, you think you can rectify it.' As would be common for Wednesday in the late 1990s, though, the good times would not last and after a poor start to 1997-98, Pleat was sacked.

His replacement was the returning Ron Atkinson. Having left so controversially in 1991 he was wary of a negative reaction from the supporters that six years previously he had let down so bitterly when he left for Aston Villa. 'If there had been a mass reaction against me and a general no-no, I'd have said "forget it,"' Atkinson said. But there wasn't. Initially chairman Dave Richards offered him a three-year contract but Atkinson wanted to see how things developed before committing himself to any longer. A contract until May was agreed.

Results generally picked up, but after a few poor performances it was reported Atkinson had his reservations over Pressman. On Boxing Day '97 he allowed a close range header from Leicester's Steve Guppy to pass over his shoulder and into the net. This came after a 4-1 loss at home to Chelsea. It was speculated the manager was interested in Liverpool's David James, whose own position was under threat from the American Brad Friedel. The rumour demonstrated how delicate the grip on the goalkeeping position can be at times. A great keeper can lose his reputation with one mistake, and with another, his place in the team. Fortunately for Pressman no replacement signing was made.

Despite a mistake on the final day of the season, when Pressman failed to keep out a late goal by Clinton Morrison at Crystal Palace, robbing Wednesday of a higher placed finish and greater prize money, his form was still such that he gained a third England B cap against Chile. This was followed by a call up to the full squad for a World Cup preparation friendly against Switzerland. He had had a good game against Chile, despite the 2-1 defeat, but he missed out on the tournament in France. David Seaman, Nigel Martyn and Tim Flowers were chosen ahead of him. 'People say if I'd moved I may have got into the England side instead of being on the fringe', Pressman has said. 'That's life.'

After the board failed to offer Atkinson a new contract for 1998-99, he left the club. Considering he had rescued the club from potential relegation it appeared a curious decision, though at least he had to some extent managed to make amends with the supporters for his sudden departure in '91. (This, some years before he damaged his reputation after dropping the 'N-bomb' on microphone during a Champions League television broadcast).

It was Atkinson's successor, the former Wednesday player Danny Wilson, who brought in Pressman's next rival for his position. After a bad performance against Leeds in late 1998, a 2-1 defeat in which Pressman fumbled a throw that led to a goal, the former Newcastle keeper Pavel Srnicek was signed from the Czech team Banik Ostrava. For the next 18 months the two fought to be first choice. Looking back, Pressman was philosophical of Srnicek's threat. 'It was never really in my mind that I was the guaranteed number one. If I had one bad game I'd be worried about losing my place.' The two had greatly contrasting styles. Pressman, we know, was brave off his line and in to the action. Srnicek was more erratic, preferring, for example, to punch the ball from safety. Martin Hodge, by this time goalkeeping coach at Hillsborough, recalls. 'Pavel had to work a lot harder than Pressman in making himself a top class keeper, while Kevin had the better technical ability. Both worked on different things to make themselves better players.'

The arrival of Srnicek proved a watershed moment for Pressman. The remainder of his time at Hillsborough would be spent fighting calls from certain fans who believed he was no longer good enough for the shirt. In 1999-00 Wednesday faced a relegation battle and were turning in consistently poor performances, none worse than the 8-0 defeat at Newcastle in September. In Bobby Robson's first game in charge as manager, Alan Shearer scored five as the Owls capitulated on Tyneside. 'It wasn't a good day,' Pressman recalled understatedly, 'a bad day at the office.'

Wednesday's defence, which had looked solid the previous season, was now far shakier. Though it was Pressman, as the last line, who was held most to blame. After the Newcastle game he was dropped in favour of Srnicek and only regained his place when the Czech was ruled out in March with a damaged shoulder. But to no avail for the team as they were relegated to the First Division.

**

August 2000, Wednesday's first game in the second tier following their drop from the Premier League. After just 13 seconds of the match at Wolves, Pressman ran forward from his goal to close down the advancing Temuri Ketsbaia. Often inclined to rush out and meet oncoming attackers, on this occasion he went too far, sliding out of the area with the ball still clutched to his chest. Rightly, he was shown the red card.

That moment set the tone for the whole season, a year in which for both Pressman and the club more went wrong than it did right. After that opening match, in which Wednesday strained to a 1-1 draw, they would go on to lose five of their first six home games, including a 5-0 thrashing by Wimbledon. Danny Wilson had been sacked towards the end of the previous season and the run was an unwelcome start for the new man Paul Jewell.

The club had spent the early summer searching for a replacement for Wilson. Some believed the former Wimbledon manager Joe Kinnear would take over, but ultimately it was Jewell, fresh from retaining Bradford City's top level status, who was brought in. However, with £25 million of debt and a wage bill in excess of £12 million, the club would struggle to find him the funds he needed to bring improved results.

Because of the financial difficulties, where some costly Premier League contracts still had to be honoured but no players of similar calibre could be brought in, the line-up for that season was based around a curious mix of experienced top level players, youth products and lower league signings. One line-up comprised Des Walker and Andy Hinchcliffe, Steven Haslam and Alan Quinn, and Ian Hendon and Ashley Westwood from those respective categories. There were a few highlights of the campaign, notably the first Sheffield derby in seven years where in front of over 30,000 in the League Cup Wednesday won 2-1 in extra time thanks to a brace from Efan Ekoku, but that was as good as it got.

With the club struggling and Pressman's performances drawing increasingly vocal criticism from the fans, he declined the club's offer of a testimonial that January. The previous month a horror mix up between him and Walker against Stockport, in which both players had failed to clear an ambling through ball, had gifted the victorious away team one of their four goals that day. Afterwards Pressman reportedly received a deluge of hate mail. 'When you get letters saying you are the weakest link, it makes it pretty clear to me the fans hate me,' he said. 'Some fans have written saying I'm not fit to wear the shirt and it is fair to say I'm certainly not the most popular guy at the club. There are some who have accused me of costing Wednesday their place in the Premiership. These days when I go out I can hear the boos start when I am picking up the ball. Then there are the ironic cheers when I get a backpass.'

Sometimes Pressman did struggle, but repeatedly he was exposed by naive defending and was perhaps unfairly dropped in favour of the on-loan former Wednesday reserve Marlon Beresford. During his four games the team failed to win, culminating in a 4-1 defeat at Wimbledon, after which Pressman regained his place. Later, with Wednesday now bottom of the table, Paul Jewell was sacked. Peter Shreeves, still on the coaching staff following his spell as caretaker manager less than a year earlier after Danny Wilson's sacking, was again promoted to the job. Reinstating Pressman was his first act. Shreeves, with another relegation battle on his hands, moved to add experience to a youthful midfield, bringing in the Norwegian Trond Egil Soldvedt on loan from Southampton and Carlton Palmer from Coventry. Thankfully results improved and Wednesday moved towards safety.

2001-02 was similarly traumatic with the club again clinging perilously onto their place in the First. Pressman held onto the shirt for the majority of the season, dropping out only through injury, missing the League Cup semi-final second leg against Blackburn Rovers. In that cup run Wednesday had beaten Premier League Sunderland, then Crystal Palace and Watford. In the first leg of the semi at Hillsborough they went down 2-1, and though not fancied for the return at Ewood Park, still gave a brave performance in Blackburn, scoring twice through Soldvedt and Ekoku, but ultimately succumbing to a 4-2 defeat (5-3 on aggregate). The following year, however, after occupying the relegation places for much of the season, Wednesday were relegated.

In the third level, although a few signings had refreshed the squad – Robbie Mustoe, Terry Cooke, Adam Proudlock and later Mark Robins among those brought in – it was largely the same team that had come down which again disappointed. Under another new manager in Chris Turner (he had taken over from Terry Yorath who had replaced Shreeves), the Owls were most unimpressive, finishing 16th and just three points above relegated Grimsby Town. It was Pressman's last season with the club.

That year he had spent long periods out of the team because of injury, losing his place to Ola Tidman, a young Swedish keeper bought from Stockport. Tidman played the first six games of the season, failing to keep a clean sheet, before being replaced by Pressman. He lasted just five games before again succumbing to injury. David Lucas was signed on loan from Preston, the first of two spells he had with the club that year, and played a handful of games. But ultimately it was Pressman who saw out the season – and his career at Hillsborough – as the club's number one. It wasn't a happy time, though. 'To be honest I didn't enjoy my last 12 months with Wednesday', he said in grim retrospect. 'In fact it was probably the least enjoyable of my 20 years at the club.'

Pressman was released at the end of 2003-04, a great anti-climax after so many years of service. His legacy was aptly summarised by *The Guardian* when they wrote, 'His brand of loyalty borders on self sacrifice. He was booed by his own fans when the team leaked goals . . . and was deprived of the trust to try to turn England U21 and B appearances into a full cap.'

After Wednesday it was on to Leicester where he briefly competed with Ian Walker, then on to short spells at Leeds and Coventry. Aged 39, he signed for the Irish League side Portadown, commuting from England for every match and turning in a series of matchwinning performances. 'I could have easily just sat at home and not bothered,' he said. 'But I wanted a challenge and something to test me.' When he retired he took up coaching roles at Scunthorpe and Bradford City.

4

Derek Dooley

1950-1953 (player)
63 appearances, 63 goals
1971-73 (manager)

If Wednesday had to select a 'Roy of the Rovers' figure, Derek Dooley would be top of the list. His scoring record – 47 from 31 matches in one league season – is legendary, unheard of in the modern game. The fans treasured him, his powerful style, huge stature, persistence and awkward grace endearing him like no other player of that era. Like Roy Race, 'Melchester Rovers' brave, battling, boisterous, battering ram,' he was 'thunderboots', chasing every ball, 'galloping after shadows to turn them into substance'.

He was a gentleman of the game, well-mannered, sporting, optimistic, brave, playing always with a smile on his face and quickly became a hero to the fans. When tragedy came, his career truncated by a tragic accident that ultimately cost him a leg, the outpouring of public sympathy was extensive and sincere. Bravely, he fought back, carving a career for himself as a football administrator and later, when the club's fortunes were down, becoming manager of the first team, an appointment designed to inspire a similar reversal in fortunes for the club that he had helped bring as a player.

1951-52 began with great expectation for Wednesday. The team was required to challenge for promotion, ensuring a swift return to the First Division after relegation the season before. As it began, however, the side struggled in front of goal, and while the club had several talented attacking players – Redfern Froggatt, Dennis Woodhead Jackie Sewell – none could fill the centre-forward role effectively. Manager Eric Taylor, increasingly troubled by the lack of end product in this area, looked elsewhere for a solution. Charlton's Charlie Vaughan was considered, but their manager Jimmy Seed, a captain of Wednesday in the '30s, refused to sell. In frustration, Taylor even turned to winger Walter Rickett, one of the smallest players at the club. Some critics called it desperation.

In October '51, Taylor selected Dooley for the home game against Barnsley. Hopes for the game were low. Wednesday had won only three of their first ten matches, having embarrassingly conceded seven at Bramall Lane against Sheffield United, plus another five at home to Rotherham. The previous week Dooley had played for the reserves against Bolton Wanderers and scored four. He was worth a try. Against Barnsley he carried on from where he had left off against Wanderers, scoring two as Wednesday won 2-1. The *Green 'Un* celebrated with the headline, 'He'll Dooley Alright at Hillsborough'. The win turned the season and began a glorious spell for the young striker. 'I had to admit,' remembered Dooley in his autobiography, 'that right from the start of the Barnsley game I felt things were going to work out for me.'

***

Born in the Pitsmoor area of the city, Dooley had been brought up a Wednesday fan. His heroes were two greats of the 1930s, Jackie Robinson and Walter Millership. His father had been a notable full-back in the local amateur leagues and been offered a trial by Bradford City, though he turned it down because he couldn't get time off work. As a player his son was a fast, energetic and enthusiastic forward. He played for his school in the arena of secondary modern vs. grammar, where hardness was cultivated and admired. He gained the nickname 'Wild Yong Dirk' because of his physical and carefree attitude.

When he left school Dooley started work as an apprentice deaf aid mechanic, looking around for a team to play for in his spare time. He found one at the local branch of the YMCA. They played him at left-back and centre-half but he wanted to be further up the field among the scorers. A few months from his 16th birthday Dooley took his first steps into the professional game, invited to play for Lincoln City reserves. In one game fate schemed to bring him to Wednesday's attention. Lining up as the opposing centre half that day was Millership, his hero from the '30s. Having being run and barged by the young flame-haired striker all afternoon, he reported back to Eric Taylor of the 'most awkward centre forward I've met . . . just like a ruddy great tank.'

A month later Tommy Walker, another Wednesday veteran, was sent to watch Dooley play for Sheffield and Hallamshire against Doncaster (at the time his appearances weren't limited to Lincoln). Dooley scored four and the club wasted no time in signing him up as a part-time professional. He was elated. 'Eric Taylor was the best salesman Wednesday ever had but I didn't need anyone to "sell" the club to me. The prospect of playing for Wednesday was something I had never considered remotely possible and when it happened it was like a miracle.'

In the early weeks of 1950, after two-years of National Service, Dooley returned to focus on Wednesday. His future in the game was still uncertain so he resumed his apprenticeship while continuing to play part-time. He would eventually sign full terms but made only two appearances for the first team over the next 18 months, flopping on both occasions. The first of these games came against Preston North End at Hillsborough in March. Wednesday had won only once in their previous six matches, thanks in part to a lengthy injury list, and their promotion bid was faltering. Dooley had a bad game and unsurprisingly was dropped the next week. 'No one was more aware than me that I lacked finesse and still had a great deal to learn in terms of pure football skills,' he remembered.

In terms of raw attributes Dooley had all he needed to succeed. But they needed to be honed. Richard Sparling's words in the *Sheffield Telegraph* of his early development echoed the opinions of many at the time. 'If he is willing to work hard and consistently he can remove his deficiencies and become a power. Dooley has everything in his favour – years, physique and a gift for shooting.'

The arrival of Alan Brown as coach in 1951 would transform his fortunes. Brown was a former Huddersfield and Burnley centre-half, a tough figure who quickly became one of Dooley's biggest supporters. Although not an easy man to know, Dooley admired the new coach and the two soon forged a mutual respect. Brown worked patiently with him, spending endless hours on the training pitch alongside the young player to help improve his striking techniques. In particular they worked on exploiting one-on-one situations against an advancing goalkeeper. 'Many of the goals I went on to score in the 1951-52 season stemmed from what the papers invariably described as "typical Dooley bursts down the middle."' he said.

Brown also put pressure on in training, knocking balls in quick succession in front of Dooley, from the left and the right, so as to improve his balance and co-ordination, and first time kicking ability. Brown's guidance continued on the match days, too, often providing him with advice on where he had gone wrong in the game. 'I doubt if anyone did more to encourage my development and improve my game,' Dooley recalled of his tutor.

Starting with the Barnsley match in October 1951, he then went on a remarkable run in the Wednesday side. A goal against Queens Park Rangers demonstrated that his performance three weeks before was not a fluke; five in the second half against Notts County that he might be something very special. In the seven games after that came 16 more, among them each of the four in the win against Everton that took Wednesday to the top of the league for the first time that season. Very quickly Dooley became a hero of Hillsborough and there was talk of an England call-up. Despite a few setbacks in the New Year, when the derby was lost to United and Bradford Park Avenue put them out of the FA Cup, Wednesday, helped significantly by Dooley's goals, were on course for promotion.

He soon became the subject of attention from outside Sheffield, some of it unkind. Was he a flash in the pan? Was his style too ungainly and awkward, based too much on speed and physical strength rather than real technical ability? 'I think that most people in the game accepted and applauded the fact that I was simply using the best use of my strengths,' he said. 'They knew I played hard but fair . . . I would run, I was fast, and once I was on my way, if a defender stood there I would knock him down . . . Naturally I took a lot of verbal stick from opposition supporters at away grounds.'

Promotion was eventually secured in 1951-52, Dooley's record standing at an astounding 47 goals from 31 appearances. Expectations for the next season were fairly high. Wednesday stuttered though, collecting only one point from their first five games. Dooley took a month before he managed to score. Soon he was dropped from the side. The First Division, he found, was a much tougher environment than the Second.

He decided that the best way to rediscover his goalscoring touch was to play in the reserves. Eric Taylor agreed and added Dooley to the line-up for the next reserve game at Hillsborough against Sheffield United. When word spread round the city a crowd of nearly 10,000 turned up to watch him score two in a 3-1 win. He attributed that sudden change of fortunes simply to the psychological effect of reverting to his old pair of football boots. The next week, he bettered his haul with a hat-trick against Liverpool reserves.

The success of these two appearances earned him a recall to the first team. Though he failed to score against Tottenham, he managed a strike in a 2-0 victory against Middlesbrough in September. After that the team went on a ten match unbeaten run that lifted them off the bottom of the table. While not as prolific as before, by February Dooley had notched 16 and sat top of the scoring charts with Bolton's Nat Lofthouse.

The critics who had accused him of lacking technique now had a new-found appreciation for him. The hard work he had put in with Alan Brown had paid off. 'Dooley's recent form had shown how studiously he was adding to his physical advantages a keener positional sense, neater ball control, and a more elastic understanding with his colleagues', wrote *The Guardian*. No one, however, knew what tragedy lay ahead.

***

Valentine's Day 1953 was a horrid day. Heavy snow in the region had blocked major roads to the extent the Wednesday players had to make their way through the Pennine hills to Preston by rail. Although most of the snow had been cleared from the Deepdale pitch, it was still icy and dangerous come kick off. The hosts worked well to beat their visitors, harrying and stifling them while holding a high defensive line to thwart Dooley's 'fearless' bursting advances. 'Preston played the offside game very effectively', recalled Dooley. 'To beat it we had this move worked out. Whoever got the ball had to release it very quickly, before the Preston defence could move up. Albert Quixall released the ball from well back, and I chased it.' The resulting clash with the North End goalkeeper would end Dooley's career.

'George Thompson, the Preston keeper, hesitated and then came out . . . I'd run from the halfway line . . . I connected with the ball just as George stuck his leg out and caught me just above the ankle.' In one cruel moment, Dooley's life was altered forever.

After two days confined to a hospital bed it was discovered his potted broken leg had become infected by gangrene. There was no choice but to amputate. 'I thought my world had collapsed,' said Dooley, 'football was my life. So when I lost my leg I thought, "Well, I might as well snuff it because I've not got a lot to live for."' Public sympathy was enormous. Together the *Sheffield Telegraph* and *Star* started a Shilling Fund that raised over £2,700. It bought a house for him and his new wife. Two years later his testimonial at Hillsborough drew a crowd of 55,000 people. It was a match that coincided with the official opening of the ground's new floodlights. Beforehand the lights had been set to half power. As Dooley walked onto the pitch, they turned to full. A gala send off.

Life moved on and job offers came. The chance to run a Stones pub (turned down); a 12-month contract with a national newspaper as a match reporter (accepted). He then took a job as a telephonist at Gunstone's Bakery. He stayed there for ten years, rising through the ranks. Importantly, he maintained his contacts at Wednesday, in particular with Eric Taylor, who offered him and Hugh Swift (another player whose career had been cut short by injury) the opportunity of working part-time with the club's junior team. Almost a decade after the Deepdale game, a first tentative step back into football. In 1962 he once again became a full-time employee of the Owls. A Development Fund had been set-up to raise money for the club and Dooley was chosen as its organiser. Then, when Danny Williams was sacked as manager in early '71 Dooley was the surprise choice as his replacement.

The offer was irresistible, putting him back at the club's centre. Wednesday were having a bad time in the Second Division and the board hoped that Dooley, as a powerful, imposing figure, could be their talisman again and reverse the decline. Attendances at Hillsborough had dropped to around 12,000 and the place needed a lift. But with limited experience, would he have the necessary skills required of a manager? 'My approach', he said not long into the job, 'has been the same as it would be in any situation. I treat the players as I would like to be treated if I was one of them. I want to be firm, but fair. That's how it must be, there's no other way.'

He brought in players he thought could entertain the dwindling Wednesday crowd. Midfielder Peter Eustace, a member of the 1966 FA Cup final team, came back from West Ham and Willie Henderson, an old-fashioned winger and Scotland international, was also signed. Henderson soon endeared himself to the fans with his skilful and confident displays. 'Willie was like a breath of fresh air, a wonderful tonic on and off the field,' remembered Dooley. 'He had a terrific rapport with his team-mates and several of the lads hero-worshipped Willie as much as any of the supporters.'

After securing Second Division status at the end of his first season, Dooley began the next in promising fashion. 11 games in and Wednesday led the table. That challenge soon faded, however, not helped by a goalkeeping crisis around March. Dooley lost both his senior keepers, Peter Springett and Peter Grummitt, to injury and as the transfer deadline had passed, the League refused permission for an emergency replacement to be brought in. Trevor Pearson, a local amateur called up from the reserves, was used instead. The closing form of that season was not good, but Dooley remained positive, 'When I viewed the situation in the context of the circumstances I didn't feel we had done too badly,' he remembered. 'I reached the end of the first [full] season convinced we had made more progress than the statistics suggested and was confident that all we needed was a bit of fine tuning.'

1973-74 began as poorly as the previous season had ended. By December Wednesday were struggling near the bottom of the table. Attendances had once again dwindled. In October a virus had swept through the club and over the next two months the squad was decimated when more than 15 senior players were affected. 'At one stage I had thirteen players available for selection, including two goalkeepers,' he said. 'I couldn't honestly say that all those capable of standing were really fit. When I look back on that painful phase I cannot help but feel I made the wrong decision in choosing to play down the depth of the crisis we faced. Frankly even some of the directors seemed unable to comprehend the extent of the problem.'

Dooley was sacked on Christmas Eve. Understandably devastating, it wasn't entirely unexpected. Earlier that month chairman Dr Andrew Stephen had departed along with board member Keith Gardiner. Both Dooley and the secretary Eric Taylor were wary of the changes brought by the new chairman Matt Sheppard and the board members Bert McGee and Roy Whitehead. Dooley in particular was left in the cold as to what was going on in the boardroom. 'I don't know what their thinking was . . . The sudden changes in the boardroom had created a mood in which the new regime no doubt felt that they had to act decisively and quickly. The irony is that whether I was unlucky or not to lose my job, it would have long been forgotten . . . if the board had chosen a different moment to sack me. As it is, for many Wednesdayites and in the club's history, Christmas Eve will forever be synonymous with my sacking.' After attending one match in 1976, he vowed never to return to Hillsborough again, the pain of how he was treated too real, and only relented on derby day 1992.

He then turned to the other side of the city, returning to football administration when he accepted an offer from United to become their commercial manager. He went on to become a director then chief executive, before retiring in 1996. Three years after that he was persuaded back to take over as chairman of the football club. In 2003 Dooley was awarded an MBE for services to football. He interviewed Neil Warnock, the manager who eventually would return the club to the Premier League.

As a player Dooley had come to and left the game a boy, his flame burning brightly and quickly. 63 games, 63 goals. When he died in 2008, aged 78, the people of the city paid warm tribute. 'Derek was Sheffield's greatest ever sporting legend', said United's chairman Kevin McCabe, 'one of only a few people who achieved the quite incredible feat of winning the utmost respect of football supporters from both sides of the Sheffield divide.' When the sweeping new Shalesmoor road was completed later that year one part was renamed Derek Dooley Way – the link from Hillsborough and Wednesday to central Sheffield and United. Today a smiling, waving statue of him stands outside Bramall Lane.

5

Nigel Worthington

1984-1994
417 appearances

Along with being among the proudest moments of any footballer's career, an international call earns great respect for that player's club – sending the signal that they can produce and nurture an individual of the highest quality. For Wednesday the emergence of such a player has been somewhat of a rarity. Only a few have become active internationals while at Hillsborough, fewer have gone on to collect more than a handful of caps. Of note were Ron Springett, England's goalkeeper for 33 games between 1959 and '66, and Nigel Worthington, the Northern Ireland full-back who earned 50 caps over his ten years as a Wednesday man.

Between 1984 and 1994 Worthington featured in two promotion seasons for the club, played in the League Cup success of '91 and contributed to the double run to Wembley two years later. He was part of two distinct Wednesday sides, Howard Wilkinson's tough, up and coming outfit, and Ron Atkinson and Trevor Francis' more cultured attacking force. Throughout those periods he delivered consistently reliable performances down the left of the pitch. Despite his slight frame, he satisfied both the defensive and distributive functions required of a top level full-back, confident and adventurous on the ball while upright, strong and expert in the tackle. Endearingly named 'Irish' by the fans, the grey haired defender excelled at the club and quickly became a club great.

In May 1983, after five full seasons in charge of Wednesday, Jack Charlton resigned as manager. The Owls had come sixth in the Second

Division when promotion had been expected. After failed attempts were made to lure Nottingham Forest's Brian Clough and Watford's Graham Taylor to the club, the little known Howard Wilkinson was brought in from Notts County. A Wednesday player in the '60s, he was now a promising and determined young manager who had built his reputation at County, coaching the side to the First Division under the guidance of elder statesman Jimmy Sirrel. Wilkinson's appointment, if not expected, was fitting; an ex-player and fan with the skills to deliver using only limited resources. He was ready for the fresh challenge Wednesday would bring

With time running out before the start of the new season, and with little money to spend on new players, Wilkinson had to make best with what he had inherited. From the beginning it was evident he would adopt a different strategy to his predecessor Charlton, even more rigid, even more disciplined and more tactically minded. His approach was based on a high work ethic, an almost unrivalled level of fitness (certainly in that division) combined with just enough flair and skill to overturn more talented opposition. Under him Wednesday were the fittest, strongest and best organised outfit in the league. As a consequence his team could maintain a high intensity game for 90 minutes, outlasting even the most formidable opposition.

Wilkinson's Wednesday played a 5-2-3 formation. The wing-backs Lawrie Madden and Mel Sterland were deployed either side of three central defenders, Mark Smith, Mick Lyons and Peter Shirtliff. Two midfielders, Gary Megson (son of Don) and Gary Shelton, sat in front of them. While three strikers, Tony Cunningham or John Pearson, Imre Varadi and Gary Bannister, worked a line across the top of the pitch.

Despite the manager's restrictions in the transfer market, imposed initially through time but then through a shortage of cash, Wilkinson soon realised he had to make a change at left-back. Lawrie Madden was more naturally a centre-back but had been used on the left for much of the season. Although he had equipped himself well, the feeling was that to best deploy the wing-back system someone different was required – namely, a player of similar pace and engine to Mel Sterland, who operated with great effect on the opposite side of the field.

The answer was Worthington. In 1981 Wilkinson had paid

£125,000 to bring him to Notts County from the Northern Ireland side Ballymena. 'Howard was at County when I first signed and I'd spent two years with him,' says Worthington. 'I had a good relationship with him and the moment I knew he was interested I couldn't get to Sheffield quick enough.'

'Working with Howard and knowing the way he worked I was very comfortable with that. County needed the money and from a career point of view it was a very good move. Wednesday were a big club and seemed on the up. The potential crowd size and everything . . . the whole thing sold itself. A fantastic club. It was very much a feeling in the right way.'

Worthington slotted into the side well, complementing Sterland on the right. Both were defenders who could prevent the opposition from playing but who had the ability to attack. Importantly as well, their defending capabilities up the field meant the ball could often be retrieved in an attacking position, thereby switching the play from back to front in an instant. 'Mel had fantastic energy up and down that side. I was very fit and full of running, too. I did my bit defensively but could do the attacking as well. We were a good match for each other.'

Quickly he managed to cement his place in the first team. 'You always need solid individuals', says Howard Wilkinson, 'people who are role models. And though Nigel didn't say much to begin with, he was just that. He was on time, did his work, was conscientious about everything and was coachable. He listened and learned, and had the determination to improve himself. That aspect of his nature particularly impressed me.'

By the time Worthington arrived at the club Wednesday were well on their way to promotion, though results through Christmas 1983 temporarily undermined their chances of an automatic promotion place. A Boxing Day defeat to Grimsby was followed by a home loss to Middlesbrough, and a draw at Carlisle ended their long period at the top of the table. In late January they faced promotion rivals Chelsea at Stamford Bridge. With much riding on the occasion, Wednesday began direct and purposeful. An early shot from Gary Megson was saved marvellously by Eddie Niedzwiecki in the Chelsea goal, then Gary Bannister's effort was cleared off the line by Nigel Spackman. But it was Chelsea who took the lead, Mickey Thomas on his debut.

He then got another, 2-0.

In the second half Pat Nevin pounced on the ball after a Martin Hodge fumble to make it 3-0. Wednesday came back with a couple of goals , but it was too late. The 3-2 defeat held them in second place and meant they would play catch-up for the rest of the season.

New arrival Worthington played in all but one of the last 15 games of '83-84. Wednesday won ten of these, conceded just nine and managed to hold on to their promotion place. They lost just once at home and won ten times away, regularly grinding down their opponents before nicking a goal to take the points. In fact, around half of their wins came by a single goal, among them the 1-0 victory at Newcastle in the run-in (Gary Shelton's brilliant overhead kick the difference that day), and Crystal Palace at Hillsborough (Mel Sterland's penalty securing the long-awaited promotion). After a 14 year absence, Wednesday were back in the First Division.

One week after the season ended Worthington made his debut for Northern Ireland in Swansea against Wales. The team was in one of its most successful periods having famously upset hosts Spain 1-0 in the World Cup two years earlier. In the lead up to the 1986 World Cup in Mexico Worthington became a regular for Billy Bingham's team and started two of their three group games in the tournament. Over the next 11 years he played for his country 66 times, 50 of those coming while with Wednesday.

In 1984-85 the Owls were able to pull off surprise wins against Liverpool (2-0 at Anfield) and Manchester United (2-1 at Old Trafford). At one point they reached as high as second in the table. Playing largely the same way as in the previous promotion season, Wilkinson's team, it appeared, adjusted to the higher division with ease. They eventually finished eighth, Worthington playing in all but four of the league fixtures that year. 'There was a great team spirit and camaraderie in the side at the time,' he says. 'We were fit and committed, and what we achieved that year was fantastic.'

The following year brought further improvement, fifth place this time, the nine-game unbeaten run that began in September helping the club to their highest placing since 1961. If not for the ban on English teams following the Heysel disaster, it would have meant European football the next season. They also advanced well in the FA Cup. Wins over West Brom, Leyton Orient and Derby County set-up a quarter-final with fellow league high flyers West Ham United.

At this stage Worthington's long-term position in the side was under threat. Glynn Snodin, a left-wing-back with a good goalscoring record, had been signed from Doncaster Rovers the previous summer. An equivalent to the marauding Sterland for the left-hand side, Snodin got in to the team when Worthington had earlier been injured. While he never managed to repeat the scoring exploits of his time with Rovers – just one goal in his two years at Wednesday – he provided Worthington with a great challenge at left-back.

'I had no issue with Glynn's signing,' says Worthington. 'He is a super lad, and bringing in new players is part of the manager's job. Competition is a very good thing. I had a few bumps and knocks and Glynn got a good chance in the team. When I was back the two of us played in the team for a period of time, before eventually I slotted back in to my usual position.'

'To his credit,' remembers Howard Wilkinson, 'Nigel did what you would have expected of him. He took it on the chin, knuckled down, turned up for training, did his work, was as conscientious as ever, and saw off the opposition.'

For the West Ham quarter-final, Snodin was injured so Worthington (before having fully seen off his rival) took his place. It was his first match since New Year's Day 1986 and he got the winner in the 2-1 win, a low, hard deflected strike sending Wednesday through to the semis.

The reigning First Division champions Everton were next at Villa Park. Worthington, though, missed out through injury, taken off at home to Liverpool the week before after he had hurt his knee and fallen awkwardly following a challenge from Steve McMahon. 'It was around the halfway line,' Worthington explains. 'I did my left medial ligament which put me out for about a month. I was hugely disappointed that I wasn't able to play in the semi. It was a big disappointment not to be involved. With Wembley looming it would have been the biggest moment of my career up to then.'

In the opening exchanges of the game Wednesday looked most likely to score, Gary Megson having two early headed attempts on goal. In the second half, the score still 0-0, ping pong football emerged as Everton changed their strategy to match the Sheffielders' more direct and physical style.

After a battering in the first half, Everton came back firmly into the game and took the lead through Alan Harper who lobbed Martin Hodge from the corner of the box. The Owls then countered, Snodin's first time cross headed on by Paul Hart for Carl Shutt to flick past Bobby Mimms. 1-1 and Wednesday were back in the game.

They had a few more chances, but there would be no more goals in normal time. It would be Everton who got the winner in extra time, Graeme Sharp shooting first time from a diagonal ball to send the Merseysiders to Wembley. 'Some of the hardest men in football were reduced to tears in the dressing room', said one Wednesday player afterwards.

In the years after 1985-86 Wednesday slid from fifth in the First Division to 13th, then as Wilkinson struggled to improve his squad, 11th. By 1988, having experienced continued pressure from the increasingly frustrated fan base, and with little funds to help him build on what he had achieved up to then, the manager left to join Leeds United where more money was provided for players and success followed. His assistant Peter Eustace took charge of Wednesday for a few months but his time was unsuccessful. After him came Ron Atkinson.

Atkinson immediately transformed the atmosphere of the club. Though his team suffered relegation at the end of 1989-90, his first full season in charge, he subsequently set the club on a far more positive course. He changed the training regime – rigid to more relaxed, with days off given to the players – and the team's style of play – direct to fluid. Thanks to the Wednesday chairman Dave Richards pledging to carry on paying the same good wages to the squad following relegation, batting away approaches for their signatures from other teams, the unit was kept together for the crucial upcoming promotion challenge.

Through the signings made by Atkinson, like John Sheridan, Carlton Palmer and John Harkes in midfield, Wednesday were able to attack smoothly, providing great entertainment for the fans and good ammunition for the finishers, David Hirst and Paul Williams. In defence new faces replaced old. Mel Sterland was allowed to join Glasgow Rangers for £800,000, some of which was spent on the Swedish right-back Roland Nilsson, £375,000 from Gothenburg, and Peter Shirtliff, a centre-back who cost £500,000 to bring him back to the club from Charlton. Later Viv Anderson was added on a free transfer from Manchester United, supplementing an already strong group of defenders which had at its centre the captain and 'heart and soul of the Wednesday side,' Nigel Pearson. It was an elegantly formidable team.

Yet Worthington may not have been involved. After Wednesday failed to win any of their first five games of 1989-90 he made a transfer request – despite having signed a new contract only the previous season which reputedly had made him one of the best paid players in the First Division. He expected better of the side in which he played and wanted out. Atkinson was happy to let him go, but only when an adequate replacement could be found. That November he spent £400,000 on Swindon's Phil King, a solid left-back who, like Worthington, had a good attacking instinct.

Ultimately Worthington stayed on, so Atkinson shrewdly opted to use the two in tandem down the left. If not by design, Worthington in front of King brought happy results for the side. 'It was good for me when Phil arrived,' Worthington later recalled. 'I did think he was signed to replace me but that's when your inner soul comes out. I've never had anything against another player coming in for the same place in the side. Its healthy . . . keeps you on your toes . . . That's when you think, "Right, I'll bloody show you."'

The general style of Atkinson's side saw the play spread wonderfully across the expanse of the Hillsborough pitch, taking advantage of the significant available space to create chance after chance. 'Play, play, play was all he wanted us to do,' says Worthington. He and King had their part in it. When one attacked the other dropped back to cover, thereby maintaining the back-four. Together they offered a more robust defensive barrier than the traditional full-back and winger pairing ever could, doubling up against oncoming dangers. Meanwhile, in attack, the music of their overlapping provided an underestimated threat, two defenders each able to advance effectively, in tandem and with surprise.

'Obviously my number one position was at full-back,' he says. 'But Ron was quite clever in playing us both. We'd looked at it in training. He thought it would work. He stuck us together and it did. Phil would come flying past me and do his attacking thing and me, as a natural full-back, would sit in there and deal with things until he came back.

Likewise he would do the same if I attacked. It was a situation I really enjoyed.

'We had a fantastic relationship, too. We got on well and that's important because if you get on with people something will work out. Phil and I on that left side between us were as good as anything in the league.'

Both started the 1991 League Cup final win over Manchester United, Worthington protecting the back four from left midfield, working with King to thwart the attacks from the Reds. It was Worthington's free kick, a lofted ball into United's box that was headed out by Gary Pallister, which fell into the path of John Sheridan and brought the winning goal. 'The ball had floated in from my kick. When it left John's foot there was a lot of hesitation and expectation. It was baited breath as the ball headed towards goal. Is it going wide? Thankfully it banged in to the post and rattled in to the back of the net. There was a lull in the atmosphere for a moment when you looked to see if it was going in. But it did. In you go, thank you very much. The noise was phenomenal. A fantastic feeling.'

The following season, 1991-92, King was voted the club's Player of the Year as Wednesday came third behind Leeds and Manchester United. Unfortunately he missed much of the next season through injury, and when the winger Andy Sinton arrived for £2.75 million from QPR, King was loaned to Notts County. Worthington then replaced him at left-back. King later joined Aston Villa where his injuries returned. He went on to make only a handful of appearances for the Birmingham club.

Worthington himself would soon be out of Hillsborough as well, sold to Leeds in 1994, joining up with Howard Wilkinson for a third time. 'I had 10 great years at Wednesday, probably the highlight of my career,' says Worthington. 'But Howard came calling again. I had spoken to Trevor Francis about a longer term contract, but he wasn't comfortable in doing that. Howard offered me two years, so I went there.' The fee of £375,000, set by the pre-Bosman tribunal that determined the value of out-of-contract players, was well short of Francis's £1.3 million valuation. His replacement, the pedestrian fellow Ulsterman Ian Nolan, cost £1.5 million from Tranmere Rovers. He never even came close to matching the quality of his predecessor.

Worthington stayed at Leeds for two seasons before moving

on to First Division Stoke City. His first managerial role came soon after that – player-manager of Blackpool. He spent a couple of years there followed by assistant manager postings with Wilkinson and the England under-21's; then with Sammy McIlroy and Northern Ireland. When Bryan Hamilton left Norwich in 2000, the club turned to Worthington, who had been Hamilton's assistant. Within a few years he had taken them to the Premier League. He later worked for Milan Mandaric in his pre-Wednesday days at Leicester City, keeping them in the Championship in 2007. Then he took the Northern Ireland job, replacing the outgoing Lawrie Sanchez, taking his country through two qualifying campaigns (World Cup 2010 and Euro 2012) before resigning in late 2011.

On three occasions he might have taken over as manager of Wednesday. First in 2001 after the departure of Peter Shreeves. Again in 2006, shortly after he had left Norwich (Brian Laws ultimately given the job). And again in 2009 when Laws was sacked. Despite the speculation, however, Nigel Worthington as Wednesday manager never materialised. On the first and third occasion he was still employed by Norwich and Northern Ireland; on the second, while apparently in the running, he turned down the club's advance. 'The biggest time was just after I'd left Norwich,' he says. 'After 24 years of playing and managing I'd decided to give myself six months off, to relax and have a bit of family time. But then Wednesday came on and asked me if I wanted to speak to them. I thought about it, but at that time it just wasn't right. I continued with my promise to have that break. That's the closest I came to the job.

'The other couple of times it came up I was in a job, and when I'm in a job I like to stay loyal. I would love to be the manager of Sheffield Wednesday one day. Whether that will happen or not, I don't know.' Considering the lack of success enjoyed by other former Wednesday players who have taken the job over the past 15 years or so – Danny Wilson, who failed in the Premier League and Chris Turner, who failed in the First and Second Division – it may not have been such a great move anyway. The role's high expectation and, until 2010 when Milan Mandaric bought the club, lack of resources, has done greater damage than good to managerial reputations. At least Worthington's 10 years of excellence as a player for the club have not been allowed to dim because of it.

6

Howard Wilkinson

1962-66 (player)
22 appearances, 2 goals
1983-88 (manager)
2010-11 (chairman)

On being appointed Wednesday manager in June 1983, Howard Wilkinson walked into the club that meant so much to him and surveyed the task before him. There were just five weeks to go before the start of the season and he knew little of his new team or backroom staff. To be fully prepared for his first game, away to Swansea City, he had to work fast. Though confident in his abilities, the challenge of managing the club he supported as a boy and played for briefly as a young man was huge; his new employer's wanted promotion from the Second Division as quickly as possible. In those weeks he set in place the coaching regime that would provide the springboard for success. It won him the respect of the players and fans, along with the ire of the national press.

'I came in for the first time and thought, where do I start?' says Wilkinson. 'I remember thinking; I don't know the first thing about the players. I was ringing them up asking them to come in so I could get their faces in my head, to try and find out something about them. At the same time I had to put together the pre-season training schedule and work out how we were going to play. I knew I had two years to get it right. If we were still in the Second Division by then it would have been "on your bike."'

When his Wednesday team took to the field in South Wales on the opening day of 1983-84, it already bore the hallmarks of the typical Howard Wilkinson side. Strong, disciplined, with an engine that could sustain a haranguing pressing style. They won at the Vetch Field that day, captain Mick Lyons heading in Gary Megson's corner. It started a run that would keep them near the summit of the table all season, concluding with the promotion that had been demanded. It was a campaign short on flaws, underpinned and driven by the 'Wilkinson Way.'

That style was an adaptation of the POMO (Position of Maximum Opportunity) method adopted by several other clubs of the time. The ball would be pressed quickly and relentlessly upfield, mostly on the flanks and in the penalty area, often after a long pass. These were areas where, logically, it was viewed that most goalscoring opportunities were created.

POMO was developed by Charles Reep, a Navy Lieutenant who began objectively analysing football matches in the early '50s. He argued that as 80% of goals came from moves of three or less passes, the ball should be moved forward as quickly as possible in order to maximise the number of scoring chances. In the '80s the FA's Coaching Director Charles Hughes furthered the theory, stating that five passes or less was a more suitable number. Wilkinson, Dave Bassett at Wimbledon and Graham Taylor at Watford achieved great success through the tactic, helping their respective teams sail up the Football League in the 1980s.

Wilkinson first became aware of POMO while manager of Notts County. After their promotion to the First Division in 1980, he realised that in order to compete at that higher level his players needed an edge. They were, he says, good on the ball but opposition teams quickly learned how to counter their attacks. They needed a change. 'It was on a wet night in Bolton,' he remembers, 'I drove up with Jimmy Sirrel [County's Director of Football] to watch a cup match against Watford. I saw it being used in a very successful and attractive way. Lots of attacking play, time in the opponents' defending third, crosses from good wide players, lots of shots, lots of goals. I thought, why not?'

At Wednesday the ball would be sent quickly from defence, often bypassing the midfield who were required to press and support the three strikers working a line across the field. They would work along the front, chasing passes, closing down defenders and making chances. 'I used to explain that in a sense the three were tied together by a rope which stretched two thirds the width of the pitch. If the ball was on the left, one had to be wide on the left and so did the other two. The far right striker had to be about level with the far post. The rope is pulling you. If we lost the ball, if it was on their left, you had to get over. The rope is pulling you.' It contributed to the overall strategy of pinning back the other team, leading to a relentlessness volley of attacks and chances.

Sheffield Wednesday 2 Chelsea 1
Second Division, Hillsborough, 17 September 1983

To some the legacy of Reep and Hughes was to produce footballers that lacked technical skills and were ignorant of prettier alternative playing strategies. 'As you watch the average Wednesday player,' wrote one paper of Wednesday in the 80s, for instance . . . 'over-developed torso, under-developed between the ears – interminably pumping the ball into the air like a mortar launcher, you feel overwhelmed by a prehistoric nightmare that can only get worse.' And today their ideas continue to come under criticism. Yet, as the Football League supports 92 professional clubs, the less skilful and flair-filled teams will have to find another way to compete. When utilised correctly, POMO helped bring results for Wednesday and those who played in a similar way. 'I don't blame people for being disciples of the knowledge they generated,' says Wilkinson.

Central to the success of POMO was a high level of fitness. Wilkinson revolutionised a fitness regime which had been *comparatively* lax under his predecessor Jack Charlton. The stories of Wilkinson having his players embark on long runs in harsh conditions – and of unconditioned players struggling to keep up – are well known. But they worked. It was a well thought out strategy that achieved the fitness levels required for a 90 minute game of football. 'I stole the idea from my former manager Alan Brown,' explains Wilkinson. 'The training ground at Wednesday was not the most attractive place to be five days a week, and we were on the edge of some glorious and interesting countryside, so I thought it was a good idea.' Though tough, it was never running for the sake of running. 'I hadn't just picked it out of the sky,' he says. 'It had a scientific basis and was part of our strategy for winning matches. As I explained to the players, the first 15 minutes was a warm up, the final was a warm down, the middle represented the time you were on the pitch. In a match you only work for an hour, even though the game lasts 90 minutes. So it allowed the players to know, psychologically, that they could cover anything that was thrown at them during a match.' Almost half of the club's victories in 1983-84 came through a single goal. That fitness was vital for killing off those tight games, lasting to the end, concentrating to the fullest.

After promotion that year, with their play unchanged but the standard of players improved, Wednesday did well in the First Division. Lee Chapman, an endeavouring centre-forward, replaced Tony Cunningham, sold to Manchester City for £100,000, and Brian

Marwood, a promising player bought from Hull for £115,000, replaced Gary Bannister who had gone to Queens Park Rangers for £200,000. Though initially struggling with the change from Third to First Division football, Marwood soon adapted to the pace. He lay slightly deeper and freer than his predecessor Bannister, and by drifting into dangerous areas he brought a new, arguably improved dynamic to the Wednesday side. Other incomings included Mark Chamberlain, Glynn Snodin and Andy Blair, the latter replacing Gary Megson who went the other way in a swap deal with Nottingham Forest.

Unsurprisingly 1984-85 was not the stroll the promotion campaign had been, with Wilkinson's team often finding themselves penned back by the division's better forwards. Nevertheless, Wednesday still managed to start well, a 3-1 home victory at Nottingham Forest along with excellent wins at Anfield and Old Trafford showing they were a worthy addition to the division. In the end they finished eighth.

They improved dramatically the following season. Mentally tougher and more aware of the physical needs of the league, Wednesday began brightly and after five games sat second in the table. By November, still in the top three, they faced a tough test with the visit of Manchester United, unbeaten in their first 15 matches of the season. In front of a crowd of 48,000 at Hillsborough the Owls gloriously came away 1-0 winners, Lee Chapman's header from a corner beginning United's championship collapse (after that they won only 9 of their remaining 26 matches). Though Wednesday also fell away from the title race, the momentum of their FA Cup run, climaxing in the semi-final defeat to Everton at Villa Park, helped them finish well. Only two games were lost out of their last ten – sadly one of them was the Everton game – as fifth place was achieved.

***

Wilkinson's association with Wednesday had begun aged 18 when, after being spotted playing as a winger at amateur level, he was signed as an apprentice by manager Vic Buckingham. His parents had encouraged him to go to university, but football was his choice. 'Wednesday offered me a contract,' he says, 'so did Leeds United. Vic came to our house, as did Leeds' Don Revie, and I have to say Revie's pitch was much more forceful. His motivation and enthusiasm was better than Vic's, so was the money Leeds were offering. But being a Wednesday fan, I went with my emotions.'

Under Buckingham and his successor Alan Brown (a great teacher in Wilkinson's eyes) he had only a small role in the first team. His first appearances came in 1964-65. A few more followed the year after. But eventually he dropped out of the picture. 'Bottom line,' he says, 'I wasn't good enough to be picked every week.' He moved to Third Division Brighton in search of more regular opportunities. The change in environment came as a shock. 'Brighton were still locked in to traditional practices, the opposite of Wednesday. The manager [Archie MacAulay] believed training was a walk on the beach, a few stretches, then out for a steak.' But at least he got more games.

When he was 26 Wilkinson decided he wanted to become a manager and one of the coaches at Brighton, Steve Burtenshaw, was running a coaching course. 'Steve came in the dressing room one day and pinned a note on the notice board advertising a preliminary course.' With little else to do with his evenings, Wilkinson went along. 'I was hooked. By the end of the second session I was thinking to myself, this is making sense of something that sometimes seems like a mystery. It's actually about applying some logic to the game.'

He left Brighton in 1970 and enrolled on a Physical Education degree. He then became a teacher, playing for and coaching Boston United part time. Managed by fellow Sheffielder and Wednesday fan Jim Smith, Boston were going through one of their better periods and with them Wilkinson won two non-League titles. His first full-time role came with Notts County in 1980. There he worked as coach under Jimmy Sirrel who, in his role as Director of Football, took a less hands on approach to training, leaving that to Wilkinson.

After helping keep County in the First Division the young manager began attracting interest from other clubs. West Brom offered him the manager's job, but he turned it down believing his next club should be one which had the resources and potential to compete with the best in the country. Not long after that the Wednesday job came along. 'I'd got a phone call from a good friend, Frank O'Gorman [a director at Sheffield United]. I was about to leave for a holiday in Spain and he said, "would you fancy being manager of Sheffield

Wednesday? I was speaking to someone at the club and your name cropped up."' Wilkinson, the Wednesday fan and former player, of course, accepted.

***

Despite the impressive finish in 1985-86, Wednesday seemed to lack sufficient technical ability to allow a complete abandonment of the long ball tactics that since promotion had worked so well for them. As a consequence, players who relied on the ball being played to their feet, like Mark Chamberlain, found to their frustration they were not receiving it as often as they would have liked due to the defenders' urge to hit the long ball. Blocked out of the game, such players would appear uninvolved and ineffective.

Wilkinson was well aware of the problem and went to some lengths to change the system. As one of his new signings, Paul Hart, recalled, 'At our first meeting he told me he felt some players were abusing the long-ball and hiding behind it, and said my brief was to add my experience to encourage a different approach. To a degree, it worked, but it was a culture shock for me when I came, because at Leeds and Forest we had defended deep, never played offside, and passed it.' 'After the 1986 semi-final . . . we switched to a back four and started working on centre halves-coming to the line and joining in', recalled Hart. 'I remember playing the ball into Brian Marwood's feet which surprised him because nobody had been doing that.'

The shift in style was taking time to be realised and the pressures of renewing the squad took its toll on Wilkinson. He was not helped by the club's choking transfer policy and wage structure that prohibited the big signings that may have propelled them to the very top (but at the same time may have damaged them financially). 'I wanted the Wednesday fans to know and understand my dilemma. But a sense of duty to my employers prevented me from publicly exposing a policy I knew in the long term was shortsighted. I explicitly recall on three separate occasions explaining at board meetings the imperative need to review financial planning, outlining the path I thought the club should be heading down.'

At Notts County he had been content to manage with few resources. But at Wednesday the reticence of the board to invest appeared to affect him. Not least because he unfairly developed a reputation for being unable to bring in the big name players. He realised that if the club were going to progress further, a far higher quality of player simply had to be sourced. 'I tried to persuade the board to change its philosophy, to give me more money to pay better players. But they wouldn't. I don't hold it against them. That's what the chairman believed, and Bert McGee was a very good chairman. Eventually I went in to the board meetings thinking it's just going to be more of the same.'

Wilkinson left Wednesday for Leeds United in October 1988. His frustrations with the situation at Wednesday had been kept relatively quiet and so the move came as a major surprise. Leeds were bottom of the Second while Wednesday were seventh in the First. The initial contact was made to Owls chairman Bert McGee who gave United permission to talk him. After a protracted negotiation period he agreed to the move. 'People were amazed, just amazed when I went to Leeds,' he says. 'The interview lasted about three weeks because I wanted to be sure their board were committed to understanding the pathway to success.'

At Leeds he enjoyed substantial backing to re-establish them as a force in English football. In his first season the wage bill of his Second Division team was £200,000 higher than Wednesday's (a substantial figure in those pre-Premier League days), and he was given £1.7 million net more to spend on transfers. An early signing was Gordon Strachan, made in direct competition with his old club. Believing they got their man, Wednesday were once again snubbed in favour of a more attractive financial package elsewhere. Leeds were promoted the following year (1989-90) and won the First Division in '92. That year their wage bill stood at £4.5 million. Wednesday, who finished third and had by now adopted a looser policy, still paid nearly £1 million less.

Through his time in Leeds Wilkinson repeatedly looked to players who had previously proved themselves for him at Hillsborough. To add to John Pearson and Glynn Snodin who were there when he arrived, signed by his predecessor Billy Bremner, Wilkinson in turn brought Carl Shutt, Lee Chapman, Imre Varadi, Mel Sterland and also Chris Turner on loan from Wednesday. In 1992 he returned to sign the young centre-backs David Wetherall and Jon Newsome.

Both made their mark in a Leeds shirt and perhaps upset the Owls' future defensive prospects. He later also bought Carlton Palmer (admittedly a post Wilkinson-era man) for a club record £2.9 million as a replacement for David Batty.

Five years after that title win Wilkinson left Elland Road. He went on to take a role with the FA as Technical Advisor. He encouraged the involvement of managers in the international set-up as preparation for potentially one day taking the England job, something he had experienced himself in the '80s. 'At that time I was a young whippersnapper,' he remembers. 'When Ron Greenwood got the job he invited me and some others, Bobby Robson, Brian Clough and Terry Venables to join him. He wanted a kind of Club England, wanted people involved throughout the system and supporting him in his work.' When Bobby Robson took over, he offered Wilkinson the role of assistant manager.' I turned it down because I wanted to earn my spurs at club level.'

He wanted it later though. 'When I was at Wednesday I was supposed to be the next England manager. And when I was at Leeds I was supposed to be the next England manager. It was not seen as the poisoned chalice it is now. If you were good at what you did, where did you go? So yes, I would have wanted the job.' And his time with England did come. In-between Glenn Hoddle and Sven Goran Eriksson's spells in the job Wilkinson was twice caretaker of the full team. On the first occasion he led England to a 2-0 loss to France at Wembley in 1999. Then, after Kevin Keegan resigned as manager in late 2000, he took charge again for a 0-0 away draw with Finland. After that he went on to spend a short, unsuccessful time with Sunderland, trying to help them off the bottom of the Premier League.

Seven years later he returned to Wednesday as Technical Adviser to the then chairman Lee Strafford. When Strafford resigned in 2010 he became interim chairman, tasked with keeping the club out of administration long enough for investment to be found that would clear the £33 million debt pile. It was not an easy time, he admits. 'It was one of the hardest periods of my life,' he says. 'People glibly talked about putting the club into administration, but that was something to be avoided at all costs. Doing that is not the right thing unless you absolutely have to . . .'

As rumours of various takeovers were sounded, mostly from suspicious consortiums that each came ultimately to nothing, some fans began to question whether Wilkinson and the Chief Executive Nick Parker were doing enough to attract investors. On one occasion they were accosted by a mob of supporters after a match at Hillsborough, interrupted and sworn at as they tried to answer their questions. 'It was just a struggle,' he says, 'complicated massively by all sorts of interrelated, fringe myths and fantasies, half truths and mistruths. You had people swearing at you, and you think, I've just spent ten months of my life, stopped the world and 24-7 dealt only with this.

'Quickly it became one of those very very clear situations, it became a matter of saving a life.' Every day the situation was getting deeper and solutions were becoming more desperate. Thankfully, though, the club was finally rescued from probable administration by former Portsmouth and Leicester owner Milan Mandaric. '[It's] one of the most important days in the recent history of our great club,' a relieved Wilkinson said at the time. 'Our trials and tribulations have been well documented, but I can now see a brighter future for Sheffield Wednesday.'

7

Jimmy Mullen

1970-1980
263 appearances

Boxing Day 1970 was a memorable day for Jimmy Mullen. Wednesday were struggling in the Second Division and travelled to Hull in desperate need of a win to stabilise their league position. It was a match the young debutant that afternoon will never forget. 'We were four-one up,' he remembers, 'with three minutes to go – and it finished four-all. If the referee had played another minute we'd have been beaten.' It was the first in a series of turbulent events that would mark Mullen's career as an Owl, a decade in which he rose from youth player to captain while the club struggled through a prolonged period of great instability.

Mullen was born in Jarrow, the north east town with a long and proud radical history. Once home to the famous Palmers Shipbuilding Company, it was one of many working towns that straddled the River Tyne all the way to Newcastle. In 1936 the closure of the shipyard prompted its workers to down tools and march to London in protest against poverty and unemployment. It was in this environment that early in his life Mullen's ability as a footballer would manifest itself.

Like many players of that era who would go on to become professionals, Mullen had a conventional childhood. 'I loved football. I was always out in the back lane on the streets, on the lanes of the terraced properties that led up from the shipyards, we played all day until darkness until when your mother came and dragged you off home.' On the wet, muddy north east playing fields he yearned to be at the centre of the play. 'I classified myself as a midfielder,' he says. 'I was all left foot, and some people thought I should play on the left wing, but I wanted to be on the ball all the time, to be at the centre of the action.' He soon impressed and was invited to play for local sides based in Bolden Colliery and South Shields. By 16 he had progressed to Hedworth Celtic in the under-18 regional league, an arena known for its physical, unforgiving teams. 'In the north east it was fine if you were a footballer, but if you couldn't handle the physical side of it you were quickly found out.'

Though aware that scouts would often come to watch matches at that level, it nonetheless came as a shock when Alec Barker, Wednesday's scout in the north east, turned up at his house one day. 'We'd seen Alec at the games and I recognised him immediately,' remembers Mullen. 'I was standing there shaking in my shoes.' After reassuring his parents that football was the career path he wanted to follow, he accepted Barker's offer of a trial game. 'I got injured in that match but had played well.' After a period of recuperation he was given a second chance. 'They didn't think I had the pace to be an attacking midfielder or a left winger so I played left centre-back. I'd won most of the headers and played the ball well. The week after I was offered an apprenticeship.'

Of course, the experiences of an apprenticeship footballer were vastly different in the 1960s to what they are now. Accommodation was basic. Mullen lived on Leppings Lane with Dennis Lymer, also from Jarrow, and along with their daily training, had to work for the club. Before a match day the seat covers on the North and South stands had to be folded neatly and packed away before being put back on the Monday morning. Other tasks included cleaning the senior players' boots and the toilets, laying out kit and repainting the stands each summer. There was strict discipline in place, each apprentice aware that if their work was not completed satisfactorily a punishment would soon follow.

A month after signing professionally, Mullen made his debut at Hull. Soon after that the manager Danny Williams was sacked, joining Alan Brown and Jack Marshall as the latest in a growing list of Wednesday bosses who had tried but failed to return the club to their success of the early '60s. Williams' final record was poor, just 17 wins in 18 months in charge. After relegation in 1969-70, with no sign of a return to the First Division, the axe fell. Yet although Williams' record was poor, he is remembered well by Mullen. 'He gave everything, stuck to his northern roots and could make us laugh,' he says. 'He was always "de-da" this and "de-da" that. He often used to say himself, "Won't be long 'til I'm on beach t'down Bournemouth."'

The appointment of Derek Dooley as Williams' successor came as a surprise in the city, his special connection to the club trumping all reservations of his suitability. Unlike his predecessor, he had no real coaching credentials so ceded those responsibilities to former Wednesday players Gerry Young and Ron Staniforth, though he was still a presence on the sidelines during training and matches, despite his disability. In Young in particular Dooley saw a senior player not long retired who could communicate easily with the players, so let him get on with it.

One of Mullen's earliest memories of Wednesday was watching the '66 FA Cup Final defeat to Everton. Of the players that day it was Young, a fellow Jarrow product, who caught Mullen's eye (possibly because of his failure to trap the ball that led to Everton's winner). Now at Wednesday, Mullen would be trained by Young on a daily basis. 'I remember he was sat on the bench once when we were playing Aston Villa. The Villa striker gave me an elbow and my nose was bleeding. Gerry said, "Welcome to the centre-halves' world." He was a big inspiration.' Also helpful to Mullen was the Welsh international Peter Rodrigues. 'I learnt a lot from him. After one loss in particular I was being pretty vocal, Peter came up to me and said "We're all hurting inside. There's no need for that. Sometimes it's best to just sit there and do nothing."'

In the main Wednesday performed somewhat unspectacularly in the league under Dooley. He had 16 games of the season left when he was brought in and, with no money to sign players, the best he could hope for was safety (something he achieved with a 15th place finish). 1971-72 saw a small improvement, one place higher than the last. But the team was inconsistent, wins by narrow margins and mixed runs meaning they never troubled the top reaches of the table. New players like John Holsgrove, Brian Joicey and Dave Clements played well, but it proved too early for the players to make much of an impact.

A welcome perk of that season was the arrival of Pele and Santos for their second match in a decade. It proved one of Mullen's most cherished memories as a player. 'I'll always remember that Tommy Craig said something to the referee at half-time. About a minute from the end, I was marking Pele from a free kick. Tommy came back into my position and shouted me to "get in the hole, get in the hole." Being a young dumpty idiot I left him. No sooner had he taken the kick, the ref blew his whistle, and Tommy grabbed Pele and got his shirt. If he had blown when I was marking him it would have been me that would have got it instead. It was probably the only time in his life that Tommy came back to his own penalty box.'

Dooley's third season proved as frustrating as the first two. While the team briefly flirted with top spot, they fell away to mid-table. And after three years in the Second Division, it seemed Wednesday might be losing sight of a return to the First.

'We just didn't see it coming,' Mullen recalls of Dooley's sacking on Christmas Eve 1973. 'Every Christmas before we went home we had a tray of sherry and port brought into the dressing room. The directors used to come in to say thanks and wish us a merry Christmas. But that year the trays were taken away and we were told that Derek had been let go. It was a complete shock.' The timing was shameful and, as Mullen says, considering that the team had spent much of the season in the top half, surprising. The team had been strengthened and the mood of the squad was said to have been positive. Going into early October they sat second, having briefly led the table the previous week after a 3-2 win at Hillsborough over Huddersfield. But then a virus gripped the club, costing Dooley up to 15 of his first team players at any one time. Their form collapsed and as a result he paid the price.

Replacing Dooley was Steve Burtenshaw, a man who was well recommended from his spells as coach at Brighton and Arsenal, who placed a strong emphasis on keeping possession. 'He called the ball the pill,' Mullen recalls. 'Run after the pill. Come on lad, look after the pill.' Under Burtenshaw, in pursuit of a winning formula, the line-up consistently changed, the only constant being his wish for his side to play in an attractive way. The players, however, didn't appear to possess the skill to implement his plans. 'It seemed to get worse,' says Mullen, 'and we had no luck.' The team would play well, have good possession, yet fail to create enough chances. Meanwhile their opponents, as so regularly is the case in such circumstances, would break, score and take the win, inflicting another narrow defeat on the Owls.

Though the team continued to struggle, Mullen was growing in stature as a player. He was playing more regularly and gaining appreciation among the Wednesday supporters as a hardworking member of the team. Other managers began to notice him. An enquiry was made by Ron Saunders at Aston Villa, but rejected by the club. 'If I'd gone to Villa, who knows where my career might have taken me?' He stayed and was relegated with Wednesday at the end of 1974-75, the faltering side finishing bottom of the Second Division having collected a measly 21 points. Like Dooley and Williams before him, Burtenshaw was sacked by the board. 'He was there one minute and gone the next,' recalls Mullen.

Now a Third Division club, there seemed no end to the prolonged fall which since the late '60s had enveloped the club. Attendances had collapsed below 10,000 after that disastrous relegation season and the club was losing £2,000 a week. A 'Save our Owls' campaign was launched by the *Star*, aimed at attracting back the crowds. Posters, badges, car stickers were produced in large quantities. But goodwill could not disguise the fact that what was required were improved results on the field.

'I used to walk down to the stadium with the fans,' says Mullen, 'and you could feel they thought that the club was in decline. It needed stability.' Succeeding Burtenshaw into the increasingly impossible manager's job was Len Ashurst, the former Sunderland full-back recruited from Gillingham as a young boss With a thin budget Ashurst faced a huge task; instantly he was under pressure to find the required voice to inspire and find the right blend of players for Wednesday. Years before Mullen had watched his new manager play at Roker Park. Now he was interacting with him on a daily basis and, after a rocky start, would eventually become his captain. 'Len was a no-nonsense type. Discipline was everything. He knew exactly what he wanted from his players.'

Yet after losing his place to Gordon Simmonite, who made his one and only appearance for Wednesday away to Chesterfield, Mullen began to question his future. 'Ashurst told me that I was not playing as well as I could.' He requested a transfer but was turned down. Then, curiously, within a fortnight he was given the armband. 'I'll always remember that. It was a midweek game. We turned up, he pulled me into the trainer's room and told me he wanted to make me captain. I couldn't believe it. It was something I'd dreamt about my entire career.'

Wednesday continued to struggle in the league. Ashurst had only been able to bring in one other staff member, the fitness coach Tony Toms, and as such bore most of the responsibility for the team's fortunes. He took the training, did the scouting, and the managing. As the last game of 1975-76 approached, midweek against Southend, there was a feeling round Hillsborough that the club might drop to the Fourth Division. 'I remember turning up for the Southend game and thinking, I'm the captain, I've got to show the example,' remembers Mullen. 'I was giving it big licks about it being the game that mattered.' In front of a 25,000 crowd Wednesday won 2-1, goals from Eric Potts and Mick Prendergast saving the club from the ignominy of the fourth tier. 'We all promised that we wouldn't get in the same position again.' But they did.

Following a bad start to 1977-78, in which Wednesday failed to win any of the first 10 league games, Ashurst was sacked. A succession of managers had come and gone, each with different styles and approaches, but none proved to have the ability required to stabilise the club. Mullen had played for them all. Now, though, someone bigger, better was needed.

Jack Charlton was that big name, a figure whose appointment was the beginning of a generally brighter era for Wednesday. On his first Monday in the job, in front of a boardroom packed with players and staff, he outlined to each person there how important they were in reversing the decline. He addressed some of the players in person, one of them Mullen. 'Right,' he said to his fellow Geordie, 'the number six from Saturday. Can you put your hand up? You're captain as well aren't you? Well, that's not going to change.'

The new manager had two goals: improve the quality of the side and win promotion. With the legalisation of club lotteries schemes in 1977, Wednesday for the first time in a while found themselves with some additional cash for players, and Charlton was able to shop around for some additions. Andy McCulloch came from Brentford for £70,000, an imposing forward who could run down the middle and intimidate defenders, and Terry Curran from Southampton for

£100,000. The latter was a major coup for the club, dropping as he did from the First Division to the Third. It would be his job to play off McCulloch and create space for the team in which they could play. To help, Brian Hornsby, another creative ball player, also arrived from Shrewsbury for £45,000.

Mullen meanwhile continued in his role as captain but was given a new position in the team, moved from centre-back, the only position he had known as a professional, to holding midfielder. His task was to shield the defence and nullify the danger from advancing centre forwards. 'Invariably the ball would be in the air and I'd head it away. That was all Jack wanted', explains Mullen. 'He didn't want me to get the ball down and try to play. He wanted me to stop the supply and get it to the midfield players, then they could play.' Such was his success in that new position, he played there for over a season-and-a-half.

As Charlton moulded his team and brought a more relaxed atmosphere to the club, insisting the players called him Jack rather than boss, Wednesday steadily improved. And the epic FA Cup run against First Division Arsenal in 1979 demonstrated how far they had come since the new manager's arrival as Wednesday took the Londoners to four replays before succumbing 2-0 at Leicester's Filbert Street.

Still, for all the improvements under Charlton, life could be difficult for players if they didn't keep in line. Before the famous 'Boxing Day Massacre' of 1979, the 4-0 victory over Sheffield United at Hillsborough, Mullen's frustration at being asked to play out of position led to a confrontation between the two. 'Leading up to the game I had been playing left-back. And I hated playing there. I was sulking because I was going to play left-back, I didn't want to. I wanted to play in my position. We had two practise matches leading up to the game and I had mucked about a bit, so Jack came up to me and said, "Do you want to play on Saturday?" And I said "No". So he told me to get lost. I shouldn't have done it but I'd talked my way out of the team. I've regretted it ever since.'

During his final season at Wednesday Mullen drifted in and out of the team. The young defender Mark Smith was maturing into a great prospect and Mullen found it increasingly hard to beat the challenge posed by him and others such as Mick Pickering. In the promotion season of 1979-80 Mullen made only 18 appearances. Afterwards he was offered an improved two-year contract and the opportunity to assist Maurice Setters with the reserves. 'It was a chance to learn from Jack, and to get on the ladder for the coaching side of things. But then Ian Porterfield at Rotherham came in.' Porterfield offered the opportunity of first team football, something Charlton was less able to do, so Mullen felt he had little choice but to move. 'I felt as if I was in my prime and I wasn't ready yet to dedicate my time to coaching.'

At Rotherham he found success again, winning the Third Division in his first season. 'My first year at Rotherham was a continuation of my final year at Wednesday really. We had big crowds and some great players, a balanced side and fantastic team spirit.' Two years later he moved to Cardiff where he joined up with Len Ashurst once again. When Ashurst left to manage Sunderland in 1985 he was put in temporary charge, experiencing his first taste of management. He would go on to have a varied career in the role, including a notable five-year stint at Burnley in the '90s that included two promotions. His most recent coaching role came with Ronnie Moore at Rotherham.

8

Redfern Froggatt

1943-1960
538 appearances, 165 goals (including wartime)

'I'd just got in the first team,' says Don Megson. 'Before one game I'd gone over to the door on the South stand, where you went with your tickets to give to your friends and family. I was stood there and saw Redfern. It was only about three weeks since he'd gone. He was stood at the door with the punters waiting to get in. He said he'd got no tickets, so I gave him mine. I thought to myself "You're only in this game when you're in the first team."'

***

The 1950s is a particularly romanticised period of English football. It was, we are reminded, a time when the game was more in tune with its working class origins, when men were men, the tackling uninhibited and, say some, the play unsophisticated. It was also when pitches quickly became muddy swamps and, until Hungary demolished them 6-3 at Wembley in '53, people could state with some confidence that England was the greatest footballing power in the world.

Two memories of those different days remain particularly vivid. First the kit, heavy sponsor-less shirts with lapels and cuffs, baggy shorts and large socks over shin pads that appeared as if balloons wrapped round a player's ankle. Second, the loyalty shown by players towards their clubs. Due to the enforcement of a maximum wage and an undeveloped transfer system, that gave clubs far greater control over players' movement than they have today. There was little impetus, save for the pursuit of on-field glory, to move on. As a consequence there existed many long associations between players and clubs. From youth to senior level, numerous individuals stayed loyal to a single team.

Of the Wednesday players of this time, Redfern Froggatt best represents this figure. He spent 20 years at Hillsborough, 'a devoted one-club man,' scoring and creating countless goals, making hundreds of appearances, always battling hard to retain his first team place. A versatile and elegant forward with death control of the ball and magnificent passing ability. With a brylcreemed rocker's quiff, he was a light of the early post-war period, a 'gentleman', 'the type of player,' said one former team mate, 'any club would want in their side.'

Froggatt was born in Sheffield in 1924, son of the former Wednesday captain Frank. From an early age Redfern dreamed of playing for the Owls. 'I was always a Wednesdayite,' he said, 'but this wasn't particularly because my father played for and captained the club. It was simply that going to a school overlooking Hillsborough inspired my dream of one day wearing the famous blue and white stripes.'

His road to professional football was similar to many other players of the era. While playing for the nearby YMCA he met 'Pop' Bennett, a local trainer who dedicated his time to mentoring the young players in the city of the day, among them Derek Dooley and later John Fantham. After his team won a tournament at Millhouses Park, Froggatt was spotted by the Wednesday scout Cyril Hemmingfield and was offered a chance to train with the club. 'After the final,' Froggatt recalled, 'about eight scouts from professional clubs invited me for trials. The only one I was interested in saying "yes" to was Mr Hemmingfield'.

He made his debut in 1943, home to Grimsby Town, replacing the bursting 'goal machine' Jackie Robinson, a club great and a hero of Froggatt's, who lit up the Wednesday side with his energetic forward play. As a boy Froggatt would kick a ball around Hillsborough Park with his friends. With the great ground just in sight, sneaking into view from behind the trees, he would imagine himself as Robinson. 'I was the "Great Robbo"', he said. 'Many was the time I saw him collect a ball on the halfway line and go through everyone before planting the ball in the net.'

Following his debut, Froggatt played 90 times through the truncated wartime seasons (when fixtures were fewer and the Football League regionalised). After, as the country emerged from conflict, and with Robinson soon to be sold to Sunderland, Froggatt played more frequently for the club. Wednesday, like the rest in the League, had to rebuild. Only a few players remained from the cut-short 1939-40 season, among them Robinson and the goalkeeper Roy Smith. A talented local youngster like Froggatt, then, 'displaying promise of a quite extraordinary order', was vital to the rebuilding process.

Playing as a deeper lying forward, he brought intelligent and 'subtle' play to the side, operating all along the front positions (at one point or another he was used at inside- and outside- forward, on the left and right sides). He drifted dangerously, creating space for the other forwards, as he drew the opposition away from the busy middle upfield. With the ball he could make measured and accurate passes, short incisive cuts through the opposition's defence, or longer crossfield balls to advancing team mates. Froggatt's fine first touch enabled him to stop a ball dead, giving him a split second and the upper hand over his pursuers that, when coupled with his open vision, allowed him the extra fractions and space within which he could execute his next move. This slowing down of the play gave time, not just for himself, but for the whole forward line to get up into place.

By 1949-50, following steady and consistent improvement in those first few post-war seasons, Wednesday were promoted to the First Division, runners-up to Tottenham and playing in front of crowds that averaged over 40,000 (in terms of attendances it was the club's best ever era). 'I don't think there is anything in the world better than that great cheer when you run out on the pitch at Hillsborough', he once said. 'It tingles you through and through.' Froggatt was key to the team's success of the time, contributing a goal nearly every other game, setting up many for others. Wednesday lasted only a year in the First, however, finishing second bottom in '51. It was the start of a pattern of relegations and promotions that became the unwanted feature of that decade – the yo-yo-years. Four ups and three downs in all. Sadly, despite possessing such individual talents as Froggatt and later Derek Dooley, Albert Quixall and Alan Finney, Wednesday struggled through these years to build a side capable of establishing itself at the top level.

Back down in the Second the Owls went on to clinch the second of that decade's promotions, taking the title thanks to goals from the electrifying Dooley and Jackie Sewell, an inside-right who had joined the club from Notts County towards the end of the previous campaign. Sewell's transfer (£35,500, a record in Britain) came following a move for Sheffield United's Jimmy Hagan. United had accepted, but the player turned Wednesday down. Sewell himself came with great pedigree and later played in England's famous defeats to the Hungarians in November 1953 (6-3) and, six months later in Budapest, 7-1. His deadliness in front of goal failed to save the club from relegation in 1950-51, but the 23 he added to Dooley's tally a year later justified his massive cost.

For Froggatt, though, Sewell's arrival had 'hit [him] down a notch', said one observer. Coupled with the emergence of the blond wonder boy Albert Quixall, Froggatt had found himself reduced from first teamer to attacking deputy. At inside-forward, his preferred position, Wednesday, it was said, were 'overburdened with riches'. Always the professional, though, Froggatt continued to work hard, setting a good example to the other less experienced players while waiting for a regular place back with the first team.

Despite being in and out of the Wednesday first team, Froggatt received recognition from the FA selection committee. Beginning in the autumn of 1952 over a seven month period he made four appearances for England. His debut came against Wales at Wembley, followed by games against Belgium (he impressed and scored a header from a Tom Finney free-kick) and Scotland. His last game came against the USA in the Yankee Stadium, New York, at the end of a gruelling month long tour of North and South America in '53. The game was the first meeting between the two sides since England's shock 1-0 defeat to the Americans in the World Cup in Brazil three years before. Because of heavy rain the match had been postponed by a day, moved from Sunday to Monday. Only 2,000 were there to see the game in the cavernous famous baseball stadium. England won 6-3. Froggatt, playing alongside his cousin Jack (the 'inspiring . . . dynamic' Portsmouth defender), scored his second and final goal for his country.

Despite the recognition from England, Froggatt still found it a challenge to get a game for Wednesday. Around this time his loyalty to the club was well tested, and on a few occasions he might have moved away. Tottenham, Newcastle, Sheffield United and even Fiorentina (one of the strongest teams in Italy at the time) were each said to be interested. *La Viola* would go on to win the Serie A title in 1956, followed up by four second-place finishes and a European Cup final appearance. Froggatt's presence in the Italian game would have been a rarity . Because of the very strict rules on foreign players, if one did sign it would be because they were a big name, a promising talent or had somehow found a way in through an agent. Leeds' John Charles was a few years from moving to Juventus and at the time only a very small handful of other Brits were playing in the country.

Unlike in England, there was no salary cap in Italy. A move could have brought Froggatt great riches. When Charlton's South African born striker Eddie Firmani joined Sampdoria in 1955, he was paid £100 a week. By contrast in 1953 the average wage of a footballer in the Football League was £8. A factory worker, admittedly undertaking more strenuous and probably less satisfying work, earned £11. Even if Froggatt was among the 15% of players' who were earning the League maximum of £15, a move to Italy would have changed his life. 'Football was a game of the working class, for the working class, by the working class', writes Gary Imlach in *My Father and Other Working-Class Heroes*. 'One thing it wasn't was a golden passport out of the working class.' For Froggatt, Fiorentina may have been.

In the end, despite his struggle for a first team place in Sheffield, he stayed. 'My father had said to me, "If you ever get in with Wednesday, stick with them." And I was determined to do just that . . . I never wanted to play for anybody else.'

His father, Frank, had been a great influence on him. '[A] dour tackler', and 'fine header of the ball', Frank had spent six seasons at Hillsborough between 1921-27. In his last two years with the club he was made captain. In the last of those, after six years outside the top level, Wednesday were promoted from the Second Division as champions. Their leader Frank played in all 42 games as his 'band of triers' worked all season to keep pace with the leaders, eventually cantering to the title over the last quarter of the season. (At home to Blackpool on the final, celebratory day, one man in the crowd entertained his fellow fans with his cornet playing, perhaps the first incarnation of the Wednesday band which was formed in the 1990s). The 1926 promotion was the beginning of a very fruitful era for the club. Inspired by the signing of the experienced forward Jimmy Seed from Tottenham, Wednesday went on to win the League in 1929 and 1930. Five years after that they won the FA Cup. The team had two brilliant wingers in Mark Hooper and Ellis Rimmer, plus the excellent England defender Ted Catlin.

Frank Froggatt died in 1944, sadly missing most of the games his son played for Wednesday. 'My only regret', said Redfern, 'was that my father's death . . . meant he didn't live to see me start to make the grade.'

In 1955 Jackie Sewell was sold to Aston Villa and Froggatt again found himself back in the Wednesday team. He and Albert Quixall's goals filled the gap left by Sewell and drove the Owls to another Second Division title. A couple of seasons later, though, in 1957-58, the club were again relegated, for the third and final time of the decade. Thanks to a flu epidemic that had wiped out much of the playing squad early in the season, they had stuttered and, even when the illness had left the squad, barely improved their position. Goals from Quixall, Roy Shiner and Froggatt gave promise that year, as did the late season arrival of the excellent new goalkeeper Ron Springett, but it wasn't enough to put things right.

Happily the managerial change made at the end of that season which saw Harry Catterick replace Eric Taylor marked a dramatic change in the fortunes of the club. Froggatt was the only man to have played in every one of Taylor's years as manager and, in an astute move of Catterick's, was made captain as the team raced back to the First Division. While promotion was expected of what was a talented and promising squad, the manner in which it was earned indicated Wednesday would not have as much trouble as they had previously endured back in the First Division – a good points total with a more robust and tighter defence, a wider spread of goals and a better style of play providing this promise. Froggatt had a fantastic season, scoring 26, a career best haul that included a five-minute hat-trick against Sunderland, and the promotion-clinching winner against Liverpool. 'The team', he said, 'was shaping into perhaps the best one I played in'.

He began the next season as first choice. 'I was 35,' he remembered, 'but felt much younger, and was really enjoying my football. Unfortunately, I developed some cartilage trouble, and when the manager signed Bobby Craig in November, it started the countdown to the final whistle.' As the Owls flew in the First under Harry Catterick, Froggatt spent the final two years of his career predominantly playing in the reserves, talking his younger team mates through the games, passing on the welter of knowledge he had accumulated over a long career; setting a flawless example of technique and, perhaps more importantly, behaviour. Colin Dobson, a young winger who graduated to the first team in 1961, remembers his influence. 'Redfern was very good to me,' he says. 'Out of all the older professionals playing in the reserves he always took the time to speak to me and give me advice. I liked to attack and he was always willing to encourage that.' By the early '60s, with first team opportunities dwindling even more, Froggatt retired from the game. A great loss to the club.

In 1962, almost 20 years since his first appearance for the club, Froggatt was granted a testimonial against Ajax. A great evening under the lights of Hillsborough to finish a great Wednesday career. For his 20 years of service he received a silver statue of himself, given pride of place on top of the television in his Lodge Moor home. He died in 2003. 'A good man all the way through,' says Don Megson, 'the nicest man I knew in football.'

9

John Sheridan

1989-1996
244 appearances, 33 goals

On April 21 1991 Wednesday ended their 56 year wait for a major trophy with a 1-0 win over Manchester United in the final of the League Cup at Wembley. Haranguing, frustrating and containing their talented opponents all game, they held on magnificently to the 37th minute lead given to them by midfielder John Sheridan. The unforgettable miracle of winning the cup complemented the promotion to the First Division earned a few weeks after and remains one of the happiest recent memories of Owls fans.

Promotion came on the penultimate day of the season, a fine 3-1 win against Bristol City confirming their place back in the top division at the first time of asking following the surprise relegation the year before. As the players completed their lap of honour around Hillsborough, each could reflect with pride on a wonderful year. Ron Atkinson's stylish team was showing signs of significant potential with a brand of solid and well balanced, attractive football. Importantly, in David Hirst, Carlton Palmer, Nigel Worthington, Nigel Pearson, Roland Nilsson and John Sheridan, the ever-present orchestrator in midfield, they had the talent to easily adapt to life back in the First.

After a previous setback with Brian Clough's Nottingham Forest, 1990-91 had been a significant rehabilitation for Sheridan. Having been brought to Forest from Leeds United to replace Neil Webb, who had left for Manchester United, Sheridan would go on to make only one start for the club. Clough quickly decided he was not the player for him. 'He can't tackle! He can't head! He can't run! What the fuck have I signed him for?', the Forest manager is alleged to have said of his new man.

Sheridan was certain of the kind of football he liked to play, and how he worked best on the field. And though Clough had a similar playing philosophy, in Atkinson Sheridan found a manager who fully appreciated his talents. He would settle at Wednesday almost immediately, driving endless attacks and providing a great goalscoring threat which helped them to glory that April day at Wembley.

Wednesday's journey to that final had been memorable. After replays in the third and fourth rounds against Swindon and Derby – John Harkes scoring a long range strike past Peter Shilton in the latter game at the Baseball Ground – a quarter final victory at Coventry, courtesy of a Nigel Pearson header, set up the semi with Chelsea. In the first leg at Stamford Bridge the home side spurned several chances, Chris Turner in the Wednesday goal making impressive saves from Dennis Wise, Gordon Durie and Andy 'Tactics Truck' Townsend. Wednesday then unexpectedly took the lead, Sheridan's free kick down the line to an overlapping Worthington, who crossed for Peter Shirtliff to head in. A mistake in defence nearly allowed Wise to equalise but Wednesday held on and doubled their lead. Sheridan's long ball to Hirst, moved back to Phil King, who fed Paul Williams, who gave it back to Hirst to calmly sidefoot home for 2-0.

In the return leg in the cauldron of Hillsborough Wednesday quickly doubled their aggregate lead. First a Pearson header from a lovely Sheridan corner. Then Wilson put the tie beyond doubt (if there was any by that point). Shirtliff's free kick found its way to Carlton Palmer in the box. Palmer headed on to Wilson who hit first time towards the corner of the goal, the ball curving sharply past David Beasant for 4-0 overall. Graham Stuart got one back for the visitors but it came in vain as with less than five minutes to play a Steve McCall ball was controlled by Williams who calmly placed the ball into the net. With a 5-1 aggregate taking Wednesday to the final, fans invaded the pitch to share in the celebrations with the team.

The Wembley game was masterfully executed by manager Ron Atkinson. A loose training session was held in Hyde Park (trees for goal posts) before a more serious outing at Bisham Abbey spent running through the tactics of the match readying the team for the threat of United. On the coach was some Scouse funny man amusing the squad, lightening their mood and relaxing their minds ahead of the intense 90 minutes to come. Then out on to that famous pitch.

Turner. Nilsson. Pearson. Shirtliff. King. Harkes. Wilson. Worthington. Williams. Hirst. And Sheridan.

Wednesday dominated early on, Nigel Pearson commanding in the centre of defence, Nilsson and Harkes keeping the exciting United winger Lee Sharpe at bay. Then the goal. On 37 minutes, an unstoppable Sheridan bullet from the edge of the box. Too powerful for Les Sealey as it hit the post with a dull clunk before landing in the net. 'I knew I had struck the ball well', said Sheridan, 'but I thought the keeper had saved it'; 'I said to Carlton [Palmer] before the game: "If I score I'll come running straight for you." So I ran straight to him . . . He wasn't playing [due to suspension] and had to have a few drinks before the game to settle himself down. He was half drunk.' After the goal, while United held the majority of the possession, the Owls held their lead.

In the second half Wednesday managed to take over some of the play, Williams feeding Worthington whose shot was blocked before going close himself. Then Turner made a fantastic save from a Brian McClair header to keep Wednesday in front. With Mark Hughes unable to find a way past the wall of Pearson (the Owls captain rightly won Man of the Match for his performance), and with Lee Sharpe fading, it appeared Wednesday would stay ahead.

The minutes plodded on before finally the referee's whistle blew. Music to the ears of the Wednesday fans – confirmation of Atkinson's miracle. The cup was going to Sheffield. As the players climbed the famous steps to receive the trophy, they could be sure the better team had triumphed. For the goalscoring hero Sheridan, it was a massive moment. 'For a Manchester lad, playing against Manchester United in a cup final when a lot of my mates were supporting the other team was a big thing. To win and score was a great feeling.'

***

'I'd spent most of my career in the Second Division with Leeds,' Sheridan once recalled. 'When Howard Wilkinson came in I didn't really fit into the way he wanted to play. He wanted us to battle our way out of the Second.' The new Leeds manager wanted a midfielder that could support a more direct style of football (a style he of course had employed with success at Wednesday). '[But] I'm not a player who'll run around. I'll put my foot in but I don't win many tackles or headers. I feel as though I don't give the ball away easily – that's my strength.' These strengths were not particularly appreciated at Nottingham Forest either. Brian Clough expected him to win those headers and make those tackles. 'I thought it [moving to Forest] would be a great move. They played the passing game, football I liked. Everyone wanted me in the team. Clough had it in his mind that he didn't want me in the team, so that was that.'

In November 1989 Wednesday were bottom of the First Division with only six points from their first 11 games. Ron Atkinson, not that long in the job, decided to take strong action. He spent £500,000 on Sheridan and another £775,000 on Phil King and Roland Nilsson. Sheridan made his debut away to the club he had just left, helping his new club to a 1-0 win. It was only Wednesday's second of the season. The next match against Charlton proved transformative, Wednesday unleashing a much-needed, effective attacking dimension to their game. They won 3-0.

Still, they appeared to lack the consistency to overcome their poor start to the season and, thanks to a terrible run-in, ended up relegated. The squad was kept together for the following season. Many of the players, Sheridan among them, were impressed enough by the determination shown by the board not to let the best players leave, and by Atkinson's confident pledge to return the club to the top level, and decided to stay. 'Ron had given me the chance to play first-team football [and] I was happy there,' Sheridan recalled. '[He] was the best manager I played under, the best man-manager and just knew how to treat players, to get the best out of them. We had some very good players, who all got on with each other, and an amazing dressing room.' And though the team which was retained in the Second was strong, few could have predicted how successful 1990-91 would turn out.

The campaign began in impressive fashion. Away to Ipswich Wednesday were ahead within half an hour through Williams' sublime volley. Peter Shirtliff added another to ensure the 2-0 win. The following week at home to Hull it got better, David Hirst scoring four in a 5-1 demolition. The good form continued into September,

Sheridan scoring from 30-yards to take the win at Charlton. Atkinson's team attacked as a unit and with pace, their swift and crisp passing stretching the pitch and their opponents. The goals came effortlessly, and at the heart of it was Sheridan. Rarely was an opportunity made that did not include him in some capacity.

Notably, that side was built around partnerships. Hirst and Williams up front. Phil King and Nigel Worthington on the left. And Sheridan and Carlton Palmer, who had formed a good understanding, in the centre of midfield. 'He [Palmer] was the runner of the team and I was the passer', said Sheridan, 'so we suited each other.' Palmer, the motor of the midfield, would often become involved in the attacks, too, winning possession before manoeuvring into an advanced position from where he could deliver effective final weighted passes to the forwards. He went on to win 18 England caps for Graham Taylor's England while at the club. (Sheridan himself caught the eye of the then Republic of Ireland manager, Jack Charlton. Charlton took him to Euro '88 in West Germany, World Cup '90 in Italy and USA '94, where he played in all four of their games, including the famous opening victory of the group stage against Italy in New Jersey in which he hit the crossbar.)

Wednesday's good start to 1990-91, just like it had been in the promotion year campaign of 1983-84, was dampened by some uninspiring mid-to-late season form. In December there were five draws and, after a recovery, three defeats in a row as the finishing line approached. In April they worryingly lost 2-0 to mid-table Oxford United, Sheridan missing a penalty before slipping on the ball to help gift the visitors their second. His reward was voracious heckling from the crowd. 'The fans were expecting us to win every game at home', he said. '[I]n the Oxford game . . . The crowd got a bit frustrated. I didn't expect it.' Perhaps they could see the Owls' promotion hopes slipping away.

Just over a week later Sheridan was again at the centre of events against Blackburn, though this time his involvement brought a happier outcome. Within a minute of Viv Anderson's 54th minute equaliser, he hit a 20 yard drive past goalkeeper Bobby Mimms. 20 minutes after that he got another from the penalty spot, celebrating with the players before the now rapturous fans.

'That is probably the game I remember the most . . . When I scored the first goal I was in two minds whether to do something to the crowd. But scoring was the best way to answer it. With the penalty I felt as though I was on form. Everything was going right for me.' It started the most decorated month of his career, ending with the League Cup win and promotion.

At the end of that successful 1990-91 campaign, Ron Atkinson left controversially for Aston Villa. Trevor Francis was appointed his successor, his first season in charge beginning in exhilarating fashion. After an opening day defeat to Atkinson's Villa, wins over QPR, Everton and Manchester City, followed by a 3-2 victory at home to Manchester United in October, calmed the nerves the team might have had upon their return to the top tier.

Although Wednesday were now performing well in the League and already had a strong squad, Francis felt an additional, more experienced striker could help the club kick-on further. In September 1992, Mark Bright arrived from Crystal Palace in exchange for Paul Williams plus cash. Before that happened, though, Sheridan and company might instead have had a certain Frenchman to supply.

By early '92 the career of Eric Cantona was already filled with incident and, after early promise, now seemed to have stalled. He had failed to settle after a French record 22 million francs transfer to Marseille in 1988, and spent time out on loan to Bordeaux and Montpellier. His efforts there impressed the Marseille owner Bernard Tapie and he was brought back in 1990. However, after failing to take to the ways of the manager Raymond Goethels, he was transferred to Nimes. In one game for them he was sent off after throwing the ball at the referee and received a four game ban. Put in front of a disciplinary commission to explain his actions, Cantona in turn called each member of the panel *idiot*. The ban was extended to two months.

After a temporary retirement from the game, he began looking abroad for opportunities. A meeting was arranged in Paris between the agent Dennis Roach, a friend of Gerard Houllier, (at that time assistant to France manager Michel Platini), Wednesday's Trevor Francis (a client of Roach) and club secretary Graham Mackrell. The meeting led to a trial in Sheffield. Due to icy weather conditions and snow covering the Middlewood training ground his only viewing came against the American side Baltimore Blast in a five-a-side match at the newly-built Sheffield Arena. Cantona scored a hat-trick but the club failed to make Nimes an offer. They wanted to see him for a few more days but he politely refused. 'He [Francis] never doubted my worth . . .' said Cantona, 'he knew I hadn't played for a month and a half. We trained indoors. He wasn't able to make a judgement for himself.'

At Leeds, however, Howard Wilkinson was willing and able to make the plunge Wednesday couldn't. The Frenchman went on to play a peripheral, but nonetheless significant, role in Leeds' title win that season. He scored three times and made nine starts, his presence creating 'a celebratory mood' at Elland Road, 'which contrasted with the debilitating nervousness at Old Trafford', and his play changed the course of a game. On their way to the title Leeds picked up 13 points in their last five games in contrast to Manchester United's four. In Sheffield, Trevor Francis remained philosophical about the one that got away. 'I don't have any real regrets. I was aware that he had some problems. But I don't think it could ever have been possible for Eric Cantona to stay with us.'

Though Wednesday never really looked to have a chance of taking the title in the spring of '92, they did manage to stay within touching distance of the top two. Going into their penultimate game at Crystal Palace they were within two points of the leaders and, had Leeds not won earlier that afternoon against Sheffield United, Wednesday might still have been in with a chance of the title. At Selhurst Park Sheridan's deep cross was met by Williams to put the visitors ahead, but with moments left a long ball into the Wednesday box was picked up by Mark Bright who chipped the ball over the advancing Chris Woods to make it 1-1. That was how it stayed. It didn't matter anyway, Leeds' earlier win moving them out of the Owls' reach. After Manchester United lost to West Ham later that afternoon, Leeds clinched the championship.

In his first season as manager Francis had guided Wednesday to their best league placing for years. The future seemed bright. He continued to build his side, the signing of Chris Waddle assuring Sheridan that he was at the right club. 'It showed what the club was trying to achieve', he said. 'He [Waddle] was obviously a big name and he was frightening that season.' Waddle added to

Sheridan's own class in midfield while others, like Carlton Palmer, Danny Wilson and John Harkes, worked hard around them to win the ball and get it to them. In 1992-93 Wednesday finished seventh, reaching the two cup finals.

Sheridan had spent a considerable part of 1991-92 out with injuries. He had surgery on his knee that summer to rectify the problem, meaning he didn't make his first appearance alongside the new man until October '93. While Sheridan went on to play well for the remainder of 1992-93, his feeling was that something was not right physically. 'I think I hurried my return because I wanted to play with him [Waddle]. I was okay in the matches themselves, but the reaction afterwards was not what it should have been.'

It was in the later years of Francis's reign, and under his successor David Pleat who took over in '95, that the team then began to fall. 'After the two cup finals, one or two players left too early', Sheridan recalled. 'The team was slowly slipping away.' Pleat, despite admitting Sheridan was the best passer of the ball at the club, saw him and his style of play as expendable, rarely picking him. 'A bit of a strange man to be honest', Sheridan said of Pleat. 'When he first came in I was always in the team but when anything used to go wrong, I was the first one he seemed to leave out.' May be if the manager had been less reticent to use the flair of Sheridan and Waddle, which had given the team so much in previous years, he might have done better for the club.

Sheridan's departure did, therefore, not come as much of a shock. After a loan spell at Birmingham City he joined Bolton Wanderers. He didn't request a transfer but accepted he was no longer part of the manager's plans. 'When I moved to Bolton in late 1996,' he said, 'I just walked out of the door as if I was going home like on any other day in the previous seven years. But I knew I wasn't coming back tomorrow, and somehow it was as if that didn't matter to anyone. Nobody said thank you . . . I felt so disappointed.' Such a low key departure for the hero of Wembley '91.

In 2003 he returned to Hillsborough with Oldham Athletic, helping them to a 2-2 draw. By the return fixture their manager Iain Dowie had left and Sheridan was in temporary charge. Oldham won 1-0. He reverted back to coach when Brian Talbot took over but two years later was given another chance. After three years in charge of the Latics he joined Chesterfield, leading them to promotion from League Two in 2011 and, a year later, the Football League Trophy, with an attractive brand of play – Sheridan style.

10

Harry Catterick

1958-61

In 1958, after 16 years in the combined role of manager and club secretary, Eric Taylor and the board decided it best he move aside. From then on, he would concentrate on his work in the offices of Hillsborough, surrendering the full responsibilities of management to a younger, more qualified man. The era of those like Taylor, who combined first team and administrative duties for their club, was nearing its end. Many clubs were taking steps towards having someone for the players – methodical and focused on maximising their performance levels – and someone else to serve the business side off the club – innovative with good commercial sense.

Initially, it was not obvious who should occupy the role at Wednesday. Taylor had held the job for well over a decade and the club's hierarchy had no experience of appointing a manager. Attendances were down and there was considerable boardroom unrest. There was no real profile of someone who would best suit the role. The only thing certain was that promotion back to the First Division in 1958-59 was a priority and that appointing the wrong man could prove time wasted.

One of the first to be approached was Tottenham's Bill Nicholson, at the time only a coach with the north London club. But he opted to stay put, promoted as their manager not long after. Next, it was rumoured, was Barnsley's manager Tim Ward, but that proved unfounded. Then, seemingly out of nowhere, came Harry Catterick, manager of Third Division Rochdale. He got the job.

At 39 Catterick had spent most of his playing career at Everton before starting in management in 1951 at Crewe. Later, in cold, damp Rochdale he had achieved middling results with limited resources. Players were signed on frees and coaches doubled as groundsmen, cutting the grass, marking out lines on the pitch and painting the stands. Frustrated with the lack of options available to him, he nevertheless stabilised the team after a rocky start. In his first season in charge he oversaw the club's worst ever opening to a season; then in the second, a 17 game winless run. Catterick's third season, however, was more promising as Rochdale secured their entry into the inaugural Third Division (when it was split into northern and southern conferences before 1958-59) following a series of impressive performances which had seen them rise as high as fourth.

It was possible that, with that last, relative success in mind, the Wednesday board felt moved to make their choice. (Or maybe, he just gave an impressive interview?) Nonetheless, the appointment came as a surprise: to the local media, the fans and even the Rochdale directors. Catterick, though, was ambitious and knew he was ready. 'I could go on living in comparative ease in the soccer backwoods of Rochdale,' he said. '[But] when a man loses the will to accept a challenge he loses everything.'

His impact upon arrival at Wednesday was immediate and extensive. A quiet man who shied from the media, his disciplined approach soon endeared him to the players and fans. In turn he rewarded them with success unknown in those post-war years. During his near-three years in charge Catterick won the Second Division, reached an FA Cup semi-final, took the club to fifth in the First and in 1960-61 ran Bill Nicholson's great Tottenham champions close all season, before surprisingly decamping to Everton.

Yet for all his success with the club, his brief stay in S6 was, they say, mired by clashes with his predecessor Eric Taylor – the two holding different opinions of how Wednesday should progress. Catterick wanted to invest in the playing squad, Taylor seemed more content with building up the first class facilities at Hillsborough, creating a lasting legacy of improvement that would benefit the club and its community for years to come. That Catterick ultimately lost in his battle against Taylor is indicative of how his legacy became dulled over time, eclipsed by memories of managers with more extrovert personalities. It seems a great pity, then, that his time with the club along with his subsequent successes with Everton have to some degree become lost. Certainly his achievements with the Owls deserve recognition.

***

Previously the manager's job at Hillsborough had combined the role with that of club secretary. Before 1950 it was common for a coach to be left to supervise training, with an office man taking responsibility for team affairs, picking the side, bringing in players and choosing tactics. At Wednesday the first man to hold such a position was Arthur Dickinson who acted as honorary secretary between 1891 and 1920. After relegation in 1920, Dickinson persuaded the directors that a professional manager was required and Bob Brown was given the role. Brown would go on to capture two successive League Championships, in 1929 and 1930, before ill health forced him to resign. Succeeding him was the former Aston Villa man, Billy Walker.

Walker had only recently retired as a player and was a leap forward in terms of approach to the job. He took an active interest in tactics and coaching, and oversaw the renovation of the club's training facilities with Turkish baths and new equipment introduced. He also brought in special diets for the players. During practice games Walker would stand in the broadcasting box at Hillsborough and shout out instructions to his players through a megaphone. Sometimes he would take to the field to explain tactics.

This new approach initially worked. Wednesday won the FA Cup in 1935, but league results declined so he resigned in late '37. The former Scottish international Jimmy McMullan replaced him, but with the outbreak of War, footballing operations were pared down. He was released from his contract in 1942.

Succeeding McMullan was Eric Taylor who had joined the club as office junior in 1929, gradually working his way up to assistant secretary. At the time of his promotion to manager he was working in a reserved occupation in the steel industry. Under his guidance Wednesday reached the final of the wartime Northern League Cup. Afterwards, in the 1950s, he oversaw a series of promotions and relegations from the First Division.

Taylor's limited involvement in team affairs seems quaint by today's standards. He didn't take to the training field, having had no experience in that area as a player (though he would spend most free nights scouting players and the opposition). Before every match he would meet the coaches who reported back to him the results of that week's training. Working on this information, Taylor would then consider each player's suitability for the team that week. Come match day, there was no team talk or half-time dressing room intervention, only a sporting rallying cry of 'good luck and make sure you enjoy yourselves' before the team ran out.

Harry Catterick, meanwhile, had been an apprentice marine engineer while playing football at amateur level for Stockport County and Cheadle Heath Nomads. As a striker he impressed enough to earn a move to Everton in 1937. His time there began in the reserves, playing alongside the ageing but still brilliant Dixie Dean, before making his debut for the first team three years later, sidekick to another great, Tommy Lawton. He had to wait until 1946 and the resumption of the full Football League schedule before making his proper debut. Despite some impressive appearances he was hampered by a series of injuries (including two broken arms) which restricted him to only 59 appearances over the next five years.

Upon his arrival at Wednesday the players quickly noticed a positive change from Eric Taylor. Dressed immaculately in fine suits and waistcoats, and with an accent that betrayed the classless inflections of elocution lessons, Catterick wasted no time in stating the style of play he wanted to introduce, and the type of team he wanted. '[A]ny system I adopt will have as its aim a combination of skill and power, and will be dependent on peak physical fitness.' he said. '[The] First thing needed is a tight defence . . . no defender can be brilliant in distribution until he has won the ball.'

Like Taylor, he was not a training ground manager, but was able to command the respect and devotion of his players. The defender Peter Johnson soon recognised the new manager's abilities. 'He knew the game and could not only assess the strengths and weaknesses of individuals and teams – he could also communicate that knowledge to his own players. He understood footballers and knew how to handle and get the best out of them.' Catterick was aware of the influence he could have on them, and how over-exposure to him could work against him. Always he was careful to give fresh comments to keep them motivated. 'People think that the manager can go into the dressing room at half time, match after match, and motivate the players,' he once said, 'but that is a fallacy. If you constantly come out with the same formula, they soon grow sick of it.' When he did speak, though, it mattered. Tom Eggleston, a coach under his charge, recalled his approach 'When you'd had a good game he would congratulate you, saying something like . . . "I thought you should have done this, but you've done things right and it worked out."'

Catterick's first full season in charge, 1958-59, began well as the team raced to four wins from their first five games in the Second Division. They scored 24 goals in the first eight matches, culminating in a 6-0 thrashing of Sunderland at Hillsborough with Redfern Froggatt scoring a hat-trick. The match would be the forward Albert Quixall's final appearance for the club before his record move to Manchester United. The comprehensive nature of this win, along with Catterick's willingness to do without one of his most talented players, cemented the feeling that Wednesday could go far under their new manager. With a strong defence and fluid attack, his side notched over a century of goals that promotion year, eight players breaking the ten-goal barrier. Thanks to the 5-0 home drubbing of Barnsley in the final game of the season they secured the title by two points. 'All smiles again!' read the matchday programme that final day as the new manager had returned the club to the First Division.

Like most teams of the day, Wednesday deployed a 3-2-2-3 system. Two full-backs, three half-backs and five forwards. Don Megson and Peter Johnson at the back linked to Tony Kay and Tom McAnearney by the centre-back Peter Swan. When Megson or Johnson pushed up with the ball the other would move across to cover the penalty area. Swan, a 'stopper' centre-half whose job it was to defuse the threat of the opposition centre-forward rather than build the play, would drop back to cover the advancing full-back. That left Kay and McAnearney to build the play from the middle.

In attack, the wingers Alan Finney and Derek Wilkinson would drift back, hugging the sidelines to receive clearances from the keeper Ron Springett and the full-backs, before dribbling up the line or passing to the inside forwards Bobby Craig and John Fantham. They would lurk between the midfield and the box, shuttling up and down, awaiting possession from the backs before rolling forward to link up with the strong central pivot of Roy Shiner, who would either hold up the ball, make diverting runs to create space for the inside-forwards, or strike on goal. That front five, observed the great sportswriter John Arlott, attacked in arrow formation, causing havoc with their economic swift movements and inter-passing. Catterick's Blue Arrows.

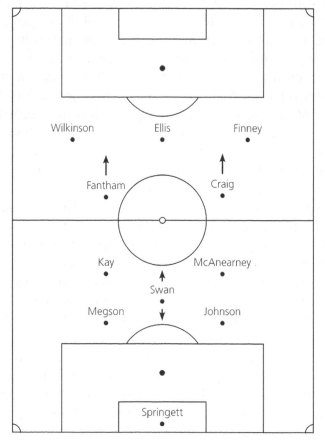

Sheffield Wednesday 5 Arsenal 1
First Division, Hillsborough, 19 December 1959

Training had been altered, too. Left largely to the coaches Maurice Lindley and Tom Eggleston, much of the lapping and sprinting of Taylor's era was supplanted by tactical work and set-piece preparation.

This freed Catterick to concentrate on broader match plans, based on the detailed surveillance of upcoming opponents. 'Once he had the people in place he let them get on with it – obliged them to get on with it', wrote Gary Imlach of Catterick's later time at Everton. Still, despite his relative absence from training, he retained full control over his squad. 'He rarely materialised at training-ground level, but from his corner office on the first floor he could see all the parts of Bellefield [Everton's headquarters] that mattered; the slightest change in the angle of the blinds in his window was enough to quicken the pace down below.'

Catterick demanded hard work and full, considered preparation from his players ('work them hard,' he would tell his coaches) and gained a reputation as a fierce disciplinarian. 'Preparation for the game was about a winning attitude, going out there and fighting for each other,' he once said. His coach Eggleston remarked, 'Catterick knew what he wanted from his team, and was determined to get his players to perform. He was a hard man . . . who spoke with a lot of authority. If you retaliated to a challenge, conceded a penalty or got sent off, he'd be into you.'

'Harry was a disciplinarian,' remembers Don Megson. 'We once got hammered by Aston Villa at home, and after the match he brought us all in and he ordered us all in to play against the reserves on the Sunday. Ron Springett [who lived in London] said that he was going home. Harry replied by telling him that if he didn't, he would never play in the team again.' The Wednesday manager also demanded punctuality. At Everton every player at the club from the England internationals down to the apprentices had to sign in each morning on a massive blue ledger. After a certain time the pencil was replaced by a red pen. Anyone whose name could be read in red received a fine.

He did have a softer edge, however. After Wednesday secured a 7-2 victory away to Manchester United an FA Cup replay Catterick wrote a heartfelt letter to Ronnie Briggs, United's young goalkeeper who had been drafted in after the senior keepers Harry Gregg and Dave Gaskell were ruled out trough injury. In the letter Briggs was assured that he had a bright future in the game and should not let one bad performance get him down.

Catterick's second season at Wednesday, 1959-60, brought further progress. Back in the First Division, they achieved their highest league placing for 25 years: fifth, just six points behind champions Burnley. Early form had been indifferent, but as September came a few changes to the first team were made that would see things improve. Roy Shiner, scorer of so many goals in the previous three years, left for Hull, the youngster Keith Ellis filling his place at centre-forward. Also, Bobby Craig, a skilful ball playing inside-forward arrived from Scotland as a replacement Redfern Froggatt.

On Craig's debut Wednesday gave one of their best performances of the season, beating league leaders West Ham United 7-0 at Hillsborough. John Fantham, Keith Ellis and Alan Finney each scored twice, Craig getting the other. Over the next four matches the team notched another 14, helping underpin a long unbeaten run that pushed them up the table. They were, said *The Guardian*, 'cleverer, faster and more determined' than many of their opponents.

Though Wednesday played a very effective game at that time, on occasion they were caught out. In the FA Cup semi-final of '60 against Blackburn, a game in which Wednesday were firm favourites to win but lost 2-1, Catterick decided his team would be most effective by hitting long balls up to Ellis. Ellis, however, was kept quiet all game by the Blackburn centre-half Matt Woods, and as the match progressed, with the Owls forward having little effect, nothing was done to change the plan. 'I think we'd have won the game if we'd played the ball on the ground more,' remembered Peter Swan. 'Instead we had to keep sending it up over the top to Keith and it just didn't work out.'

1960-61 was the culmination of Catterick's efforts to make Wednesday a true force in the English game. As the only serious challengers to Tottenham that season, his side reflected in their play the hard discipline and careful adventure instilled by their manager. 'They were a hard dour side,' Bill Nicholson recalled of his Spurs side's visit to Hillsborough that year. 'I knew it would be difficult to win. It was the most physical encounter we had experienced, and we lost 2-1 . . . I did not complain. As I left, I shook my fist in jest at Harry and said: "When you come to us, we'll give you more of this!"'

After defeat in the return fixture to Tottenham in April, Nicholson was proved correct. Catterick, though, was not present, having resigned with five games of the season remaining. Wednesday were still mathematically in contention for the title when he left, and there was a sense he might have taken the club on further still, given the time and greater resources, but it wasn't to be. We now know that he most likely left because he was unhappy at being refused funds to sign Hibernian's England international striker Joe Baker. Catterick was acutely aware that to jump that final hurdle the club would have to invest in such quality. Baker was a prolific striker and would have acted as a more skilful replacement for Keith Ellis, who, while accomplished in the air, was limited with his feet. After a transfer saga that lasted over a year, during which Eric Taylor refused to authorise a move to Wednesday, Baker, eventually joined the Italian side Torino for £75,000, much to Catterick's frustration.

By then the rift between Catterick and his boss Taylor had became irrecoverable. 'It was Catterick's misfortune,' admitted his former player Jim McAnearney, 'that he and Eric Taylor didn't get on. If Taylor said black, Catterick said white... a situation developed whereby Catterick tried to get Taylor out – which was a mistake because at the time nobody could shift Eric Taylor.' '[He] had a wall around him,' said another former player, 'and Catterick couldn't move a brick.'

Ten days after leaving Wednesday Catterick was appointed manager of Everton. He took over from Johnny Carey, who had been sacked by chairman John Moores during a taxi ride to the Football League's annual general meeting. Moores, the founder of the Littlewoods Pools company, was able to give Catterick the spending power that Wednesday couldn't. It brought great success: two First Division titles and one FA Cup. After the frustration of Sheffield, Catterick was home and had the backing to build a winning side. His first match was at Hillsborough. It finished 2-1 to Everton.

'Catterick's brilliance', wrote Gary Imlach, whose father Stewart had coached for Catterick, 'lay in buying and blending'. In then came big name signings like Gordon West, Dennis Stevens, Johnny Morrissey, Alex Scott and, for a massive £55,000, Wednesday's Tony Kay. Once blended, those new players drove 'The Millionaires' Everton on to their first title for 25 years in 1962-63. Over the next 12 years further honours followed. The FA Cup in 1966 (3-2 over Wednesday) and a second League success in 1969-70.

When he moved to Merseyside, Catterick swapped his rivalry with Eric Taylor for another, with Liverpool's Bill Shankly. Heavily linked with the Liverpool job before Shankly had been appointed in '59, Catterick was a complete contrast to the fast-quipping Scot, his media image being dour and uncooperative. 'Harry's nature is to be withdrawn and cagey,' Shankly remembered. 'He was just as intense as me and was hell-bent on winning, but he did things in a different way. Possibly he tried to do things in a more diplomatic way. I used to call him "Happy Harry" . . . he called me "Rob Roy."'

Catterick's authoritarian approach and harsh disciplinary methods, including weigh-ins of players to monitor their physical condition and a lock on the TV in the players' lounge, proved unpopular with some, while the increased media attention greatly exposed the peculiarities in his character. When live televised football was introduced, he saw it as a threat that would reveal too much about his players and tactics to the watching opposition. He attempted to forge an anti- TV alliance with Liverpool. It was only in 1967 that Everton first appeared. He used to name his team in alphabetical order rather than 1 to 11 so that people would have to work out how the team would line up.

Later, despite the success he brought, his selection choices came to cause friction with the Everton supporters. When he dropped their favoured son Alex Young for Joe Royle in a league match at Blackpool, Catterick was attacked, knocked to the ground, by a group of fans. 'At the time we had little or no chance of winning any trophies and there were a number of youngsters in the reserves who I thought would make the grade,' remembered Catterick of the incident. 'This group of people wanted to vent their feelings on someone and, as at every club, it is the manager who takes the stick. They closed in on me and I was quite deliberately kicked to the ground. The incident certainly gave me some moments of deep thought afterwards'.

Catterick suffered a heart attack in 1972. Although briefly returning to his post at Everton, he was ultimately replaced by Billy Bingham. Three years later, having tired of the vague consultancy role which he had been given with the club, he moved on to Preston where he stayed for two years. He died in 1985, suffering another heart attack shortly after watching Everton draw 2–2 with Ipswich at Goodison Park.

11

North Stand

1962-

Walking through the park or down Wadsley Lane, Herries or Halifax Road, approaching Hillsborough stadium on alternate Saturday's, Wednesday fans can share their feelings of excitement, optimism, possibly dread, for the 90 minutes of football ahead. For many, talking with friends and family, glancing around at their fellow supporters as the stands appear through the brick and leafy scenery, this may be the best part of the day. How wonderful then that the setting at the end of that walk is one of the older, finer English grounds: large, beautiful blue stands, decent facilities and a pristine pitch. However the Owls' may be fairing, the winning setting happily remains.

In the 1960s Eric Taylor, now freed from his managerial responsibilities, was able to focus solely on his secretarial duties with the club: directing commercial activities, arranging player contracts, improving revenues (he introduced club mascot Ozzie Owl whose image was used to market merchandise to the fans) and developing the stadium. While his reign as manager had been lengthy and his record reasonable, his skills were far better suited to that other, administrative role. Taylor brought floodlights to Hillsborough in advance of most other clubs. He also attracted the FA, hosting the Cup semi-finals, and Pele's Santos, twice (plus many other foreign teams from central Europe and the USSR). Such was Taylor's reputation, the North American Soccer League once attempted to entice him over the sea to help develop their League. Their lucrative offer was politely turned down, the loyalties of the man whose house was painted blue and white lying firmly with Wednesday. 'Once a Sheffield Wednesday man, always one', he said.

Taylor thought a lot about stadiums. He advocated multipurpose venues that would serve both club and community, every day of the week and not just every other weekend. At Hillsborough he built a revenue-generating gymnasium and South Stand restaurant – sound foresight considering what most stadiums have today. He also proposed that same city clubs should build new, shared homes, achieving improved economies through split construction and running costs. A joint stadium for Wednesday and United, he said, could even be linked to town by a monorail. Of course the notion of such an arrangement was not (and is unlikely to be) entertained in Sheffield, the rivalry of the two clubs too immense to allow it. So his focus remained on the Wednesday ground, on turning it into one of the Football League's best, a Wembley of the north, 'fit for the biggest and the best.' When the magnificent cantilevered North stand opened in 1962, he had succeeded.

At Hillsborough the style and scale of its four contrasting stands sets it apart from many others: the vast Kop and South, and the tired-looking West Stand with its out-of-place, roofless corner. But it is the North, running the length of the pitch, which most impresses. '[A] sleek, instantly recognisable icon from the 1960s', writes the stadium expert Simon Inglis, 'as fresh and vibrant as the day it opened.'

Realising a new stand was needed to replace the aged structure which had stood on the north side of the ground since 1900, Taylor commissioned the Sheffield firm Husband & Co. to come up with a pioneering design for a new structure that could be realised for £130,000 (although the final cost came in £20,000 higher). The funding came in large part from the issue of debenture shares which along with giving a reasonable yield offered the owner the right to purchase a ticket for any match held at the ground, including the Cup semi-finals. Sadly for manager Harry Catterick, this money could not be used to enhance his playing squad.

What Husband delivered was of outstanding quality. The North's grand cantilevers and girders, stretching out from its back, strongly support the acre of aluminium roofing – from the outside a good while can be spent admiring these steel claws. The roof gives comfort, cover and, somewhat uniquely for the time of its construction, unobstructed views from every seat. While the curving solid concrete walkways provide wide rounded access to the stand's top half (protruding elegantly from its back, they add good drama to the stroll, or if kick-off has been missed, a breathless pelt up to your seat). Off these grey corridors and up the narrow stairs into the light, to the rows and rows of the stand and the sight of the green Hillsborough pitch. From up here, there is no better view, no better place to be, as the North's steep gradient provides a fine angle on the playing surface, affording a feeling of you almost being on top of the game (a feature acknowledged as integral to the best atmosphere-generating stadium design).

The roof, vast though it is, hugs the top line of seats helping capture and retain the noise from the crowd underneath (even if its height initially caused the pitch to deteriorate due to a lack of wind circulation). The atmosphere on the Kop is probably more vibrant but thanks in recent years to the arrival of a boisterous element towards the Leppings Lane side, the North can create a decent racket of its own. Broadly speaking, too, there are far fewer tiresome, moaning voices found there than opposite on the South. A happy place. Where else would you rather be?

The stand sat as part of a wider development of the city in the 1960s. The introduction to *Sheffield: Emerging City* (published '69) describes an 'ever-changing' Sheffield, 'emerging into a richer future.' It mentions the other buildings that had appeared on the skyline that decade: The University Arts Tower and Hallam Tower, and the brutalist Park Hill and Hyde Park housing complexes. And the North, with its similarly unique and groundbreaking design, helped represent the extent to which the city had moved on after the devastation of the post-war years. It gained a wider influence, too. In 1962 Manchester United released plans for a similar group of stands, beginning with the construction of the United Road side. Today Old Trafford is cantilevered all around, as are the magnificent Leazes End and Jackie Milburn structures of St James' Park, Newcastle.

***

Before they moved to the Hillsborough area in 1899 (known then as Owlerton), Wednesday's home was in the city centre at Olive Grove, and before that London Road, Myrtle Road and Sheaf House.

When their lease expired a move became necessary. Although the preferences of the supporters were split evenly between Owlerton and Carbrook as the club's next home, the committee opted for the former. Wednesday moved across town – as did the Olive Grove main stand, brick by brick.

There wasn't much in Owlerton at the time. A nearby barracks (now a supermarket), some houses, lots of grass and, at the time, no tramway. It wasn't until 1903 that the district actually became a part of Sheffield. But, it had a growing football stadium, with its transplanted stand and three other basic structures and Wednesday's determined fans became used to venturing across town for their football (in that first year, 1899-00, 4,000 to 13,000 was the range of their league attendances).

Improvements to the ground took place in later years. In 1914 a stand designed by Archibald Leitch – the Scottish architect responsible for many fine football structures in the early 20th century, distinctive for their criss-cross steel fronted balconies (see Sunderland's old Roker Park) or roof top gables – was built on the River Don side of the ground. Leitch is responsible for Fulham's brick-backed listed Stevenage Road stand, and the now demolished Trinity Road structure at Villa Park. Wednesday's cost £18,000 and gave an extra 5,600 seats, a front standing paddock and distinctive golden ball on its roof. A fine Leitch offering to oversee the best days of Wednesday before the war. By the '60s, however, Hillsborough required some uplift. So Eric Taylor built the North.

Once construction had finished in '62 Taylor revealed his grander ambitions for the entire stadium. 'We would have liked to have done even more,' he said, 'to have extended our new stand to all four sides of the ground.' A scale model of how this would look was displayed in the city, perfect symmetry of three other similar stands enclosed at each corner. A superb, seamless vision that would have remained uniquely impressive today. Though as Taylor admitted at the time, the plan was 'completely beyond our finances'. The model ground never fully materialised.

If not quite in line with what Taylor had hoped, Hillsborough continued to be upgraded. The World Cup came to England in 1966 and, for three of its games, Sheffield. That meant the building of a new two-tiered West Stand, funded in part by an FA grant. With Villa

David Hirst takes a breath while anticipating his next opportunity at goal
© Steve Ellis

Wednesday Man, Don Megson. 442 appearances over 11 years, many of them as Owls captain

Megson makes an acrobatic interception

Kevin Pressman
marshals his defence
© Steve Ellis

Derek Dooley, original goal machine
© Steve Ellis

Immortalised outside Bramall Lane,
Dooley waves forever to his city
© Louis Clay

Pensive. Howard Wilkinson surveys his
team's performance from the dugout
© Steve Ellis

Reunited following their spell at
Notts County, Wilkinson and Nigel
Worthington celebrate on the
Hillsborough pitch
© Steve Ellis

'Time for a dash up field?' Worthington takes the ball on for a run
© Steve Ellis

Jimmy Mullen had many ups
and downs during his 10 years
prowling the Owls defence
© Steve Ellis

Loyal Redfern Froggatt,
spent his entire career with
Wednesday, 1943-60
© Steve Ellis

Following his brilliant Wembley winner against Manchester United, John Sheridan lifts the League Cup in 1991
© Steve Ellis

Though still a hero of the fans, Sheridan was rarely utilised by manager David Pleat and ultimately had to leave the club
© Steve Ellis

Harry Catterick's Blue Arrows. His team won promotion to the First Division in 1959, and may have won it two years later if not for the unstoppable Tottenham double winners

After disagreements with the club's hierarchy, Catterick left Wednesday in April 1961. The Owls finished the season runners up to double winners Tottenham Hotspur
© Topfoto

The North Stand, Hillsborough

Designed by Husband & Co. of Sheffield, the cantilevered stand, with
its steel girders, aluminium roof, and curved walkways, was one of
the earliest – and finest of its kind in the world

Eric Taylor's vision. A model unveiled in 1963 showing how the ground may
have looked if finished in a similar style to the North
photo picturesheffield.com

After years in the dark, Jack Charlton began to turn the club's fortunes
© Steve Ellis

Paolo Di Canio. His stay at S6 was brief yet memorable. His skills were dazzling . . .
© Steve Ellis

. . . his impact significant. Following his sending off, the Italian's push on referee Paul Alcock proved the tipping point that accelerated a great decline for the club
© Steve Ellis

Wednesday's number one. Ron Springett tips the ball away from danger

. . . England's number one. Springett
with one of his 33 international caps

Albert Quixall, teenage sensation,
beats his man
© Steve Ellis

Le Magicien –
Chris Waddle
© Steve Ellis

Waddle celebrates with
David Hirst and Mark Bright
© Steve Ellis

Des Walker tussles with Mark Hughes in 1994
© Steve Ellis

Everton's Gordon West takes the ball from Johhny Fantham in the 1966 FA Cup Final. Wednesday had led 2-0 but a comeback from the Merseysiders denied them the trophy that day
© PA Photos

Cardiff 2004. Captain Lee Bullen celebrates promotion back to the Championship
© Steve Ellis

Roland Nilsson. One of the finest sights ever in a Wednesday shirt . . .
© Steve Ellis

Park, Hillsborough shared the six Group Two fixtures contested by Switzerland, Spain, Argentina and West Germany.

In front of big crowds at Hillsborough the Swiss lost 5-0 to Germany and 2-0 to Argentina. For that first game it was said 10,000 made the journey from Germany – a few thousand of whom were even there a week later to cheer on the Swiss against Argentina. Those two giants (Germany and Argentina) advanced comfortably to the quarter finals, Argentina going on to beat Spain, before losing to England in a bad tempered semi-final; Germany remaining in the city to beat Uruguay on their way to defeat in the final.

Hillsborough remained a highly regarded stadium well into the 1980s. It had hosted 13 FA Cup Semi-finals in the years before the World Cup and 16, plus a replay, afterwards. Understandably its reputation never recovered following the 1989 Liverpool-Nottingham Forest tie, the blackest day in British football when 96 lost their lives. A range of unforgivable factors contributed to the disaster, among them the failure of the city council to update the club's safety certificate (to incorporate changes of the stand's layout – for instance the earlier removal of crush barriers) and Wednesday's inadequate safeguarding. The stand had an insufficient number of turnstiles for the people entering it, helping cause the crush outside. Poor signage meant fans were drawn to – and forced down – the terrace's central pens, and there was then no means of accurately measuring the numbers within them. It did *not* happen because of drunkenness or yobbishness from the Liverpool supporters [those who continue to believe otherwise should consult Lord Taylor's Interim Report].

Four years after the disaster, per Taylor's final report that set the minimum criteria for a stadium's facilities, the Kop had its capacity halved when it was converted fully to seating. Still, the huge terraced bank, covered in 1986 by a £1 million roof to protect its blue sea of spectators from the Sheffield elements, remains a fine sight when even half full today. Between 1993-96 the South stand also saw big change as the club prepared for the European Championship. A new roof was installed, followed by a row of executive boxes and an extra tier of seating, taking the ground partway over the passing river. The stand, said chairman Dave Richards in the club's accounts, was '. . . one of the finest facilities in the Premier League'.

As the World Cup had been 30 years before, the Euros were a

grand occasion for the country and the city. While England were entertaining us against Scotland and the Netherlands at Wembley (before scraping past Spain on penalties, then losing to Germany by the same means in the semi), Sheffield and Nottingham played host to Group D of Portugal, Turkey, Denmark and Croatia. Flags hung from the lamp posts on Penistone Road, visiting supporters played football with the locals in Hillsborough Park and Croatia, competing in their first international tournament since becoming an independent state five years earlier, overcame the holders' Denmark a in glorious fashion.

That June Sunday 33,000 happy Danes, Croats and English, many with beer in their bellies, were enjoying the beating Yorkshire sun. Denmark had drawn their opening game with Portugal but Croatia, also winners in their opener against Turkey, were set to storm. Ladic.

Stimac. Jerkan. Bilic. Stanic. Prosinecki. Boban. Asanovic. Jarni. Vlaovic. And Davor Suker.

After a cagey half of few chances – the Laudrup brothers of Denmark involved in many of them – the game came to life in the second. Suker's through ball with the outside of his foot found Stanic, running into the area where he was brought down by Peter Schmeichel. Suker converted the penalty for his first of the day. Great passing in their midfield then saw Croatia take a hold of the game. After Denmark had come close, hitting the post after an increasingly rare break, they conceded another, Asanovic feeding Suker at the edge of the box. Suker turned his defender and crossed from the left to find Boban at the far post for 2-0. 'It is like an explosion when we break', said Boban afterwards.

After that came the real delights of the day from Suker. First, having spotted Schmeichel off his line, he tried an cheeky lob from around the halfway line, saved by the Manchester United keeper, before scoring one of the best goals the old ground has seen. After the Danish keeper had come up for a late corner to try and help recover his team's deficit, a quick punt from Croatia's half found Suker who, running on in to the area, poked a magnificent chip over Schmeichel's up-stretched hand and into the net. Poetry from the Sevilla man.

For the tournament the pristine South Stand was almost full and bustling. Today, though, it serves more as a reminder of Dave Richards' period as chairman – physical representation of the decade of financial mismanagement he oversaw. The redevelopment cost many millions (£15 million, said the 1995 accounts, had been spent on the whole stadium in those years). Yet the expense, combined with increased investment in players (through escalating wages and transfer fees) contributed to a growing debt problem. It had reached £18 million by the end of '96 and would later prove ruinous for the club – the pain of it felt well into the non-Premier League years. The South looked pretty good then. It looks pretty good now. And probably its facilities are necessary for many modern supporters (certainly it helps generate substantial corporate revenue). Perhaps, though, if so much was to be spent on it and the rest of the redevelopment of Hillsborough, a similarly costly recruitment drive of players should have been curtailed. Or vice versa?

Since then the ground hasn't changed much. There was talk of expansion during the brief chairmanship of telecoms entrepreneur Lee Strafford between 2008-10, when Hillsborough was put forward as a possible venue for England's bid to host the World Cup in 2018, but that's about it. That bid required a number of potential host cities and stadiums from which FIFA would have selected their preferred choices. Strafford's plan was to upgrade and expand the ground from its current 39,000 seats to the required 44,000. He wanted to fill in the gap between the North and Kop, add a row of boxes to the former and build a new, pillar-less roof over the latter. The West would be revamped, too, eradicating the very visible image of the 1989 disaster (the middle tunnel through which the Liverpool fans were swept) while an 'education facility' for local learners would be constructed behind the North.

The scheme was costed at £22 million, supposedly to be funded by government grants and 'club revenue', presumably the future extra money raised from the new boxes and increased matchday spend. But England lost out to Russia – cueing the expected xenophobic reaction – and so the plans were never realised. The episode cost Wednesday and the Sheffield tax payers hundreds of thousands of pounds.

Probably it will be a while before more significant change takes place at the old ground. Understandably, since his takeover in 2010 Milan Mandaric has channelled his funds to the first team, not stadium redevelopment. Yet, save for a new coat of paint, is there much need anyway?

Many famous stadiums and stands have been removed from the British landscape over the years, replaced with unimaginative and unadventurous off-the-peg identikit bowls, like the homes of Middlesbrough, Derby, Leicester and Southampton. And it is strong testament to Eric Taylor and the North's designers Husband & Co. that the iconic structure they devised still so finely serves its dual function of holding thousands of Wednesday fans, while looking rather nice at the same time. Capacity is more than sufficient for current levels of crowds and even though the West admittedly requires a facelift, the Kop and South are fine.

All the while the magnificent North remains conspicuously grand; both aesthetically and architecturally. The jewel of Hillsborough.

Since its opening the North has stood witness to a great many Wednesday moments, some good, others less so. A World Cup. Don Megson's debut, and farewell. Howard Wilkinson's Second Division promotion winners, Ron Atkinson's, too. Cushions thrown on the pitch in disgust. Roland Nilsson. The birth of the Premier League. Rampant Croats. A falling referee. Jack Charlton's resurgent men of the 1970s and early '80s. For many, Hillsborough is home. The North, ever present since 1962, one happy part of it.

12

Jack Charlton

1977-1983

Jack Charlton was a World Cup winner in 1966, held many honours with Leeds United and had become a successful manager with Middlesbrough. In 1977, having taken 'Boro to the First Division and relative success, he resigned, believing he could take them no further. It seemed likely that he would secure another role with a high profile side. Instead, he came to Wednesday, a Third Division club with dwindling crowds and no money, a club seemingly going nowhere. Somehow he found the task of restoring the Owls to their prior, higher position too great to resist.

In '77 Wednesday were at a significant low. Relegated to the third tier two years before, and with little hint of improvement, they were staring nervously down at the Fourth Division. Derek Dooley's sentimental, albeit disappointing spell as manager had been endured, as had further ignominy under Steve Burtenshaw. And while Len Ashurst had gone some way to reversing the slide – his team finished mid-table in 1976-77 – there wasn't much suggestion of an imminent improvement.

The opening nine games of 1977-78 were grim. Successive 1-0 defeats at home to Shrewsbury and Peterborough sat among a winless run of eight. Memories of the previous season's comfortable finish (eighth) had quickly evaporated as the dire performances turned the fans away. Gates began to drop below 10,000 and many already concluded that relegation was inevitable.

Ashurst faced an uphill struggle. His staff was stripped to the bare minimum, meaning most of the coaching work was left to him, and because transfer fees were out of reach, with loan players relied on heavily, he found it hard to coax much from his unsettled side. After another defeat in early October, away to Preston, he was sacked. In a throwaway remark he recommended Jack Charlton as his successor.

A few days later, Wednesday's biggest crowd of the season so far witnessed a 1-0 win over Chesterfield, Tommy Tynan getting the important goal. Ken Knighton, an ex-player and by now a member of the coaching staff, had been put in temporary charge of the side and was said to be interested in the job. Sat opposite his dug-out midway up the grand North Stand, however, was Charlton, surrounded by fans pleading with him to join the club. The performance on the pitch, while not great, suggested to him at least some hope. Wednesday had decent players, he thought, along with a great stadium and passionate fans. A sleeping giant.

After Middlesbrough, it was the challenge he sought. To start again in the lower leagues and work back up. At full-time he walked round the pitch to the director's box and afterwards emerged as the club's new manager, tasked simply with avoiding relegation that season. One step at a time. 'No other job has interested me like this', Charlton said. His appointment would prove one of the most significant in the club's history, an inspirational figure brought in to awaken the Owls from a decade-long drift.

Aware of the task ahead – 'It's going to be a long, difficult job', he said – Charlton knew he had a lot of work ahead of him. He was now in charge of Third Division players of limited ability and, through training ground drills and set-piece preparation, worked quickly to galvanise the group into a well organised unit capable of winning matches. While the training was more prescribed than it had been under Ashurst, it was somewhat more relaxed. He insisted that his players call him 'Jack' and he proved loyal to them. Crucially (despite his abrasiveness and tendency to forget their names) they would work for him.

Though never a regular presence at training, the players were under no illusion about the level of work expected of them, or what their specific role would be in his side. Charlton instructed his coaches to work the squad hard, and the players to learn and refine their carefully set duties. You will do this . . . and this . . . then this, was the approach. 'The less choice you give a player,' he said, 'the more likely he is to make the right decision.' There would be no veering from his word. It was only in attack that Charlton allowed a little more expression. 'Only when the ball was in the last third of the field were our players allowed to decide for themselves how to play', he explained.

Progress was steady. In December '77 Wednesday sat bottom of the table having won just two league games since his arrival. They had managed only a few goals, and added to that were embarrassingly knocked out of the FA Cup by non-League Wigan. After that, though, performances began to pick up as Charlton's straightforward demands began taking effect. Entering the second half of the season, Wednesday won five consecutive home games, they would lose only three of their last 23. By the end Third Division safety was achieved with some comfort – 14th position from a low of 24th representing a great turnaround.

To get out of the Third, however, Charlton realised he needed to significantly enhance his squad. He needed tougher players; even more harder-working players. Publicly he was unconcerned over the lack of resources available to him, and so picked up the targets he could afford: ones that could fill specific roles in his side. In came midfielders Ian Porterfield and Brian Hornsby, the latter bought to inspire more creative play, and the goalkeeper Bob Bolder. The biggest coup was the signing of Terry Curran from Southampton. His signing in particular was a testament to the high regard the manger's name carried

Curran was a player in his prime, a forward who had been considered for the England squad, who in moving to the club had, like Charlton, dropped down two divisions. At Southampton Curran was having an ineffectual season and was persuaded to move north. He brought exciting play and, most importantly, goals. Sometimes he was used wide, then later, when Charlton reverted from a front three to a two, centrally. It is from here that he did most damage. As his manager explained, 'he [Curran] was accustomed to turning quickly and on the ball . . . taking on defenders, as wingers do. He played the same way after I'd moved him inside . . . central defenders, unused to that kind of situation, were wrong-footed over and over again.'

For most of 1978-79 the team again sat in the bottom half of the table, though this time they were never troubled by the prospect of relegation. The signs were that Charlton, slowly, was building an effective and hard-to-beat team. That year Wednesday 'would sneak a goal and then defend like mad' – nine of their 13 victories came by a single goal – as again they finished 14th. Their robustness was put on show to the nation in the FA Cup as they took Arsenal to four replays in the third round. Five games, one at Hillsborough (before which the visitor's 'keeper Pat Jennings was pelted with snow balls from the Kop), one at Highbury and three at Leicester's Filbert Street. The fifth game ended 2-0 to the Londoners. But after a great show from Charlton's side, it was clear they could compete with the best.

***

Not even the kindest footballing revisionist would say the style of play Charlton imposed was beautiful. His teams, they said, hit it long, and harried and hassled with little sophistication. Yet he was a more of a developed tactician than he was credited for. He was, writes Leo McKinstry, 'fascinated by tactics and loved to think about different patterns of play.' And to varying extents, at Middlesbrough, at Wednesday, and later with the Republic of Ireland national team, he oversaw a pragmatic approach which, while rarely attractive, proved decidedly effective.

According to Roy Keane, who played under Charlton for Ireland, the team's base approach was simply to 'fire long balls in behind the opposition defence then hunt them down'. But this is unfair. Not every ball was a long punt. Many were shorter, and most well placed – even if a lot were aimed into the space beyond the defence. These passes, while somewhat direct, circumvented the midfield, leaving a fast attacker, such as Curran at Wednesday, to pick up. Often they led to a chance on goal. As Charlton said, 'it worked a charm', particularly on the international stage. When faced with a competitor potentially unused to a direct and physical game, this more direct style often provided the best route to success.

There was more to his thinking than that, though. In *Stuttgart to Saipan*, the former Ireland goalkeeper Pat Bonner outlines one of his plans, a simple but telling example of his manager's abilities. Charlton knew how one of their upcoming opponents would use a sweeper to switch the play from one side of the pitch to the other.

This enabled the winger on the opposite side to start a fast attack in the space left by the pressing team. The out-of-possession team, desperately tracking over to fill in that gap, would then be caught out and open to a swift, building attack. To counteract this, Charlton instructed his winger to remain on that opposite side, resisting the temptation to check back and cover the pressers' on the other side, forcing the sweeper to punt down the middle instead of laying it to the other side. In the middle, the ball could then be far more successfully contested by Ireland's midfield.

Before his appointment to the Ireland job, the country had never qualified for a major tournament. With the 1988 European Championships in West Germany approaching, the FAI wanted to be there. Charlton was brought in to see if he could provide a fix.

After one defeat in qualification for Euro '88, they travelled to Germany. In the group stages they beat England 1-0, drew against the eventual finalists USSR, before losing to the other finalists, the Netherlands. The stage provided Charlton's squad with sound experience upon which they could build for the next tournament, the World Cup in Italy two years later.

To get to Italy they again had lost only once in qualification and were well set for the tournament. They drew each of their three groups games but still advanced. 'We beat England one-all, we lost to Egypt nil-all, an' we drew with the Dutch. That's not bad is it?' surmised one character in Roddy Doyle's *The Van*. Romania were beaten on penalties in the second round after which, they say, people danced in the corridors of the European Council's summit that was being held in Dublin the same day. Italy came next in the quarters. 'They rattled the Italians', Doyle later wrote, '. . . hounded them and bit their arses . . . They were great and I loved them . . . Then it was over'. The hosts won 1-0. Nevertheless, Charlton was becoming a hero in Ireland.

With the help of FIFA's lineage rule, whereby a player who was born outside a country but who could prove sufficient ancestry could be selected for that international team, the pool of players he could pick from opened up. Ireland's nationality law is more liberal than many other countries, it allows any person with a parent or grandparent born there to become a citizen, and because of it Charlton was able to cast a wide net – certainly he used it more than his predecessors.

Andy Townsend, Terry Phelan, John Aldridge, Ray Houghton, along with Tony Cascarino, the striker who it later emerged wasn't actually eligible – his natural grandparents, he discovered, weren't from Ireland at all – were among those selected by Charlton.

Ireland missed Euro 1992 but made it to the United States for the World Cup in 1994. The draw for that tournament put them against Italy in New Jersey, meaning a dream day for the ex-pat Irish community and the thousands of travelling fans. In the Meadowlands Stadium, its stands smothered in green and white, Ireland won 1-0, Ray Houghton's effort gliding over Gianluca Pagliuca in the Italy goal. 'I think you could have heard the stadium from New Zealand', remembers Ireland's Terry Phelan. Later on, Wednesday's John Sheridan hit the bar.

After that came a 2-1 defeat to Mexico in Orlando, where Charlton was famously disciplined for trying to get water to his players. Next came a slog of a draw back in New Jersey against Norway which put them through to the knock-outs. They lost 2-0 to the Netherlands in the second round. Nevertheless, Charlton returned to Ireland even more popular. He was given the freedom of Dublin in 1994 and was, said some, second only to the Pope in popularity there. He gave the country two more years, retiring after a Euro '96 playoff defeat at Anfield. Still, from also-rans to true competitors, in less than a decade he had transformed the footballing prospects of a nation.

Before Ireland, he had eyed the England job. He applied twice, first in 1974 when he lost out to Don Revie – the FA didn't even reply to his application. Then again in 1977 before he joined Wednesday. That time the FA opted for West Ham's Ron Greenwood. The job was something of an unfulfilled aim of his. 'I still feel bitter about it', he wrote. Of course, it proved the Owls' gain.

***

Wednesday's breakthrough to Division Two came in 1979-80. Charlton had made several important signings before the season, among them Andy McCulloch from Brentford, a target man to lead the attack, and another striker, Ian Mellor, from Chester City. The pair's sternness complemented Curran's flair and all three had a great goalscoring year. From early on the Owls were up in the top positions – sixth by Christmas after which they ignited, one result in particular spurring them to eventual promotion.

49,309 were at Hillsborough on Boxing Day '79. It is still a record attendance for that level. They saw Wednesday demolish their city rivals and then league leader's United.

As was so regularly the case that campaign, Curran was the star as the Owls romped to a 4-0 win. After Mellor's first, Curran headed in the second, set up Jeff King for the third after a run along the wing, before winning the penalty that Mark Smith converted . 'It was our best performance by far,' said Charlton afterwards, 'they all put themselves about and the way they finished was particularly pleasing to me.'

The result, one of the club's greatest, not only brought joy to the Wednesday support but impelled Charlton's team to their third place finish. After the derby they lost only once again in the league and promotion was sealed at Exeter with one game to spare. Arriving back in Sheffield from that game Charlton and chairman Bert McGee sat up in the Hillsborough boardroom long into the night, celebrating with champagne and a fried chicken takeaway.

Despite the resurgence of the team and bigger crowds, however, McGee could still only provide a limited budget for players. '[W]e work very hard over the wage structure and to keep things in control', said Charlton of the situation, 'and we've never entered the big money buying business'. Under these circumstances, then, he kept focused on best utilising the talent he had available to him, believing this to be one of the main responsibilities of a football manager. Charlton deployed Curran as a striker, and he was enjoying his best goalscoring spell for the club. Previously he had given the defender Jimmy Mullen his new holding midfield role. He also had markedly improved the game of the defender Mike Pickering, giving lessons on how to keep position and not to be dragged left or right by an opposition forward. Of course the manager was a fine defender himself, so Pickering had an expert tutor.

By now he had also begun to supplement his older promotion-winners with younger, local players. John Pearson, a tough, hardworking striker, Mel Sterland, an energetic full-back who would go on to captain the club and gain an England cap, and

Mark Smith, a centre-back whose emergence pitted Peter Shirtliff and Mike Pickering against each other for a starting place alongside him, were all introduced by Charlton. One extravagance was the purchase of the Yugoslav winger Ante Mirocevic, £250,000 from FC Buducnost, his biggest signing while at the club (he had tried for Nottingham Forest's Stan Bowles). Ahead of 1980-81 he felt satisfied with his squad.

Following promotion, the reasonable aim for Wednesday was consolidation in the Second Division. Yet following a strong start, those early expectations were soon exceeded. With Curran and McCulloch the stand out men in front of goal, the Owls had by November motored to fourth place. Even though their form did dip, and they stuttered to tenth, the season had turned out considerably better than had been expected (save for the events at Oldham when around 300 rioting miscreants earned Wednesday fans a four-game away ban and, for an equal period, the closure of the Hillsborough terraces; around 1,500 still travelled to and gained access to Derby's Baseball ground, however).

For 1981-82 Charlton left his squad largely unchanged. His younger players were playing with increasing confidence while the additions of Gary Bannister, an excellent number nine who cost £80,000 from Coventry City, and Gary Megson from Everton improved the goalscoring capability and robustness of the team. With Bannister finding the net, and the team starting to win more matches by a solitary goal – so often the sign of a side capable of achieving promotion – it was expected that Wednesday would soon make the breakthrough. It wouldn't work out that way, though.

Despite nearing the top of the table for most of that season, things fell away at the end. Defeat at Bolton on the second to last day gave the upper hand to Norwich who took over in third. To compound Wednesday's frustrations, after the Bolton defeat and the two draws prior to that against Rotherham and Chelsea, promotion was missed by just one point. It was the closest Charlton would get his team to the First Division.

Some said the fractions by which Wednesday fell short was because of the youthfulness of the team. Yet in this case such an argument was unfair. Over 42 games there was enough experience in the squad to gain the extra few points that were necessary to go up. Megson, Pickering and Curran (who in fact was surpassed by the young Pearson in goals scored) knew how to cope with the trials of such a campaign and its run-in. To blame the youth was wrong. Perhaps a better show during the three games in February, in which the team drew one then lost two; or in the last five games when they picked up only one win, would have pushed Wednesday over the line. Charlton, understandably, felt the disappointment more than most. 'To have come so close and failed', he said, 'was one of the bitterest experiences of my career'.

In 1982-83 Wednesday came sixth. There was, though, an FA Cup semi-final against Brighton. Much like the season itself, that day at Arsenal's Highbury proved a great disappointment. Against their First Division opponents the Owls had the chances to go through, but it was Jimmy Case who scored first, a swerving shot on 15 minutes hitting the back of Bob Bolder's net. Frustratingly, the Wednesday players had been warned beforehand by Charlton of his danger from such distances.

The Owls came back in the second. Mirocevic, a usually inconsistent performer since his arrival from Yugoslavia, ran in from the left to equalise with a low drive. Andy McCulloch then had a header cleared from the line acrobatically by Steve Foster. At that point it looked as if Wednesday might get another to advance to Wembley. But with 12 minutes left Brighton, breaking, took the lead again, Michael Robinson converting his own rebounded shot. Mike Lyons and Pat Heard each came close for Wednesday but it wasn't to be.

Soon after, just as had happened before at Middlesbrough, Charlton left the club. He believed he had taken them as far as he could and in failing to make that last leap he had tarnished his reign. His work during his six years at Hillsborough should, though, negate any such thoughts of failure. With limited resources he transformed the club, building a team with a strong foundation that could, and would, be built upon. Had he stayed on another year he probably would have achieved that second promotion. Instead that was left to Howard Wilkinson.

After the Owls, Charlton returned briefly to Middlesbrough before taking over at Newcastle, keeping them in the First Division in 1985. Then came those great years with the Republic. 'We are a better club for his having been here', said the Wednesday chairman Bert McGee after he left. A hero in Ireland – there is a glorious statue of him at Cork airport – his achievements in Sheffield aren't much less appreciated.

13

Paolo Di Canio

1997-98
48 appearances, 17 goals

'[L]ittle causes can have big effects', writes Malcolm Gladwell, explaining the social 'epidemics' that change and 'mark everyday life'. These epidemics, he argues, whether they be the reduction of crime in New York city in the 1990s, the sudden rush of a particular brand of footwear, or the outbreak of flu in a school classroom, can occur 'in one dramatic moment'. He calls this 'The Tipping Point', the ripples from a small event spreading to give a more significant overall outcome. For Wednesday, such a moment occurred at Hillsborough one September afternoon in 1998.

First a tug on the shirt of the Arsenal captain, Patrick Vieira. The culprit, Wim Jonk, was then pushed to the ground. Blue and red shirts converged. Among the group was Paolo Di Canio, who kicked at Martin Keown. Red mist and red card. Then he shoved the match referee. An unthinking reaction from the fiery Italian. *Little cause*. For what seemed an age, Paul Alcock stumbled backwards and to the ground. In a second, Di Canio's Wednesday career was over. More significantly for the club, though, the gradual decline that it had been sleep-walking into would accelerate in devastating fashion. *Big effect*. To that point the effects of a gradually weakening side, a manager out of his depth and a growing financial burden had been coped with reasonably well. In fact, until then none of it had seemed much of an issue.

***

Paolo Di Canio arrived in Sheffield from Glasgow Celtic just before the start of 1997-98. A skilful forward, he had used his time in Scotland to revive a career which had stuttered in Italy. At Celtic, aged 26, he was already with his sixth club, having found competition for a starting place intense at giants AC Milan, their manager Fabio Capello preferring Stefano Eranio, Roberto Donadoni or Giunluigi Lentini.

In Scotland, though, he had thrived. A change of environment, a new league and a new manager (the late Tommy Burns) all contributed to a great season of great performances. While Rangers won the title that year, their ninth in a row, there was no doubt that Di Canio was the star of the season. His delicate and accurate passing, splendid dribbling and close control, plus his 17 goals thrilled the Celtic Park crowd and deservedly he was crowned Scotland's Player of the Year. A true *fantasiti* in the green and white hoops.

After only one season Di Canio fell out with the chairman Fergus McCann over an improved contract that had been promised if he performed well. It never arrived, so he asked to leave. Bids came from clubs back home, Bologna and Napoli, but he was enjoying his new life abroad so turned to the Premier League. Eventually he opted for Wednesday, the Owls agreeing to pay £3 million plus Reggie Blinker, the illuminating but inconsistent Dutch winger rated at £1.5 million. It seemed good business for all.

To begin with the Owls manager David Pleat chose to use Di Canio on the right of midfield. Previously he'd played there for Juventus, where he was required to track back and defend. With Wednesday, though, he was free to roam forwards, joining up with the attackers, not having to work back as often. 'The best position for him was there, off the centre forward,' believes Peter Shreeves, a coach under Pleat who would later enjoy two spells as manager. 'He knew how to pull a player out of position so someone else could go in where he was.' But Di Canio was not especially happy with that withdrawn role and yearned to play even closer to the front.

The sale of David Hirst to Southampton in October '98 helped, opening up one of the two forward positions, but it was Andy Booth and another Italian, Benito Carbone, who initially played there. Carbone had been signed from Inter Milan the previous year for £3 million – half of which was borrowed from the Co-operative Bank, a worrying arrangement highlighting the club's worsening financial state – and brought flair to an otherwise rigid, if well-organised team. Eventually, though, as results declined – eight defeats from 13 at the start of 1997-98, including a 7-2 dismantlement at Blackburn – Di Canio got his way as he was moved inward to first partner Carbone, then Booth.

By November Wednesday were bottom of the table, a huge disappointment considering they had been in contention for a European place the previous season. With wins hard to find, Pleat was sacked. Arguably he had improved the squad, Di Canio and the midfielder Jim Magilton had come in that summer, but somehow the momentum built the year before had been knocked. Di Canio didn't seem to mind that much, though. 'I never really got on with Pleat', he said. 'He never explained anything to me; we just never had any kind of relationship.'

In place of Pleat came the unlikely returnee, Ron Atkinson. He brought immediate success, winning his first three games in charge, Arsenal 2-0, Southampton 3-2, and Barnsley 2-1 (before that, under Peter Shreeves' temporary charge, Wednesday had beaten Bolton Wanderers, too). The team was transformed by Atkinson's influence. They were more confident – bravely attacking opponents, believing that if applied correctly their abilities would win enough points to lift them up the table. And crucially he managed to inspire the main creative outlets of the side – Di Canio and Carbone – to perform. He said of the pair, 'I love flair, but I like it to be productive flair'. They responded with effective and efficient play, delivering many goals and assists, which at the same time was pretty to watch.

To Atkinson, Di Canio was 'the volcano'. A man who cared deeply about the game but whose passion on occasion was liable to explode into an outpouring of shouts and gesticulation – particularly if he believed his colleagues, whether on match day or in training, were not matching his efforts. Although this could be disruptive to the squad, Atkinson handled him well, managing his outbursts rather than attempting to stifle what frankly was an unstoppable trait. While to Di Canio, Atkinson was a manager whose talents he respected. 'He jokes a lot', said the Italian. 'He is funny. But he is also strong and works on tactics.' The two did still find time to disagree, however, once coming to blows during a Middlewood training session.

Clashing with the management was not something new for Di Canio. At Juventus he had fallen out with Giovanni Trapattoni over a too-brief appearance in a pre-season friendly. After that he was moved out on-loan to Napoli. Later, at AC Milan, he fell out with Fabio Capello having been substituted during an exhibition match in China. He is said to have pushed the future England manager and moved to Celtic not long after.

Such confrontation was the result of a passionate personality. As he has said, it was necessary for him to perform so well throughout his career. 'I give my best when I'm pissed off ', he said, 'when I argue with the entire world.' This side of his character may, though, have denied him a chance to play for his country. 'Certainly,' believes John Foot, author of *Calcio*, a history of the Italian game, 'he had the ability to play for Italy. It was a scandal that he didn't. A lot more, worse players than him have.'

Under Atkinson things continued to improve for Wednesday through 1997-98. Di Canio, alongside Carbone or Booth, was working well and the good results continued. At Everton in April, playing in orange and white, they gained an impressive 3-1 win, Di Canio scoring the emphatic third. Breaking from just inside Everton's half, he danced unhindered past two defenders, rounded Thomas Myhre before walking the ball into the net. The goal demonstrated the extent of his talents, his skill, control, strength and, no matter how many opposition players were around him, calmness. The upturn was also helped by a few additions – the Swedish right winger Niclas Alexandersson had come in before Christmas for £750,000, followed by Everton's left back Andy Hinchcliffe, £2.75 million, then the defender Emerson Thome on a free from Benfica in March – and the strong performers of those remaining from Pleat's time – the Norwegian midfielder Petter Rudi ('*Tutti fruiti, Petter Rudi*'), Kevin Pressman, Peter Atherton, Des Walker and Mark Pembridge. By the end they and Atkinson had assured the club its Premier League status.

1998-99 promised much for the improving Wednesday. Yet managerially they suffered a twist when Atkinson, who was committed to another year during which time he planned to groom the former Owls captain Nigel Pearson as his successor, was let go. Dave Richards, aware that Atkinson would not accept a long contract, and seemingly against the Pearson idea, wanted greater stability and so chose to release the man who had saved the club. Atkinson was shocked, 'numb with betrayal.' At the time the decision appeared to make some sense, from a long term point of view at least (if discounting the Pearson idea), but ultimately proved a great folly. Rangers' Walter Smith was heavily linked but he joined Everton. As was Gerard Houllier before he joined Liverpool. So Wednesday, searching for their new manager, did as they had done before with Derek Dooley and Peter Eustace and opted for a former player.

Danny Wilson had spent three good years with Wednesday in the early 1990s. A starter in the '91 League Cup win, he had always been a steady performer in midfield. Having left the club in 1993 to become Viv Anderson's assistant at Barnsley, he later took over from him as manager, bringing top flight football to the town for the first time in 1997-98. His team employed an entertaining style and, though the top division proved too much for them (they finished second bottom in their one and only season in the Premier League), his reputation as one of the country's more promising young managers remained undimmed and he was chosen to replace Ron Atkinson as Wednesday manager. Di Canio, however, had concerns over the appointment. 'He was considered a rising star among managers,' he wrote in his autobiography, 'but I could tell right away he lacked something... It was a total learning experience for him and in many ways he wasn't sure what he was doing.'

Wilson built carefully for the new season, making just two additions, the Argentine right-back Juan Cobian on a free from Boca Juniors and for £2.5 million from PSV Eindhoven, the lanky midfielder Wim Jonk who had just appeared for the Netherlands at the World Cup in France. The season began reasonably well with two wins from the opening five games in which Di Canio scored twice. The manager, though, was quickly growing frustrated with the performances of some of his players.

In the first round of the League Cup at Hillsborough against Third Division Cambridge United, Wednesday lost dismally 1-0. Reflecting afterwards, Wilson targeted the 'fancy dans' in his side, citing poor decisions made at the moment before a pass as the reason for the failure that night. Even though the performance of the whole team had been particularly poor, most believed Wilson was referring to the two Italians Di Canio and Carbone. 'It was a performance bordering on complacency', he said. 'We had no work-rate and team spirit. Too many players were self-indulgent and played as individuals and not for the team.' Di Canio was most unhappy with the outburst. '[P]erhaps', he wondered, 'he thinks attacking his own players in public is the way to show strength.' The second leg finished 1-1 at the Abbey Stadium, Cambridge advancing 2-1 on aggregate.

To that point in his managerial career Wilson had little or no experience of handling top players and the delicate egos that came with them. Rightly dished out or not, criticism of that nature probably would not have come from Ron Atkinson, a man with far more experience of such players. As it was, it would get much harder for Wilson. Because four days after the Cambridge second leg, Arsenal visited Hillsborough . . .

From the start Arsenal dominated, only the firmness of Kevin Pressman in the Wednesday goal keeping them in the game as he excellently denied Patrick Vieira and Ray Parlour. Then, shortly before half-time, came Di Canio's moment. After having kicked out at Martin Keown, he was sent off. 'So I pushed Alcock away . . . [and] he fell over.' The pusher stormed off the pitch, past an unmoving Wilson and down the tunnel. 'The severity of the incident is unquestionable', said Wilson after the game. 'I just don't know what went through his mind'. Di Canio, unsure of his future with the club, headed to Italy – to Terni, a town north of Rome – where he would train by himself.

In the second half Arsenal created more chances, Dennis Bergkamp missing a notable opportunity. But Wednesday clung on. With a minute left, Lee Briscoe, the young full-back off the bench for Niclas Alexandersson, was fed by Jonk at the edge of the box. He controlled the ball beautifully and chipped it over the Arsenal keeper Alex Manninger to give Wednesday an unlikely win. Understandably, the win and the goal would be overshadowed by earlier events.

A few weeks later an FA tribunal handed Di Canio an 11 match ban – three of those for the red card. He accepted the decision. 'I had a fair hearing,' he said, 'for which I am grateful. I am very, very sorry for what happened'. Yet he remained angry with Wilson and the club. Wilson for acting so quickly to suspend him; and the club for not contacting him while he trained in Terni (though the club claimed they did). Three months later, having failed to return to Wednesday, Di Canio was sold to West Ham for £1.7 million. Harry Redknapp had formed a good mix of youth and experience at the London club, Shaka Hislop, Trevor Sinclair, Steve Lomas supplemented by the exciting prospects Rio Ferdinand and Frank Lampard, and was happy to provide the volcano a clean page.

After that the Owls decline gathered pace. 12th in the Premier League at the end of 1998-99 had been a reasonable start for Danny Wilson, but there were clear deficiencies in the team. Thanks to the central defensive pairing of Des Walker and Emerson Thome, along with Andy Hinchcliffe and Peter Atherton in the full-back positions, the team had the fifth best defensive record in the division. But following the departure of Di Canio, goalscoring became a real problem. Away at Leeds in November 1998, for instance, Wednesday appeared rigid and unimaginative in a 2-1 defeat – most of their chances, including Andy Booth's headed goal, came from Hinchcliffe's dead-balls.

The year after that things deteriorated rapidly and Wednesday were relegated from the Premier League. The defence was shipping goals, 70 in all that season, and upfield it was a similar story to the previous campaign. Benito Carbone had left, sold to Aston Villa after refusing to sit on the bench at Southampton, leaving Andy Booth to partner one of the two new forwards brought in during the summer. Unfortunately neither Gilles De Bilde, a well regarded Belgian international who cost £2.8 million from PSV Eindhoven, nor Gerald Sibon, £2 million from Ajax, impressed at all. Results were dreadful – no wins until October and an 8-0 defeat at Newcastle – and the pressure was mounting on Wilson.

In February, after drawing 3-3 at Derby (having led 3-1), one player in the Pride Park dressing room is said to have remarked that the club would now be relegated, sending Danny Wilson 'berserk' according to the goalkeeper Pavel Srnicek. At that point, even with a significant number of games still left to play, there seemed little fight left in the side. A prevailing hopelessness existed at the club that appeared unlikely to be reversed. Barry Horne, the veteran midfielder who joined on loan towards the end of the season, would later reveal the full extent of the problems. '[T]he Wednesday players', he said, 'were too busy fighting each other... to properly concentrate on seeing off opponents... one by one, people started to throw the towel in. They had lost the will to fight for survival and, in some cases, perhaps didn't care if Wednesday went down.'

Di Canio, meanwhile, was performing well for his new club. Harry Redknapp, who had gained the plaudits for taking a chance on such a firebrand player, was rewarded with flowing, entertaining football helped by his new forward. As Wednesday struggled, Di Canio scored memorable goals – notably, the extraordinary mid-air volley against Wimbledon, considered one of the greatest goals scored in the League's history. When he returned to Hillsborough with the Hammers in April 2000 his every touch was booed by the despondent home crowd, by now well used to their team's poor performances. Inevitably he was involved as West Ham took the lead, feeding John Moncur whose cross led to Frank Lampard's goal. Although Wednesday recovered to win 3-1, one of their better performances that year, it failed to mask their overall inadequacies and highlighted perhaps in Di Canio what they were missing.

At Wednesday, Danny Wilson had not only to contend with his underperforming players but also unpleasant public criticism from a group of local MPs. Four of them – David Blunkett, Bill Michie, Joe Ashton and Clive Betts – held a meeting with Charterhouse, the venture capitalists who owned 37% of the club's shares, in which they expressed concern at Wednesday's plight in the league. When details of the meeting emerged in the press Blunkett and Michie showed their regret at the leak. But Betts, the man who was leader of Sheffield Council in 1989, the body which had failed to 'revise' or 'amend' Hillsborough's safety certificate before the disaster, demonstrating, according to Lord Taylor in his Interim Report, 'a serious breach of duty', remained defiantly outspoken. 'Any other Premiership club would have sacked the manager by now', Betts said; '. . . pathetic', responded Wilson wonderfully.

However, with nine games of 1999-00 remaining, a change had to be made. Dave Richards had by now left the club permanently for a job at the Premier League, and his replacement, Howard Culley, soon lost patience with Wilson. Peter Shreeves, a coach under David Pleat and Ron Atkinson, was brought back to try and turn things around. Results improved, ten points from those last fixtures, but it wasn't enough. As Shreeves admits, 'I did OK, but I didn't have enough games. If my record had been over the season we'd have finished safely above the relegation places.' Indeed, had the points rate earned in those last games been applied to the whole season then the club would have survived.

After three-and-a-half years with West Ham, Di Canio joined Charlton Athletic. He stayed for a season before moving back to Italy and Lazio, the club which had given him his debut as a teenager. The Rome club was in serious financial difficulties and could no longer afford the large wages that had fuelled their Serie A title success of 2000. That team had been built by the wealthy Sergio Cragnotti who funded the transfers of Christian Vieiri, Marcelo Salas and Hernan Crespo. Now their squad was bare, a handful of professionals supplemented by youth team players. Such was the club's destitution, Di Canio was required to take a pay cut from his Charlton contract to, it was reputed, around £5,000 per week. Money, though, was not his concern. At 36, a return to the club for whom he had previously dazzled for five years was a duty. 'The club I love . . . needed me', he said. 'How could I turn my back on them?'

At Lazio, while providing some excellent performances, Di Canio managed to court considerable controversy, on three occasions producing the fascist salute to opposition fans. First during the derby against city rivals Roma, then against Livorno (of the 'most left-wing city in Italy'), then Juventus. For the latter two instances he received a €10,000 fine and a one-game suspension. Di Canio, as is his entitlement, is a proud fascist and has been vocal in his admiration for Mussolini (the leader who was said to have been a Lazio fan). '[H]is actions', Di Canio said, 'were often vile and calculated . . . But all this was motivated by a higher purpose'. Not surprisingly this statement attracted much criticism from outside observers. As the author Tamir Bar-On notes, such comments and actions 'consciously plays (*sic*) to Lazio's hard-core neo-fascist and neo-Nazi constituencies'. And while Di Canio is not the latter – 'I am a fascist, not a racist' – they have little place in a stadium of people, most of whom are wanting to watch a game of football. As John Foot says, 'absolutely he knew what he was doing, but it was just a bit stupid and self indulgent really. Lazio is his team and some of the fans are very right-wing. He liked the attention it got him. He was making himself even more of a darling to them. But it took away what a good player he was. He could do things on the pitch that no one else could do. Then he'd do something incredibly stupid like make a fascist salute and then that's all people talk about.'

After two seasons he left Lazio, continuing his career for a couple more years with Serie C2 club Cisco Roma. His enthusiasm for the game and outstanding fitness allowed him to continue playing until the age of 40. In 2011 he was appointed manager of Swindon Town, introducing double training sessions in order to build the fittest team in League Two while enforcing a strict discipline and a high level of organisation within the club. Those doubting his commitment to such a job, with such a club, were soon won over as they rose to the top of League Two.

***

'One moment,' said Di Canio, 'can erase everything else you've accomplished in your career. I didn't kill anybody. I pushed a referee. We all know that's wrong. But it can happen.' Naturally his time at Wednesday will be most remembered for that one moment of thoughtless recklessness. While he would go on to happier times with different clubs, the one he left behind would endure many years of affliction, from which they are still battling to recover.

The push was not the cause of the club's decline, rather it *represented* the moment that decline, which had begun to stir in the background, properly began and accelerated thereafter. As Malcolm Gladwell writes in the *Tipping Point*, 'sometimes big changes follow from small events'. '[S]ometimes these changes can happen very quickly.' Of course, Di Canio's actions are not to blame for the quick change Wednesday experienced. Far greater failings were the actual cause, notably the underperformance of Danny Wilson's team (not helped by the absence of the Italian), and the signings he made subsequently. Before that the failure to hold on to Ron Atkinson in '98 and the financial mismanagement which led to the enormous, prohibitive debt pile of the 1990s and beyond, also contributed to the initial stirring of trouble. So probably it is best to remember him for the pleasure he brought.

For the 18 months in which he worked tirelessly to entertain the club's support, providing the graceful turns, close skill and seemingly unending moments of inventiveness, helping turn an average team into an at times attractive attacking unit. For those few years Di Canio was fantastic to see. What followed him on the Hillsborough pitch was not.

14

Ron Springett

1958-1967
384 appearances

'That's him in the green, green cotton jersey,
prince of the clean sheets'

– Simon Armitage,
'Goalkeeper with a Cigarette'

For nine years goalkeeper Ron Springett thrilled the Hillsborough crowd with his commanding, acrobatic and fearless displays in the Wednesday goal. Arriving at the club a young man, he went on to become a crucial member of Harry Catterick's promising team of the early 1960s, helping sustain the supporters through some of the club's best years. As he grew more experienced he worked to set a fine example to the younger players around him, while continuing to give fine displays between the posts, demonstrating the many satisfactions of his game: the excellent shot-stopping, acute reflexes, and ability to pinpoint a long throw or kick to a team-mate which would provide a frequent and effective line of attack. Before Nigel Worthington surpassed him, Springett had amassed the most international appearances of any individual to have played for the Owls and doubtless he was one of the best goalkeepers of his era, 'a heart-breaking barrier to forwards', 'a rock on which a hundred teams have foundered'. The best Wednesday have ever had.

In one of his last acts as manager-secretary, Eric Taylor brought

Springett north from Queens Park Rangers in March 1958. The £10,000 fee was a substantial outlay for a relatively inexperienced, 22-year-old Second Division player, but he soon proved a sound investment. Taylor was so impressed with the impact his new keeper made after arriving that, when reflecting on the relegation that season, he believed Wednesday would have stayed up if Springett had arrived even a week earlier. Considering that four of the nine games in which he played were won, and that by the end of the season the difference between relegation and survival was only one point, Taylor may have been right.

Springett had made his debut for Rangers aged 16. He was happily settled in the Capital and so negotiated with Taylor that in moving to the club he would not have to move from his home. During the week, then, he would train with QPR, travelling to the games by rail on the Friday night before a game. Curious as the arrangement was, it allowed Taylor to clinch the deal. Sunderland were said to have been ready with a similar arrangement but, having already been turned down by Springett, he was determined to get his man.

The travelling often meant Springett wouldn't meet up with his team-mates until the morning of a game, but still he managed to settle well. 'He could walk into the group on Saturdays and you would feel that he had been with the team the whole week', said Alan Brown, one of his managers at Hillsborough. Today such a scenario is unlikely to be repeated, but back then Springett was so good it didn't matter.

Finishing bottom of the First Division in only his second month at the club was not an ideal start. It was the club's third relegation of that up-and-down decade and was a big disappointment. Injuries had been a problem – Wednesday were rarely free of them, had been particularly affected by a flu epidemic at the start of the campaign. And the goalkeeping position had proved particularly unstable. In September the first choice Charlie Pllu was injured at Tottenham and his cover, Bryan Ryalls, did not impress. Pllu returned but got injured again, damaging his ankle, so this time he was replaced by the veteran Dave McIntosh, who was similarly unsuccessful. The amateur Mike Pinner was also given a try, but he let by 21 goals in five matches, so it was with some relief that Springett arrived just before the transfer deadline, bringing at last stability to the position.

Under their new manager Harry Catterick, Wednesday were

transformed by the fresh ideas he brought and the appealing, yet pragmatic style of play he fostered. At the back Don Megson, Peter Johnson, Peter Swan, Tony Kay and Tom McAnearney together formed a daunting defensive unit, dependably backed up by the hands of Springett. 'Ron was a very good keeper,' says Megson. 'The biggest thing you'd say about him was that you trusted him. You knew he wouldn't make too many mistakes. That when he would come out for the ball he'd get it.'

Under the instruction of Catterick, Springett also had the role of beginning many of the side's attacks. He would launch the ball, well beyond the halfway line and with great accuracy, to a specific target who would then attempt to win headers and make knockdowns for others. The forwards, moving fluidly in the upper-third, might then go on to create a chance. Such was the vitality of the team that during the first season back in the top level in 1959-60, they managed to demolish West Ham 7-0 at Hillsborough. 'At that time we were mixing it with the best,' remembers Springett.

In training he worked tirelessly on his fitness and stopping, spending long hours preparing for upcoming encounters with opposition forwards. 'I studied the techniques of as many players as I could,' he says. 'I tried to outwit them, did things which I hoped would distract them or make them hesitate. As a keeper you used every possible method to try and give yourself the upper hand.' Part of this approach included keeping a small notebook detailing the penalty-taking habits of other players. This meticulously compiled record enabled him to predict, based on a player's previous strikes, where they might place it the next time. 'There was,' he says, 'nowhere near the amount of television coverage in those days, so you were lucky if you came up against someone you did have notes on. I did have one on Jimmy McIlroy, though, who I saved a penalty from in my first England game, but of course he still had to put it there in order for me to save it.'

That game, against Northern Ireland at Wembley, marked the first of 33 proud international caps for Springett. 'I'm sure', he acknowledges, 'the success Wednesday were having helped me greatly with this.' Over the next few years he gathered those appearances for his country, among them a brave outing in Glasgow against Scotland where twice, in blowing wind, he risked a broken neck to dive down on the Hampden turf for the ball, and travelled to the 1962 World Cup in Chile. There he helped England qualify from a group containing Hungary, Argentina and Bulgaria. In the quarter-finals they lost 3-1 to the eventual winners Brazil.

While England had been thoroughly outclassed against their Brazilian opposition, Springett received a large portion of the blame for the loss, mainly due to the nature of a couple of the goals he conceded. Garrincha had got the first with a header before Gerry Hitchens equalised. But it was the free kick from the former, that Springett saved but could not hold on to, that let in Vava to score. Then came Garrincha's 20-yard drive, which looked to be flying over the bar before it dipped into the net. Those goals raised questions over the Wednesday keeper's abilities. Some have since said that his shorter stature made him more vulnerable to the South American's longer shots that day, others more kindly put the goals down to the Brazilian's general superiority. But as Peter Chapman observes more fairly in *The Goalkeeper's History of Britain*, the 'goals resulted from vicious shots – one a swerver, the other a dipper – by winger Garrincha that would have eluded anyone.' Sadly Chile was not the only occasion Springett's height had made him the target of critics. As a youngster he was rejected by Fulham. 'Go away and grow a bit', they told the then 5ft 3" youngster (he would get taller). Such though was his athleticism, he could leap and spring superbly to reach all areas of his goal anyway.

A year after the World Cup and Brazil, Springett conceded five against France in Paris. Officially it was Alf Ramsey's first game in charge, even though he didn't pick the team. He made only a brief appearance at half-time, offering his thoughts on the rest of the game. 'Go on, you know what you have to do', he said. Again Springett received considerable blame for England's defeat. He had an uncharacteristically bad game – a 'nightmare' according to the author Leo McKinstry, missing several crosses in the Paris ice and snow. But as Springett later explained, 'one of them was a back pass and I didn't have a chance with the other two.' Such were the conditions that night, England's right-back Jimmy Armfield believed the game should never even have gone ahead. Afterwards the players had to dangle their booted feet in the hot water of the changing room baths just to thaw their frozen laces. Springett, they said, was frozen in the England goal that night. But so were the rest of the players.

Over the next few years his involvement with the national side faded, mainly due to the emergence of Leicester's Gordon Banks. Ramsey still rated Springett, selecting him on several more occasions between 1963 and '66, the last time a 6-1 win in Norway just before the World Cup, but it was Banks who Ramsey preferred. 'Deservedly so,' says Springett.

In '66 Springett was a non-playing substitute, ready to step up in place of Banks if he was needed. 'Just to be involved in the squad was an experience,' he says, 'one I will always cherish'. At the time FIFA did not give medals to all members of a winning squad, so he and 11 others, including Jimmy Greaves, Ron Flowers, Peter Bonetti and Armfield, left the tournament undecorated. Happily, this was put right almost 40 years later after FIFA decided to give medals to all winners from every tournament before 1974 (they had done from then on). At Downing Street in 2009 Springett and the others received their medals. 'One of the greatest days of my life,' he said.

***

Following Harry Catterick's sudden departure in 1961, Wednesday wasted no time in appointing a high calibre replacement. Ajax's Vic Buckingham, an Englishman who had spent two good years in Amsterdam, winning the title in one of those seasons, was tempted home by a great opportunity with an improving club. Over recent years, thanks to the achievements of Catterick, the expectations of the Wednesday board had risen considerably. Now the club was stable and thriving, expected to compete with the best at the top of the First Division. In Buckingham, the club had secured an astute, forward-thinking football idealist. His influence, it was hoped, would further this positive period.

As a player Buckingham had spent eight steady years – four each side of the war – with Tottenham, before taking his first managerial role with the Oxbridge amateurs Pegasus, where he instilled a quick-passing attractive game. 'I can reach their feet through their minds', he said of the University team. He later moved on to Bradford Park Avenue then West Bromwich Albion, winning the FA Cup in 1954, before joining Ajax in '59. In Holland Buckingham had worked with many skilful, highly technical players who were able to move the ball swiftly, easily and instinctively to each other. Some credit him with encouraging the early hints of Total Football – the 'interchanging positional play' symbolised by Johann Cryuff in the '60s and '70s. Though, as he later acknowledged, 'their [the Dutch's] skills were different, their intellect was different and they played proper football. They didn't get this from me; it was there ready to be stirred up'.

Fresh from his experiences abroad, Buckingham tried to instil the virtues of an attractive, expansive game with his Wednesday team. 'Go out and entertain the public', he would say as he rallied the team. His philosophy, recounted in David Winner's superb examination of the Dutch game, *Brilliant Orange*, was that 'football is a serious game but an elegant game. Possession football is the thing... if you've got the ball, keep it.' Of Buckingham, Springett recalls a manager 'totally different to any other the lads had previously worked with. He had lots of new ideas.'

Unfortunately, his team failed to match the excellent second-place finish achieved in Catterick's final year. According to the defender Peter Swan, Buckingham's continental ideas, far from being inspirational and effective, were simply 'foreign'. 'He got us to work with the ball all the time', says Swan in his autobiography. 'If we could have played how Buckingham wanted us to play, all would have worked well. But I think the mistake he made was to try and change our style overnight.' By April 1964 he apparently had also lost control of his playing squad, some of whom had been involved in certain unflattering indiscretions – the latest, Eddie Holliday's conviction for being drunk (and asleep) at the wheel of a vehicle. This apparent breakdown in discipline, combined with the general declining fortunes of the team, meant the board decided to let him go. Wednesday had been good under Buckingham, 'always within striking distance of the top of the League,' wrote Percy M. Young in *Football in Sheffield*, but never quite good or 'forceful' enough to get right up there.

After leaving Sheffield Buckingham rejoined Ajax. He lasted until January 1965, unable to recreate the achievements of his previous time there, though a few months earlier did give a 17-year-old Johann Cryuff his professional debut. He then returned to England with Fulham before moving abroad again, first to Ethnikos of Greece then briefly to Barcelona in 1970, starting the revival of a club which had been struggling for years. He was, writes Jimmy Burns, 'one of the great unsung heroes of Barca'. But he had to quit after a year due to problems with his back. He went to Sevilla two years later, then finally returned to Greece with Olympiakos.

Around the time Buckingham left the club, Hillsborough was shaken by a betting scandal unearthed by the *Sunday People* newspaper. Several players were implicated in the influencing of Football League matches in which they had played and placed bets on. Now, it was revealed, Wednesday's Peter Swan and David Layne, plus Tony Kay, by now with Everton, were involved. It stunned the club. All three were banned indefinitely from the game. All three were sent to prison. 'I was shocked when the story broke,' remembers Springett. 'But because of my arrangement of living in London I was too far away from the centre of the story to know day-to-day what it was like at the club. I do know, however, that in the matches following the incident us players put it all out of our minds and did our best to continue in a professional manner, both on and off the pitch.'

The club, damaged from the scandal, turned to Sunderland's Alan Brown as their new manager. He faced a tough challenge and unquestionably was hindered by the fallout. He was not helped either by a transfer request that had been made earlier by Springett. Wednesday could not be allowed to go through any further disruption, and losing a player of his quality could not be entertained. Thankfully, then, Eric Taylor persuaded him to stay.

The high point of Brown's time in charge was the 1966 FA Cup Final, his young team coming close to winning the trophy not held by the club since 1935. As Wednesday toiled in the league (if not for a good home record they may well have been relegated) they managed to fight their way to the final of the Cup. Reading, Newcastle, Huddersfield and Blackburn were each despatched away from home, as were Chelsea in the Villa Park semi.

In that game Springett and his team-mates fought hard on a bog of a pitch to win 2-0. The tackling was hard, Chelsea's George Graham and the Owls' Vic Mobley spending much of the game injured. Springett made a good save early on, down to his left from Bobby Tambling. Each side frustrated the other and few other chances were created in the first half. In the mud it had, said Kenneth Wolstenholme in his commentary, become 'one long, painful, tiring slog'.

The goals came in the second half. A cross from the superb John Fantham was met by David Ford who headed strongly towards goal. Danny Pugh, who, aged 18, had made his debut only a few weeks earlier, got the last touch as the ball crossed the line. After that, the game ignited. Both sides missed chances before, in the closing moments, Wednesday got their second. On the break David Ford gathered a throw and crossed to Jim McCalliog who looped a header beyond Bonetti for 2-0. 'Reaching the final was a great achievement for us,' says Springett. 'We had a young team and no one had expected us to beat Chelsea.'

In the final Wednesday, all in white, faced Harry Catterick's Everton. Before 100,000 fans at Wembley, Alan Brown's men raced to a fourth minute lead through McCalliog. He, as Fantham had done so effectively against Chelsea in the semi, roamed effectively from deep, helping orchestrate much of the Owls' play from behind the forward line. His goal came thanks to another cross from Ford, met with a first-time strike from the edge of the box.

As the first half drew on, Everton began to tire as Wednesday spread their play on the vast surface. 'We just couldn't get the ball', said their midfielder Colin Harvey. Early in the second, Wednesday's lead was doubled. Fantham broke fast from the centre circle, sailed past two men and shot towards Gordon West. The keeper made the save but could not hold it, leaving the lurking Ford to ease in the rebound. 2-0 and Wednesday were in command.

Springett, meanwhile, was also playing his part. A marvellous stop denied Mike Trebilcock, a leap across his goal to make the save. 'With less than half an hour to go, having to score three times to win, most teams would have been beaten,' says Springett. Everton looked exhausted. '[T]here was', said Colin Harvey, 'no way back. We were dead on our feet.' However, with less than 15 minutes left the win was snatched quickly and crushingly away.

Trebilcock got one back, a crashing shot. Then, moments later, Everton now vibrant and searching, he got another – 2-2 – and the lead had evaporated. The clock moved past 73 minutes . . .

GERRY YOUNG: 'The tension was really high . . . as Colin Harvey booted the ball out of defence [it] came through the air, directly to me'.

It bounced awkwardly, slipping under Young's foot. An elementary mistake for a normally immaculate performer. Derek Temple, a blue flash, nipped in from his own half.

YOUNG: 'He didn't even have to gather it, he just ran on with the ball'.

SPRINGETT: 'There was only me between Temple and the goal. My thoughts were to make it as difficult for him as I could. I didn't know what he was going to do, take me on or shoot early. So I just tried to make the goal as small as possible.'

DEREK TEMPLE: 'As I got to the edge of the penalty area I aimed for the far post'.

The ball sped into the goal. 3-2 and the Cup was lost. For Springett and Wednesday, nothing from everything.

'After the match the players did the lap of honour for the fans', says Springett. 'They had been tremendous and it was our way of saying thankyou for their support. As a senior member of the team I could see that the younger lads were very upset. But I thought the experience of losing at Wembley would at least bode well for them in the future. Personally, I knew I had the World Cup to look forward to, so couldn't let my disappointment drag on for too long. Wembley would have happy and sad memories for me.'

The following year Wednesday came 11th in the league and enjoyed another decent run in the FA Cup. Again they faced Chelsea, this time in the quarter-final at Stamford Bridge. This time they were beaten 1-0. The game was one of Springett's last for the club. In May 1967, after nine great years, he moved back to London and back to QPR. Wednesday received £16,000, and at the same time paid £40,000 to the same club for Ron's brother, Peter. 'The transfer came out of the blue,' says Ron. 'I got a phone call at home one Saturday evening from Eric Taylor and he said that Wednesday had been in discussions with Rangers. I spoke to Peter and told him that Wednesday would be a great move. I was happy with the deal because I would be back playing in London. We agreed terms and it went through the following day.' Unlike his brother Peter – eight years younger than Ron – would settle permanently in Sheffield. He was a highly-rated keeper in his own right.

Peter's time at the club was in great contrast to his brother. When he arrived Wednesday were in real decline. Alan Brown had resigned in 1968, as did his successor Jack Marshall. Tom McAnearney, a player for the club for 13 years, was put in temporary charge before being replaced by the uncelebrated Danny Williams. In 1970, four years after the Wembley Cup final, Williams took the club down to the Second Division. After being first choice in his first two years, Peter found himself in – and out of the team, first competing with Peter Grummitt, then Peter Fox. Still, he made over 200 appearances during what was a difficult period for the club. He later joined Barnsley, then Scarborough. Peter tragically passed away from serious illness in 1997.

Ron himself retired from playing in 1969. 'I spent the best years of my career at Hillsborough,' he says, 'and have fantastic memories of my time there. I met some wonderful people and made many, many friends.' A few months after he left the club, Hillsborough hosted his testimonial. A crowd of 23,000 attended. 'He gave endless pleasure', wrote Eric Taylor of the stopper he brought to Wednesday in 1959. '[A] man who has discovered the game and a mastery of it', wrote another . . . 'the best keeper Wednesday have ever had.'

15

Albert Quixall

1951-58
260 appearances, 65 goals

Always the home-grown player has captured the imaginations of football supporters. The story of local boy turned good for the club they grew up following, and were nurtured by, is a common and affecting story. Better still if, after their breakthrough, that player manages to reach the highest levels, becoming a star for both club and country. Then they are remembered for years.

Albert Quixall, who made his Wednesday debut in 1951, is one such player. For a period in that decade he had the game under a spell. The first genuine poster boy after the war, 'A symbol of his era'; 'one of Britain's outstanding artists'; 'the golden boy'. An integral member of the promotion sides' of '52 and '56, he made more than 250 appearances in league and cup, becoming in the process one of the club's most consistently effective attacking players. And in 1958 he became Britain's most expensive footballer when he moved to Manchester United, Matt Busby's first signing out of hospital following the Munich air crash.

Quixall made his debut in early '51, a draw with Chelsea at Hillsborough. With blond curly hair and baby face, shorts hitched up unconventionally high and an air of courageous aggression, Quixall was an endearing figure. He lived close to the stadium, was Sheffield's best-known schoolboy footballer of the time and, above everything else, had wanted to play for Wednesday. 'When Jerry Bronks, secretary of the Sheffield Schools Football Federation, asked me which club I wanted to go to,' remembered Quixall, 'I told him there was only one.' Another youngster making his debut that day against Chelsea was Alan Finney.

Quixall had met Finney when they were players in the Yorkshire League, quickly they became close friends. They were seen as a breath of fresh air against the backdrop of post-war austerity two young, exciting players keen to impress On the pitch, they became a dangerous combination. Frequently, Finney would give Quixall a pass from the wing and race forward to receive the one-two. By now Quixall had moved beyond the defence and was able to cut in towards goal. 'We [had] almost a telepathic understanding,' said Quixall.

However, the pair were, a mixed blessing to the team. At that point, the side had a fair quantity of inexperienced players, and perhaps because of this Wednesday were not performing so well in the league. Sometimes it is particularly unfair to blame the fortunes of the side on its more youthful elements – certainly they had sufficient skill and enthusiasm – but beyond their promise they at that point lacked the know-how to fully compete against the hardened professionals of the First Division. In Quixall's case, after his goalscoring introduction, he made only one more appearance in that 1950-51 campaign. 'I don't think I did anything wrong,' he recalled, 'but I obviously wasn't seen as the immediate answer to Wednesday's quest for someone to help in the fight against relegation.' Wednesday were relegated on goal difference.

1951-52 got off to an indifferent start for Wednesday, the opening run including embarrassing slip ups against Sheffield United, Leeds and Rotherham. Quixall was recalled to the side to try to provide some much required attacking invention (though with 26 conceded in August and September, one could argue that preventing goals was as much of an issue for the Owls). At home to Barnsley – the game in which Derek Dooley began his incredible goalscoring spell of 47 in 30 games – the season, and Quixall's career, ignited. He made 26 appearances as Wednesday ran home to the championship with an unstoppable run and an even 100 goals. The team was free-scoring, successful and with young players like Quixall and Alan Finney weaving the play, along with Dooley getting the goals, had great promise for the future.

Quixall and Dooley had played together in the Yorkshire and Central Leagues and both were appreciative of the other's talents.

Dooley was particularly grateful for his colleague's passing abilities, with many of his forward sprays landing nicely into his path. Often it was Quixall's through balls that fed Dooley's runs. (Even though the enthusiasm of the receiver meant that his ability to keep the ball under control appeared harder to him than finishing a chance.) When Dooley injured his knee at Swansea that November he had been chasing one of Quixall's passes. When chasing another, at Preston's Deepdale the following season, he broke and subsequently lost his leg. 'I was devastated,' Quixall said of that day. 'I just broke down and wept.'

By now Quixall had already made his first appearances for England. In October 1952, aged 19, he had played in a strong FA Representative line up against the Royal Air Force, then impressed enough in a game against the League of Ireland to receive a call up to the full squad. His international debut came in a World Cup qualifier at Ninian Park against Wales. England won 4-1. The next week he appeared in a showpiece at Wembley against a star studded Rest of Europe XI.

A second full cap came the following month against Northern Ireland at Goodison Park. Despite England securing their place at the 1954 World Cup in Switzerland, the press reaction to a 3-1 win was almost wholly negative. All year there had been worries that the England forward line was failing to meet expectations and against Ireland England had faded quickly. Apart from a few bursts from Stanley Matthews, none of the forwards, Quixall among them, impressed. He was dropped for the next match against Hungary at Wembley.

The next year Quixall travelled to Switzerland as one of the squad's junior members. He didn't see any playing time, but could take advice from the more experienced players, among them Matthews. '[He] was particularly kind,' Quixall remembered. 'I loved to practise with him or hear him talk football. He used to call me "son" so I retaliated by naming him "dad".

Quixall made two further two appearances for his country the following year during a short tour of the Iberian Peninsula. In the first match they were held 1-1 against Spain at the Bernabau stadium, Madrid, then four days later went down 3-1 to Portugal in Porto. It proved a disappointing end to his international career. Certainly at the time, few would have predicted he would not play for England again. Indeed, as late as 1957 he remained in the running for a place, *Charles Buchan's Football Monthly* arguing that he still had 'the makings of the forward schemer that England needs.'

Quixall's career, it seemed, had reached its first peak. By 1953-54 he was an established member of the Wednesday side, having displaced the great Redfern Froggatt, and his attacking play was becoming of greater benefit to his forward team-mates. There also came some accusations of cockiness, ones he assuredly batted off. 'They call me "big-head", he said. 'Well, if having confidence in myself is big-headedness I plead guilty to the charge.'

While the team stuttered in the league that season, barely avoiding relegation, individually Quixall shone. A run to the FA Cup semi-finals brought the most joy in that campaign. In a third round replay at Bramall Lane, thanks to a host of missed chances from the home side, Wednesday managed a 3-1 win over Sheffield United. United's star Jimmy Hagan ran the show and, with a strong wind aiding him in the first half, amazed the crowd with a succession of darting passes and runs which left the Wednesday players behind. However, after hardly touching the ball in the first half, the visitors, with the wind now to their advantage, turned the game in their favour, even after being reduced to 10 men following the dismissal of Vin Kenny. The first goal came from Alan Finney who, unmarked, latched onto the ball after Quixall's dummy. George Davies then added a second with a low hard shot into the near post. Jackie Sewell rounded off the win.

In the fourth round another replay was required, this time against Chesterfield. Cushioned by two inches of snow on the Saltergate pitch (a substantial blanket on which to be playing football), the timing and strength of Quixall's passing – long or short – helped demonstrate his superb ability in the 4-2 win that day. Though not yet a goalscorer, it was obvious that he could build attacks with ease. Chesterfield played well, Wednesday looking most dangerous when Quixall was on the ball. Working brilliantly with Finney, who himself had an excellent game, and whose centres had set-up Jack Shaw for the first, Shaw again for the second (via Sewell), then Sewell (via Shaw) for the third, he shone, twisting and pulling the Chesterfield defence about the difficult surface. After Dennis Woodhead struck the fourth, the Owls were through.

In the fifth and sixth rounds' Everton were despatched 3-1, as were Bolton, 2-0 in another replay, setting up a semi with Preston at Maine Road, Manchester. The game was a bruising encounter, North End's powerfully aggressive defenders Willy Forbes and Tommy Docherty brutally subduing Quixall, Sewell and the rest of the Wednesday forward line that day. At one point in the 2-0 defeat, the latter had to leave the pitch for ten minutes following the rough treatment he received from the pair, while Quixall emerged from one crunching challenge with his shirt in tatters.

For Wednesday the next three years were ones of both despair and elation in equal measure as they were repeatedly relegated from and promoted to the First Division. During this time Quixall's game developed significantly, 1955-56 proving in particular a transformative season. That year Wednesday once again were promoted as champions as Quixall emerged a more potent attacking force. Whereas before he had sat deep at inside forward, now he had begun getting forward more frequently, adding to the goalscoring threat of the team (and getting a few for himself). That season he reached 17 strikes, second only in the charts to the centre-forward Roy Shiner's 33. In '56-57 Quixall got 24, making him the club's top scorer back in the First. He explained his transformation in straightforward terms. 'I met Jimmy Hagan and he told me not to be afraid of going up and having a shot,' he said. 'I wasn't suddenly a different Quixall. 'I simply became more conscious of trying to score after being content for so long to try and make goals for others.'

His impressive tally that return year cemented Wednesday's highest league finish of the decade, 14th in the First. That year they had begun the strongly, gaining good wins over West Brom (4-2), Chelsea (4-0), Newcastle (4-0) and Cardiff (5-3). But each of those had come at home. On the road it was a different story as Wednesday picked up just two wins all season, shipping almost 60 goals. The following season, 1957-58, their away form was even worse. No wins away from Hillsborough all season. Not surprisingly they again were relegated. Quixall, was one of the brighter lights in that mostly forgettable year.

Publicly he cut a dedicated, ambitious persona. Early in his career he had stated his ambitions clearly. 'If at all possible,' he said, 'I want to become an automatic choice for England. I know what a task that is because one has to maintain a very high standard of play all the time. But if I do not succeed, it will not be for want of trying.' He hoped to follow in the steps of skilful position players such as Wilf Mannion and Stanley Matthews. Encouraged by other Wednesday players Eddie Gannon and Jackie Sewell, whom early on in his career he had often consulted, and despite the ups and downs of the team he was playing in, Quixall had made great progress since his debut in '51.

**

1957-58 was the season of the Munich air disaster where 23 people perished, among them eight Manchester United players, after the plane carrying them home from a European Cup tie in Belgrade crashed in the snow before take-off. It was Wednesday who provided United their first opposition in a delayed fifth round FA Cup tie at Old Trafford. United were broken; the team they fielded, a mix of youth-teamers and hastily-signed older professionals; the match, said one, the 'most emotion-charged game of football that had ever been played'.

Because of the passion of the 60,000-strong crowd, many of whom had queued for hours to stand together and mourn the absent players, and up against the determination of the assembled United side, Wednesday stood no chance. They were overrun 3-0, but of course the result was of minor consequence. The night was particularly solemn for Quixall who had been friends with several of those who had died. 'I don't think anyone who played in the game or who watched it will ever forget that night', he said. 'United ran their hearts out, and no matter how well we had played they would have beaten us. They were playing like men inspired.'

As the United manager Matt Busby fought for his life in a hospital bed in Germany, his assistant Jimmy Murphy was tasked with rebuilding the team. In the immediacy he had to put some semblance of a side together, then had to identify longer-term targets that could be signed either before Busby returned, or at least recommended to him when he did. And though Wednesday had lost 3-0 that day, and finished the season relegated, evidently Murphy was impressed by Quixall.

Probably the game was not the first time he had come to the

attention of Murphy and United. Don Gibson, a Wednesday player who had married Busby's daughter, had previously spoken of Quixall, raving week on week of his talents, heralding him as the gifted technician and an ideal man for the Reds. Quixall had also scored the consolation in a 4-1 defeat in Manchester the previous season, plus one in the 2-1 home win a few months after. When Busby returned, the views of Murphy and others at the club seemed to persuade him of the young forward's abilities.

Despite starting well under Harry Catterick in 1958-59, Quixall had already decided he wanted a move away from the club. He made a transfer request in September which was accepted. 'Last season, I could not ask for a transfer with the club being in a sinking position,' Quixall told the *Sheffield Star*. 'Now they are second from the top of the Second Division and they are doing well . . . You get looked at more in First Division football and better experience.' Busby then made his move, and for a record £45,000 Quixall was a United player. Wednesday had lost their golden boy.

His United debut came at home to Tottenham in September 1958, a difficult beginning on a bumpy pitch and in windy weather. He and his new team-mates failed to impress and were held 2-2. Quixall was prominent in early attacks but later subdued by Jim Iley, whose team went ahead 1-0, then 2-0. After that the comeback started with United's new signing at the centre of it. After Iley mis-controlled the ball, Quixall gave chase to the ball, kept it in touch, ran it past the keeper then centred for striker Colin Webster to score (he got the equaliser, too).

Sadly, the move to Manchester never really worked. It seemed his efforts and actions did not always match up to his skills. This was a problem both for his old and new club. Blessed with the ability to take control of a game, to control the course of play 'rather than being its servant,' he appeared somewhat naive of an overall team pattern.

At Wednesday reaction to his transfer had been subdued. While Eric Taylor was disappointed to have lost a player he considered one of the club's greatest, privately manager Harry Catterick was ambivalent. He saw Quixall as a luxury player, lacking in the mental and positional discipline to fit within the rigid team he was building at Hillsborough At inside-forward, Quixall was supposed to both attack and defend with great effort, making chances while rushing back to support the half-backs in midfield. But he seemed content to do as he liked. 'His failing was a tendency to take things for granted,' said Jackie Sewell, his former Wednesday team-mate. 'I often felt that he might have achieved more if he had been a better listener and shown a greater willingness to learn and work at his game. We often had tactical talks . . . but Albert was never one for analysis, and I think that's why he didn't win more caps. He was content to go out and play his own way, and never quite understood that you couldn't do that at the top level.'

A similar sentiment was revealed at United. 'While he was a delight to play with when we had possession,' remembered Wilf McGuiness, 'when we lost it the fellow playing behind him had two players to mark. Albert didn't do enough in those situations and had to be reminded of his responsibilities quite forcibly'. 'He was inclined to disappear on a bad day, and he never got a grip on a game', said the journalist Keith Dewhurst

Still, he helped United to second place in the First Division in 1959, and won the FA Cup in '63, at times showing signs of his previous excellent Wednesday form, feeding Bobby Charlton those well placed through balls as he had done for Dooley. However, following a comprehensive thrashing by Everton in the Charity Shield at the start of 1963-64 Quixall, along with David Herd and Johnny Giles, were dropped, replaced by the youth players David Sadler, Ian Moir and Phil Chisnall – the newest generation of Busby Babes who could be trained in exactly the manner United's Scottish manager wanted.

In 1964 he was moved on to Oldham, later playing for Stockport County, Altrincham and Radcliffe Borough. He became a scrap metal merchant in the Manchester area along with a friend of his son, who introduced him to the business at a time when players were threatening to strike for the abolition of the maximum wage. After the great promise of his move to United, by now Quixall's career had stalled. At that higher level for England and United (for whom his form doubtless was erratic) it appears his approach, not his raw ability, is ultimately what set him back.

He is, though, best remembered for the early style and exuberance shown as a teenager with Wednesday. In those early days he refused to believe that his career had a ceiling, or that his cultured game would ever become corrupted by absence of form. 'I play for the love of the game,' he once said. And that enthusiasm, coupled with his great belief, led to his best playing years. 'I simply cannot resist kicking a ball about, anytime anywhere. It was this love of the game that made me give up my job as an apprentice joiner so that I could devote my whole time to the game.' Looking back, he remained satisfied with his time as a player. He had held ambitions to play for his country – he did. And to reach the top level of the British game – he had, at least momentarily. 'I achieved a lot in my teens and had some great times in football', he said. 'I'm not bitter by any means. I don't think I ever stopped thinking of my Wednesday days as the best time of my career.'

16

Chris Waddle

1992-96
147 appearances, 15 goals

Third place on their return to the First Division in 1991-92 had established Wednesday as one of the top sides in the country. With cash to come from the new, moneyed Premier League, and a UEFA Cup adventure, the club was well positioned to move forward. Buoyed by manager Trevor Francis's seamless takeover from Ron Atkinson, the board was ready to provide the backing he required to improve the playing squad. Further building would surely bring the trophies the club desired. Of the signings made that summer, one in particular stood out, lifting the expectations of the fans to a new height.

When he arrived from Olympique Marseille in the summer of '92 Chris Waddle was Wednesday's biggest ever signing, a world-renowned gangling maestro of the wing and true star of the game. Though aged 31, he arrived fresh-faced and clean-cut, his spiky hair informative of the style seen on many playgrounds at the time, the un-tucked shirt blowing free as he dribbled effortlessly past his confused opponents, delivering the quick turns and bamboozling tricks that had helped make his name at Newcastle, Tottenham and in France. 'I love entertaining people,' he said, 'being a showman'. And the blue half of Sheffield came to love him for it.

If not a record breaking fee (the £1 million he cost was eclipsed by the previous year's top signing Chris Woods), the wages offered (reputedly £4,000 per week, a fortune at the time) signalled the extent to which Wednesday were able to compete with their rivals for such a skilful talent. In Waddle the supporters had a stand out superman

153

to worship, alongside their other idols David Hirst, John Sheridan and Roland Nilsson. And in turn he rewarded them, demonstrating in that first season the full breadth of his footballing abilities.

For all the pomp of his arrival, the beginning of 1992-93 was frustrating for Waddle. On the opening day at Everton he twisted his knee and was substituted before half-time. The match ended 1-1. Wednesday then stuttered disappointingly to just one win in their next six games. But with Waddle back for the Coventry game at Hillsborough, results would improve up until Christmas. Wins came against Nottingham Forest, Tottenham, Oldham and QPR ahead of a 3-3 draw with Manchester United which saw the Owls race to a 3-0 lead – one of the goals set up by Waddle's cross – before being pegged back.

As the season drew on, evidence of Waddle's class became clearer. While never the swiftest runner, when he did have the ball he was breathtaking. Like a disinterested schoolboy appears lethargic in class only to spring into action at the bell, when Waddle received possession he ignited. With the ball glued to his boot he would speedily beat an opposition player, a death feign and lightening step-over his weapon, before finishing, more often than not, with a perfectly delivered pass or shot. In the return fixture with Everton that season came one such instance – Man of the Match in the 3-1 victory, scoring one and having two fine free-kicks saved. '[H]is fantastic vision,' said his manager Trevor Francis, 'allied to the ability to place the ball exactly where he sees it in the picture, has made him undoubtedly the best player in the country'.

That year Wednesday reached as high as fourth position in the league, finishing seventh by the end, but is best remembered for runs in both the FA and League cups – two finals over three matches – and for the four memorable evenings in the UEFA Cup.

In the opening round of the latter competition the lightweights Spora Luxembourg were straightforwardly seen off at home 8-1, Waddle curling in his first for the club. That was followed by a 2-1 win in the second leg. Kaiserslautern of the Bundesliga awaited the Owls in the next round – proper opponents this time.

Wednesday went down 3-1 in Germany, Hirst's red card at 1-1 making the defeat somewhat inevitable. (Hirst had scored Wednesday's goal, with Waddle the maker, and most believed that his dismissal for a push on Marco Haber, whose play-acting led to the striker's card, had been unjust.)

Back in England a hot and fiercely vocal crowd of 28,000 spurred Wednesday to a 1-0 lead. It was, said the midfielder Danny Wilson, 'the best noise I'd ever heard at Hillsborough'. But the visitors equalised, and did so again after Sheridan had put Wednesday back ahead in the second half. 5-3 to the Germans on aggregate but a memorable experience nonetheless for club's players and fans.

By the spring of '93 the Owls had reached the two domestic cup finals. Having never won a trophy at Wembley, Waddle saw it as his personal responsibility to succeed on this stage. He had played in all nine League Cup ties to that point and, in one of his greatest performances for the Owls, guided then to the famous FA Cup semi-final victory over Sheffield United. In that overwhelmingly one-sided game, Wednesday thoroughly dominated their less splendid city neighbours and made the Blades pay dearly for choosing to not man-mark Waddle. He was able to demonstrate the full range of his talents, tormenting their defence all afternoon.

He scored the opener after two minutes. When United's John Pemberton fouled Mark Bright the two free-kick specialists of the Wednesday team, Waddle and John Sheridan, stood over the ball. 'I just told Shez to get out of the way', said the one to the other. A run up and . . . GOAL! A rifle past Alan Kelly from 25 yards. Manic celebrations from every Owl in the stands. And Waddle, with hands aloft, running off. 'For ten seconds you just lose your head', he once said of scoring a goal. Two minutes in to the semi-final of the FA Cup, he lost his head. A perfect beginning to a perfect occasion. *We are dizzy still*.

The goal was only Waddle's third of the season. Of course, he was about more than that, though. Expected to work as an auxiliary playmaker for Wednesday, he was allowed – and preferred – to drift inward on his better left foot, opening up space for overlapping full-backs, or making room for the diagonal pass or run on the inside. As the semi progressed he continued to unpick the United defence with such moves; setting up Sheridan, who had a shot saved, then Warhurst, who hit the bar. It was obvious United could not contain him. '[T]hey sought him here and they sought him there', said *The Guardian*. 'To no avail'.

The onslaught suggested nothing other than a comfortable Wednesday win, yet somehow Dave Bassett's men managed an equaliser. Just before half time Alan Cork was released one-on-one against Chris Woods. He placed the ball underneath the Wednesday 'keeper and past the desperately sliding Waddle, who had run back to help, into the net.

Thankfully in the second half Wednesday resumed their domination. Kelly in the United goal performed magnificently and was the only reason a conclusion wasn't reached in normal time. In the extra time that followed, one of his saves, an impossible one-handed stretch, somehow managed to deny Hirst. On 107 minutes, however, a Harkes' corner reached Bright's head and this time Kelly's goal was breached. 2-1 and Wednesday were through to the final.

In contrast to his winning performance in the semi, Waddle was largely ineffective in the final and replay against Arsenal (as he had been a few weeks earlier in the final of the League Cup, again against Arsenal). Identifying Waddle as Wednesday's main threat, Arsenal sought to quell his influence and, in all three games, pretty much succeeded, either marking him out of the contest or forcing him inside where he would be crowded by several deep-lying red shirts. In doing so the Gunners managed to stop his and, in similar fashion, John Sheridan's creative influence. When Andy Linighan's header crashed into the net in the last moments of extra-time in the FA Cup final replay, it meant the closing moment of Waddle's first year back in England would not be spent lifting the famous trophy, but instead sat tearful on the Wembley turf contemplating what might have been.

***

Waddle had become the third most expensive player in world football when in 1989 he transferred from Tottenham to Marseille for £4.25 million. Only Diego Maradona's move from Barcelona to Napoli, and Ruud Gullit's from PSV Eindhoven to AC Milan had eclipsed that amount. Bernard Tapie, the eccentric owner of Marseille, who was later jailed for charges associated to bribery and other financial crimes, had assembled a costly, and hugely entertaining and successful outfit. That year, Waddle became the next part of his jigsaw.

At first, integration for the Englishman was difficult. He struggled with the language, spent the first few weeks living in a run-down hotel with his wife and young child, and was exposed to a training regime far more demanding than he had been used at Tottenham. At one point he even asked to come home. '[G]oing abroad,' he said, 'was a nightmare at first.'

Eventually, though, he managed to settle. 'Whoever comes to the old Phocea takes root in its fluid, amazingly fertile soil', writes the French football journalist, Philippe Auclair, of Marseille. And Waddle settled. He learned the language, found a comfortable home, worked hard to improve his fitness and began to thrive in Marseille's team of stars. The prolific striker Jean-Pierre Papin, who looked out for him, let him live in his house for a period; the French international Jocelyn Angloma; the forward Adebi Pele; Eric Cantona, who would arrive to training on a Harley Davidson; the defender Basile Boli; and the superb Yugoslav Dragan Stojkovic. It was a great period for the club. They won three Ligue 1 titles, reached the semi-finals of the European Cup (defeated on away goals by Benfica) and, a few years later, the final (beaten on penalties by Red Star Belgrade).

Throughout that time Waddle illuminated the team. First playing behind Papin and Cantona, then later – freer – alongside Pele in behind the lone Papin. The Englishman, whether creator or finisher, was always among the goals. Papin was a particular admirer of his provider. 'I got along with all the players but had a special affinity with Chris', he said. 'He is one of the most talented and gracious players I have ever met. Once Chris was confident and physically on top, he was a nightmare for every opponent.'

Waddle's own, often sublime efforts brought plentiful rewards for himself as well. Over the keeper and a back-heel in to the net against Paris Saint-Germain. In from the by-line and a top corner strike against Toulouse. A chip from outside the area against Rennes. And best of all against AC Milan, a volley scored while concussed in the European Cup, a goal he had no recollection of. 'I must have had a bad head because I volleyed it with my right foot,' he said, 'and I never volley it with my right foot.' He was, says Olivia Blair in her essay on Waddle's time in France, 'a maverick'; 'an entertainer'. The fans, as later they would come to do in Sheffield, adored him, calling him, appropriately, *Le Magicien*.

It was a long way from the north east sausage factory where he worked while turning out at weekends for the local non-League side Tow Law. Famously, the story goes, Waddle arrived for his interview at the factory on a friend's motorbike and, unable to remove his crash helmet, simply lifted the visor and spoke through it for the duration. He still got the job. Newcastle United soon spotted him playing for Law and offered him a contract, paying his club £500 for his services. He was 20 and with much hard work his earlier promise bloomed, emerging as he did an accomplished and highly creative player for the club. Then, in 1985 Tottenham called, £590,000 moving him to the diamond lights of London.

Despite, however, Waddle's exploits in Marseille and later Sheffield, he couldn't get a game for England. His first cap had come in 1985 and he was involved in Mexico '86 and the 1988 European Championship. Going in to Italia '90 he had amassed 52 appearances and went on to enjoy a decent tournament, setting up Gary Lineker against Jack Charlton's Ireland in the group stages, before firing up in the knock-outs when given a freer role by Bobby Robson. (Robson had switched formation from 4-4-2 to 3-5-2, sparing Waddle the bulk of his defensive duties, allowing him to wander forward and cause more trouble more often.)

Understandably, thoughts of him in the white shirt have become monopolised by the memory of his missed penalty in Turin. But it would be unfair, as is often the case, to remember Waddle's international career for just that moment. Replayed many times over, the blasted effort which put England out and West Germany through to the final was not as bad as is actually made out. As Jonathan Wilson correctly observes in *The Anatomy of England*, 'His shot passed no more than nine inches over the bar, possibly less; it was, in other words, a foot from being perfect'.

After Italy he started only once more for England, against Turkey in 1991. That followed two substitute appearances against Hungary and Poland. His performance in the Turkey game was fairly standard, but certainly did not warrant him being dropped entirely from the plans of the new national manager Graham Taylor. Taylor preferred just one flair winger, so as to maintain a strong presence in the centre of midfield, which meant Liverpool's John Barnes was often preferred to Waddle. Even after his starring role for Wednesday in 1992-93, though, Taylor remained unmoved. '[I]t [is] absolutely crucial to be strong enough not to dive in and select a player who may be the current "flavour" of the month', he once wrote tellingly. 'I don't think I ever fitted into Graham's plans', said Waddle. 'He didn't seem to fancy me as a player . . . I think I knew in my heart of hearts that once he was appointed manager I wouldn't be around for long.'

***

Though the remainder of his time at Wednesday was punctuated by injuries, he still was able to put in some brilliant performances. In late 1993, in a 3-3 draw with Leeds, he scored a thunderous long range free-kick before delivering a beautiful cross for Ryan Jones who put Wednesday 2-1 ahead. The next month, in a 5-0 trouncing at Hillsborough, he tore West Ham United apart. The architect of four goals that day, Waddle repeatedly tormented their left-back David Burrows – showing him one way then the other; a drop of the shoulder one moment, a fast step-over the next. He set up the first, a corner headed in by Andy Pearce. For the second, a step inwards then a cutting ball in for Bright to finish. He scored the third himself, a run from the centre-circle and a 30 yard drive – everyday stuff for our man Waddle – before setting-up another for Nigel Jemson. For the fifth goal he rested. 'There's no stopping him in that mood', said Burrows afterwards, defeated, exhausted.

Soon after Waddle picked up another injury, troubles with his achilles, meaning that save for a substitute appearance against Chelsea in the FA Cup and a start at Old Trafford in the semi-finals of the League Cup (1-0 to Manchester United that night, 4-1 in the second leg), the rest of his season was a write off. Wednesday again came seventh in the league. In 1994-95 he missed around a half of the club's games, partly because of injury, partly because the team had been altered so much that he wasn't necessarily a first-choice pick. Francis, it was said, believed his once star signing couldn't now regularly see out the 90 minutes. During Waddle's four years at the club a substantial portion of his appearances came during his first 18 months. He started just over half of the club's league games with Chris Bart-Williams and, when not chosen at right-back, Dan Petrescu sometimes picked in his position. As with his international career,

Waddle's time at Wednesday was petering out.

When Wednesday paid Marseille £1 million for Waddle in 1992 there was speculation he might have joined Newcastle United instead, reuniting with his old team-mate Kevin Keegan who was now their manager. But he was persuaded to join Wednesday. Trevor Francis had first contacted Waddle five months before the transfer and had agreed most of the necessary terms. The transfer, negotiated and finalised in Paris by Francis and club secretary Graham Mackrell, supposedly with instruction from chairman Dave Richards to not exceed £1 million, was a very big deal for Wednesday at the time. 'I thought we might lose him,' Francis remarked, 'especially as the others [Newcastle and, it is believed, Leeds and Monaco] offered better financial packages. But he said he'd given his word and would keep it.'

Considering what happened to the club's finances in later years, however, had Waddle and the others signed around the time been worth the expense?

In *Why England Lose*, Simon Kuper and Stefan Szymanski observe that for the most part football clubs do not, and, they argue, should not make money. 'It is', they say, 'almost impossible to run a football club like a profit-making business. But that doesn't mean they should . . . be badly run'. At the time of Waddle's arrival Wednesday, guided by Richards, were embarking on a high-risk recruitment strategy to see them keep up with other clubs. Between 1990 and 2000, the year Richards left, bank borrowings had grown from £1.4 to over £16 million as increasing numbers were provided for player transfers and wages.

Richards admitted to having no great knowledge of the game, but managed still to sit on the Wednesday board for over a decade. A businessman of dubious success, he had been an employee of Sheffield-based Three Star Engineering in the '80s, rising to director then offered a position on the board at Hillsborough. He later bought Three Star when the holding company which had taken it over entered receivership. Under his guide it became loss making and closed in 2001.

When Bert McGee resigned as chairman of Wednesday in 1989, Richards took over. Up until then the club was solvent, over the previous 15 years it had on average spent only £35,000 a year on players and held only inconsequential debt. In general their prudent policy had served them well, even though it is seen as the reason Howard Wilkinson left for Leeds in '88. Under Richards, though, much notion of financial care was kicked out. In Ron Atkinson's two years in charge between 1989 and '91 the club's wage bill increased 100% from £1.7 to £3.4 million. And even though that investment had brought the tangible success of promotion and a major trophy in '91, it came at some cost.

Atkinson's successor Trevor Francis continued the outlay on both transfer fees and wages. In 1991-92 he spent net £2.6 million on Chris Woods, Paul Warhurst and Chris Bart-Williams. A year later he spent some more on Waddle and Mark Bright. The year after that, Andy Sinton and Des Walker, each costing £2.75 million, Dan Petrescu, £1.3 million, Ian Nolan, £1.5 million, Peter Atherton, £800,000, Klas Ingesson, £800,000 and Ian Taylor, £1 million, were all brought in. Naturally the wage bill rose further, to £5.6 million by 1995. So did the debt, £8 million. With the exception of Walker, Atherton and perhaps Petrescu (later sold to Chelsea for a profit), few of those signings had the quality to match the players they had come in to replace. Financially, Wednesday were drifting into trouble. Television cash from the new Premier League helped fund some of Francis's activities in the transfer market, but increasing losses had gradually bumped up a dept pile that was beginning to eat away at the club.

Against this backdrop, 13th place finish in the league in 1994-95 saw Francis ousted a year before his contract was due to expire. Many saw Waddle backed by an experienced assistant as a suitable replacement. Instead, Luton's David Pleat was appointed. Under Pleat, Waddle was in –and out of the team, the new manager preferring to use him as an impact substitute. After a season of this, he moved on to the Scottish side Falkirk.

Dave Richards, meanwhile, continued borrowing to keep up with the other Premier League clubs. Expenditure on transfers, stadium development and, most damagingly, wages all increased significantly. In 1996-97 he oversaw Charterhouse Capital's investment in the club, in which 37% of Wednesday was acquired for £16 million. Thanks to the deal, club directors, save for Geoff Hulley and the Labour MP Joe Ashton, managed to take a good windfall, on paper at least, for themselves. Richards himself made £137,960 by purchasing club shares in the lead up to the investment, aware that *some* investment was upcoming – likely imminent. This positioned him and the others well for when Charterhouse concluded their investment.

In March 1997 Richards wrote a letter that explained the detail of the deal. In the six months preceding that letter, when, according to Charterhouse and Graham Mackrell, the deal was in discussion, Richards and his fellow directors' had been buying up the shares. After the deal, the value of those freshly acquired shares rose substantially, giving, as David Conn puts it in his book *The Beautiful Game*, 'an appearance of gold-rush profiteering'. That the club was still a limited company when this was going on meant it was not considered insider trading. As Silitoe's Seaton would say, 'You don't need to tell me what's right and what ain't right'.

Unbelievably after this, Richards was offered a job with the Premier League in 2000. On the same day Wednesday had played their last game in the top level against Leicester City, Richards, in his new role as chairman of the Premier League, was handing the trophy to Manchester United. During his time with the Owls the club's overall debt had risen from £1.3 to £26 million.

But was the borrowing the club had undertaken worth the risk?

Of course Waddle and his team had brought substantial joy to the Wednesday supporters during those lovely days of '92-93 – there is no happier recent era. Yet all of it had come at great cost, ultimately proving unsustainable. And even if that later expenditure had brought success, the structural problems that contributed to the downfall of the club would still have remained (although it would have been easier to manage).

People will say this expenditure was well worth it, and that the years afterwards were not. But the two periods must sit together. Sheridan, Nilsson, Bright and Waddle worked out well for the club. Sinton, Nolan and Ingesson did not. Nor did Wim Jonk (who was said to have been on a £5,000 bonus for each game he missed through injury) or Gilles De Bilde, both members of Danny Wilson's 1999-00 relegation failures. And of course while Waddle's commitment to the club is without question, he still looks for their results, still lives in the city, still feels sincerely the pain the fans have gone through in recent years, his transfer having had to sit among those other unsuccessful signings. All those transfers represent the changing financial attitude of the club, from prudence in the late 1980s to the subsequent carelessness of Richards' time, and because of it Wednesday and its supporters suffered for a long time after. Such is the nature of today's game.

Waddle went on to play a few games for Falkirk, offered some minutes in Scotland to regain his fitness, before joining Bradford City. He then went to Sunderland, the club he supported as a boy, and had a stint at Burnley as player-manager, following that with a few games for Torquay, Worksop Town, and other local non-League and pub teams. 'I just enjoy getting my boots on', he said.

After Torquay Waddle moved back to Wednesday as reserve team coach. David Pleat had left, and when Danny Wilson was sacked in 2000 Waddle was promoted as Peter Shreeves' assistant. Though the pair's record was good, they couldn't save the club from relegation that year. Many believed they would be kept on in the First Division, but they were overlooked, Paul Jewell preferred instead and Shreeves staying on as his deputy. So Waddle left Wednesday for a second time.

Since then he has coached a little, most recently for Teversal, while commentating for radio and television. 'I was told that if I said "to be perfectly honest" one more time they'd pull the plug', he said of his initial work for the BBC. Happily though they kept faith and he is now one of the more astute, honest and listenable co-commentators around (his screams of 'no, no, no' in the background of the radio broadcast of England's trouncing by Germany in South Africa in the 2010 World Cup a notable highlight.)

17

Des Walker

1993-2001
362 appearances

If the signing of Chris Waddle in 1992 demonstrated how serious Wednesday were in competing with the top clubs in the Premier League, the arrival of Des Walker a year later strengthened this ambition. With lightning pace and excellent positional sense, Walker, the star defender of Italia '90, had won 58 England caps by the time he came to Sheffield. Now, in what should have been the prime years of his career, he was ready to rebuild the great reputation he had held at Nottingham Forest before his disappointing year in Italy with Sampdoria. Though subsequently Wednesday would sign other established international players, none would come with such a reputation as he.

Although the cup finals of '93 were close affairs, defeats in both combined with a seventh-place finish in the Premier League made clear that Wednesday had work to do if they were to progress. In 1993-94 the dismantling of the '91 League Cup-winning side continued, the experienced Danny Wilson, Peter Shirtliff, Phil King, Nigel Pearson and Viv Anderson all leaving – along with younger players John Harkes and Paul Warhurst – but the board continued to back Trevor Francis, allowing him to spend heavily on replacements. He bought Walker, who at £2.75 million more than doubled the fee paid for Waddle and Chris Woods, while Andy Sinton also arrived from Queens Park Rangers for the same fee. A highly regarded midfielder, Sinton would provide a left-sided counterpart in midfield to Waddle on the right. (In choosing a move to Wednesday rather than Arsenal, he had claimed that Wednesday was a team on the rise.) Andy Pearce was also signed for £500,000 from Coventry City.

Perhaps because of this upheaval, the season began in unimpressive fashion. Wednesday failed to score in their opening four games, a problem made worse when David Hirst suffered an injury at West Ham (part of a series of setbacks which would wreck his next 18 months). Gordon Watson and Nigel Jemson proved able deputies alongside Mark Bright, top scorer with 23, but Hirst was badly missed. Injuries to John Sheridan and Waddle also weakened the midfield. And while Graham Hyde, Ryan Jones and Chris Bart Williams covered reasonably well, their inferior talent suggested the many departures of the summer had left the squad dangerously under strength.

With Nigel Pearson soon to be sold to Middlesbrough, having not played regularly since an injury in February '93, Walker began life as an Owl alongside Andy Pearce in the centre of the back four. Though fast and strong, Walker was not that able on the ball, his job simply to prevent goals by dampening any defensive danger as quickly as possible. Pearce, seen ostensibly as a replacement for Peter Shirtliff (who moved on to Wolves disappointed to have missed out on the chance to play alongside Walker) was much the same style of player, if nowhere near in terms of class. Certainly, he could not offer an outlet comparable to Shirtliff and Pearson, who began attacks by delivering the ball to a full-back or midfielder. The decision to start with two such similar defenders proved a major flaw in Francis' planning for the season, leaving little alternatives in that area.

Despite these troubles, however, the team managed to pick up from their scoreless opening few matches and went on a lengthy unbeaten run to steady their league record, including the 5-0 'Waddle' game against West Ham and a 5-1 romp over Everton. By the end of the campaign, Walker's steady displays saw him voted the fans' Player of the Year, a happy resurrection of fortunes for the now former England man.

***

Walker had arrived at Nottingham Forest aged 16 after being released by Tottenham Hotspur and soon became a regular in Brian Clough's team. Thanks to his reliable performances the young defender quickly earned the chant *'You'll never beat Des Walker'* – a tune gladly adopted by the Wednesday fans – as he emerged one of the finest centre-halves of his generation. 'I consider myself lucky and privileged,' he once said, 'to have started my career under the greatest manager there has probably ever been. At that age he [Clough] would let you know the fundamental basics of football and it would be embedded in you for the rest of your career.'

Walker got into the England team, hardly missing a game after his debut in 1988, and after Euro '92 in Sweden moved to Italian side Sampdoria – the Genoa-based club paying £1.5 million to bring him to what at the time was the most glamorous league in the world. (The Italians had bid £5 million the summer before but Clough rejected it, triggering a clause in his contract that meant a year later he could make the move for less). Bankrolled by the petroleum tycoon Paolo Mantovani, Sampdoria had become one of the biggest teams in Serie A, champions in 1991 and losing European Cup finalists the year after. Back in England people got to see how life would fare for Walker when his debut, a 3-3 draw with Lazio, was broadcast live on Channel Four's *Gazzetta Football Italia* programme.

Walker's experience in Italy proved an unhappy one, though. He made several high-profile mistakes early that season and generally found it difficult to adapt to the different style of the League. One of these mistakes came against Torino, a weak header pounced on by Carlos Aguilera to score in a 2-2 draw. His old mentor Clough observed astutely, 'I knew the Italians would find him out. They discovered they could turn him quite easily. Their game is played with such precision, with players running off defenders and receiving the ball right at their feet – none of the long stuff that enabled Des' extraordinary pace to make him a hero.' Against Fiorentina, a game the Sampdoria manager Sven-Goran Eriksson labelled 'a disaster', more mistakes from Walker contributed to a 4-0 thrashing.

Initially Walker had been used at centre-back, but Eriksson eventually move him to the left, preferring Marco Lanna and Pietro Vierchowod in the middle. But that didn't work out. Walker's strength was winning and chasing the ball from the middle by charging out or back, not operating at full-back with all the distributive requirements that come with the position.

In February, he made two glaring errors as he failed to keep AC

Milan's Jean-Pierre Papin under control, the Frenchman scoring twice in a 4-0 defeat at the San Siro. In April, with Sampdoria 2-0 down in the first half at home to Inter Milan, Walker was taken off after another poor performance. He was dropped for the following match. Eriksson later admitted that moving him out of position hadn't worked. 'I almost knew before we did it that this would be a bad solution', said the Swede. 'Especially when he attacks, because he's not used to that position . . . The fault is not Walker's, it's more mine. It's not that he's a bad football player. Absolutely not.'

As Walker's confidence dipped, his England performances also began to cause concern. Though a star in Italia '90, he looked a shadow of that performer in the USA '94 qualifiers. In the 2-2 draw against the Netherlands at Wembley he allowed a young Marc Overmars to outpace him, and in desperation pulled him back to give away a penalty (though in Walker's defence the Dutch winger was frighteningly quick and the foul had in fact been outside the box). 'Des was devastated,' said his England, and later Wednesday, team-mate Carlton Palmer. The next month Walker's mistakes led to Poland's equaliser in Chorzow and, following a mix up with Chris Woods, almost a winner for the home side – 'do I not like that!' Graham Taylor famously despaired as Walker passed to John Barnes, putting him under pressure and forcing the back pass which led to the Pole's goal. Three days after that, England lost 2-0 in Oslo to Norway. On that occasion Walker was less at fault as he and the team struggled to adapt to Graham Taylor's last-minute tactical switch from two centre-backs to three. 'We didn't have much time to work on it,' remembered Carlton Palmer. 'I had a bad feeling about it . . . I think we all did.'

To salvage Walker's reputation and return his confidence, a move back to the Premier League seemed likely, necessary even. Manchester United and Leeds were interested but thanks to the strong backing in the transfer market Francis was enjoying at the time, coupled with his connections at Sampdoria lasting from his playing days there, plus the fact he and Walker shared the same agent, it was not a surprise when he opted for Wednesday.

***

By the end, 1993-94 was not a great season for Wednesday. After big expenditure an improvement on the previous season's record had been expected, yet with several key players unavailable through injury for large parts of the season (namely Hirst, Sheridan and Waddle) they again finished seventh. Wednesday did reach the semi-finals of the League Cup, but lost 5-1 on aggregate to Manchester United.

The following season they stuttered again, this time to 13th place, only securing their position after a win against Ipswich on the last day. The chart that year showed a six-point gap between them and the relegated Crystal Palace. But had Wednesday lost and Palace won game 42, they might have dropped on goal difference. Despite the final poor position, though, Walker continued to impress, acting as a swift and effective blocker alongside Pearce. Who knows what the outcome would have been without his steady presence at the back.

The bigger problem for the team in 1994-95 was scoring. In the opening run they struggled in front of goal – possibly, it could be argued, because of poor distribution from Walker and Pearce at the back, finding salvation only when Ian Taylor was swapped with Aston Villa for the forward Guy Whittingham. Immediately Whittingham made a positive impact, netting twice on his Boxing Day debut against Everton, 4-1 to the Owls. He then got another two in the 5-1 defeat of Coventry. If not for those emphatic Christmas-time displays, along with the run of six games unbeaten that followed, the club may have ended up in a far worse situation by the end of the campaign.

When the season was over, Trevor Francis was let go by the club after four years in charge. No longer did he appear to have that great an effect on his players; increasingly, too, he had been losing the support of the fans. Seemingly his failure to replace the older members of his squad proved most damaging as he turned a high-reaching side into relegation threatened underachievers. Certainly, Walker was a very good purchase but others, such as Ian Nolan, were too inexperienced and simply not of the same calibre as their predecessors.

With Francis's successor David Pleat in place, the search for a settled partner for Walker continued. With Pearce, Peter Atherton and Carlton Palmer having been tried before but deemed unsuitable, it was apparent someone new was required. The veteran Scottish defender Steve Nicol was signed on a free in November 1995, followed the next month by Dejan Stefanovic, the Yugoslav who arrived from Red Star Belgrade along with his compatriot Darko Kovacevic for a total of £4.5 million. Both were promising youngsters who had recently broken into their national team.

A mixture of poor performances and work permit issues meant Stefanovic initially did not look like the answer to the defensive problem. A seven-week delay in the issue of his work permit prevented him from joining earlier, meaning he didn't make his debut until New Year's Day '96. He then put in a series of indifferent performances. Pleat, fairly, made his initial assessment in light of the difficulty of settling in a foreign country. 'It takes a year to adjust to playing in England. Without [the language], a player doesn't always get the chance to express himself – he can't make a case for himself and he can't say anything to the referee. He [Stefanovic] couldn't relate to anyone.'

Over the next 12 months, after failing to meet the Home Office threshold of 75% domestic appearances, Stefanovic was initially denied a renewed permit (obtained only on appeal). With issues of his availability in mind, Pleat made another signing. In February Jon Newsome, a former Wednesday youth product who had been sold to Leeds in 1991, was brought in from Norwich City. Another £1 million and another defender who Walker had to get to know.

(Kovacevic, meanwhile, failed to settle. Though he scored twice in a 4-2 victory over Bolton, he soon fell out of favour with Pleat and by the end of the season had been sold, for a decent profit, to the Spanish side Real Sociadad. In Spain he quickly rediscovered his earlier scoring prowess and later moved on to Juventus for £15 million.)

Eventually, as Stefanovic began to settle and play more, he and Walker would go on to form a reasonable understanding together. Stefanovic could defend well and, crucially, had good passing ability, meaning Wednesday could again more frequently and effectively build their attacks from the back. As he advanced with the ball, Walker could remain back to cover – what he did best. In 1996-97, their first full season together, the pair, during the periods when Newsome was sidelined, gave a number of imperious displays. In the 1-0 victory at Liverpool, they repelled a strong Liverpool attack, that featured Robbie Fowler and Steve McManaman, to anchor Wednesday's first victory at Anfield for 11 years. Then, in a 1-1 draw home draw to Manchester United, they for the most part managed to keep Eric Cantona and Ole Gunnar Solskjaer at bay.

That season Wednesday had begun superbly, winning their first four fixtures thanks to goals from the emerging young forward Richie Humphreys. For a while, before things inevitably fell away, they sat top of the Premier League.

By the end of that year Walker began to assess his future options. It had been four years since his Sampdoria rescue and Wednesday had a new contract ready for him to sign, but he was stalling. The recent Bosman ruling had opened up the European transfer market, allowing out of contract players from EU nations to move from one member state to another for no fee, though it didn't yet cover moves *within* those member states. In early 1997 Vinnie Jones was negotiating a new deal with Wimbledon and, realising he could not move to another English club on a free, lobbied for the rule to be applied internally as well. Walker's camp looked on with interest. They believed it unfair that to benefit from the new rule he might have to move abroad again. Despite interest from Forest and Middlesbrough, eventually he and Wednesday came to an agreement and he signed a new deal worth a reputed £10,000 per week.

While Walker enjoyed his nice new contract, things weren't so rosy for the club. A poor start to 1997-98 led to David Pleat's sacking in November. His good showing the previous season had brought optimism to the club. After that impressive early lead in the league, inspired by the goals of Humphreys, they slipped to an eventual seventh. The slip continued in to the new campaign. Rumours spread that Pleat had fallen out with the playing and coaching staff – we know he was unpopular with some players – so the sterner Howard Wilkinson was touted as a potential returnee. Some also believed that Chris Waddle would be given the job, though in the end it was neither. The man chosen to again lead the Owls was Ron Atkinson.

The change produced yet another partner for Walker as Atkinson uncovered Emerson Thome, an unknown Brazilian gem available for free after playing in Portugal. Thome had interested Stoke City and Huddersfield Town, but both had been deterred by his questionable fitness. Atkinson, though, took a gamble – it proved excellent business. Over the next 18 months (from March '98) Thome and Walker played almost every game together. They formed a fine understanding with each other, helping ensure Premier League survival in Atkinson's first season back in charge and in the next year under Danny Wilson, a 12th place finish.

Soon, though, Danny Wilson's shortcomings as a top league manager became more evident. Paolo Di Canio, Wednesday's main creative outlet, had left controversially following his push on referee Paul Alcock, as later did Benito Carbone when he fell out with Wilson over his refusal to be a substitute at Southampton. The partnership of Walker and Thome also began to deteriorate (though Wilson can't really be blamed explicitly for that). Then, due to the club's worsening financial situation (the debt by now standing around £25 million), Thome was sold to Chelsea for £2.5 million. The sale was unpopular among the fans and probably he was sold for less than his worth at the time, but actually it didn't harm the defence as much as people thought it might. Peter Atherton was moved centrally to partner Walker again (he had done on quite a few occasions over the previous five years), with Ian Nolan coming in at right-back, and Wednesday conceded fewer goals in the remaining games of the season than they had during the first portion (although in total the overall tally of 70 served to flatten any hope of survival). Still, this improvement was too little too late and the club was relegated.

The summer of 2000 presented Wednesday with a big task as they adjusted to life in the First Division. While supporters expected a swift return to the Premier League under new manager Paul Jewell, it would turn into a going-nowhere year. The loss of the experienced heads Atherton, Nolan, Danny Sonner and Wim Jonk on free transfers, and Andy Hinchcliffe, Simon Donnelly and Phil O'Donnell to injury, meant Jewell had to rely on players who were either scandalously disinterested in the cause, or simply not available or up to standard. Unlike in 1990-91, there was little financial support available from the club's hierarchy and only a few signings could be made. Steve Harkness, £200,000 from Blackburn, and Ashley Westwood, £150,000 from Bradford, were both uninspiring, though the loan of Efan Ekoku from Swiss side Grasshopper Zurich proved more successful.

Behind the scenes there were problems with the team, lacking as it did the solidarity or spirit required to form any sort of promotion push. 'One of the first things I noticed', said Jewell's assistant Terry

Yorath upon his arrival, 'was the split in the camp between the British players and the foreign legion. The British lads didn't like the foreign players because of their poor work ethic . . . [and] we had to knock the two dressing rooms at the training ground into one . . . The foreigners would change in one and the British-based players in the other . . . I'd never come across anything like this in all my time in football.' In his autobiography, Gilles De Bilde wrote, disgracefully, 'The only way foreign players amused themselves was talking about money. It was the only reason we were still playing in England. In that period the Dutch players and I made a calendar. Each of us made a drawing of how he saw his future. I drew a nice villa in Spain with a waiter serving me while a plane dropped pounds over me.' Walker, meanwhile, was left to play alongside several different defensive partners, including Westwood, Con Blatsis (a loanee who appeared from nowhere one game away at Huddersfield), the academy graduates Steve Haslam and Leigh Bromby, and later, Carlton Palmer.

By now Walker was back as club captain. When first given the armband by Trevor Francis upon his arrival, Palmer and Nigel Pearson had both questioned the decision. Walker was the new man. He did not always shout or bawl, which is often considered a necessary requirement for a captain. Nor, said some, did he particularly inspire his team-mates. Would he again be able to encourage them, lead with the calm authority required of a captain and make them think about their individual and collective roles in the team? He had seemed to do OK in his first few years but when Wednesday floated perilously close to the drop zone towards the latter stages of 1995-96, David Pleat took the responsibility from him, giving it to Peter Atherton. He held it for four years, Walker only regaining the armband when Atherton left for Bradford after Wednesday's relegation in '99.

After bringing in Palmer and Trond Egil Soltvedt, Peter Shreeves, who had taken over from the sacked Jewell in February, managed to guide the side away from what was becoming a relegation fight in the First Division. The pair stabilised the midfield and the side went on a run of six wins from the next eight, the form of a revitalised Gerald Sibon also helping considerably. The Dutchman was part mesmerising, part infuriating, always looking lethargic but with the ability to pull off expert touches on the ball, to execute long finding passes and score brilliant goals. In Shreeves' second game he scored the only goal in a 1-0 win at Nottingham Forest, his long leg intercepting an ill-directed pass from Chris Bart Williams before turning and shooting low into the net from outside the area. Sibon's strikes went a long way to saving that season.

At the end of 2000-01, after eight years with the club, Walker's time with Wednesday came to an end. They simply could no longer afford to keep him on the wage bill. He spent time assessing his options. Maybe America and the New York/New Jersey Metrostars? Or Burton Albion (then managed by his former Forest colleague Nigel Clough), whom he trained with briefly? Eventually, though, after impressing manager Paul Hart, Walker returned to Nottingham Forest. He had demonstrated a good level of fitness and, of course, still had that tremendous defensive capability. Walker stayed there for two years, a low point being his own goal in front of the Bramall Lane Kop in the 2003 play-off semi-finals.

In all he is among the best defenders to have played for Wednesday. When he arrived he was a player of true international class and, while further acknowledgement did not come from successive England managers, he continued, even through difficult times, to deliver consistently for the club. *'You'll never beat Des Walker'*.

18

John Fantham

1958-1969
434 appearances, 166 goals

About an hour into the 1966 FA Cup Final, with Wednesday 1-0 up and dominating, John Fantham collected the ball cleanly from just outside the centre circle. Dashing forward, he left behind him the blue shirts of Everton 'as if they weren't even running.' Gliding on, he shot from 18 yards. Gordon West in the Everton goal saved but the rebound fell to David Ford who guided the ball into the net. 2-0 and victory for the Owls appeared certain.

Though that day would be spoiled by Everton's devastating comeback, 2-0 to 3-2 in the last 15 minutes, Fantham's electrifying run demonstrated to the nation some of his best talents. In particular, his acute control and superb pace when moving with the ball at his feet. What wasn't shown of his talents in that run, namely his stylish passing and expert finishing, was seen over the rest of the 13 years he served the club, a spell in which he gained an England cap and took a key role in the club's ventures into European competition. And although his career is marked somewhat by notions of unfulfilled potential, still he is remembered as an exciting and prolific Wednesday forward.

As a youth Fantham excelled at cricket, golf and football, possessing the key attributes of both speed and balance required of a top sportsman (in later years he would hold the course record at Beauchief golf club). Ultimately he concentrated on football, believing that the game would offer him the quickest way to the sporting career he desired. Fantham's father, Jack, had played in the '30s for Rotherham, Stockport, Chester, and Wolverhampton

Wanderers and was able to provide some pragmatic guidance for his son. 'Nobody can teach you how to play football,' he said, 'people can put you on the right lines, but they can't give you natural ability if you haven't got it.' Johnny had it.

John began playing for Sheffield and Yorkshire Boys, soon discovering a knack for getting goals. He might have joined Wath, the South Yorkshire nursery club for Wolverhampton Wanderers, but already he had begun training with the Owls and decided to stay with them. At 15 he signed up as an apprentice.

When Albert Quixall was injured before a game against Tottenham at Hillsborough in late 1958, Fantham was given his chance in the first team. Fantham was, he remembered, as 'nervous as a kitten.' When Quixall was sold to Manchester United soon after, a gap opened in the Owls' forward line and it was Fantham who filled it. (The happiness of this early run in the side sadly coincided with the death of his father. Called up for the derby against Sheffield United, a day meant to be the best of his nascent career, it instead was a day of sadness as Jack Fantham collapsed and died outside Hillsborough. 'I was always sorry my father never saw me get any of my Wednesday goals', John later said.)

The Wednesday manager Harry Catterick had been accepting of Albert Quixall's sale and it is said that Fantham was one of the reason's why – an in-house, ready made replacement. After the Tottenham game there was considerable pressure for him to carry on as he had begun. Immediately he repaid the faith that had been shown in him. Of the team's 100 goals in 1958-59, Fantham scored 12 and set up many others with his swift and precise, chance-making passing. In the two years which followed he netted another 41 times, setting-up countless others. The Owls' methodical yet flowing forward line of Alan Finney on the right wing, Derek Wilkinson then Colin Dobson on the left, combined with Fantham to make countless opportunities for himself and other forwards. As Fantham later explained 'I always had a lot of chances, I was always getting knock-downs and benefiting from their [the forwards Keith Ellis and later David Layne's] presence.'

Necessary to Fantham's successful goalscoring record was his vibrant and purposeful impulse of moving forward, always into open spaces. 'My strength', he said rather straightforwardly, 'was being in the right position . . . keeping on the move in the box and anticipating the chances.' He could return the favour, too. On the ball he was a constant danger, roaming dangerously and persistently from inside-forward, his purposeful dribbling and clever passing linking the forward play well. And he worked hard, dropping back to support the half-backs before switching forward to make the attacks. As his cup final dash later showed, he was integral to the creation of goals, along with getting them.

Despite a change of manager in 1961, Fantham continued to impress for the club. Vic Buckingham encouraged a neat passing style which arguably gave him a better platform on which to shine. In Buckingham's three years in charge, Wednesday would enjoy two spells in European competition, the Inter-Cities Fairs Cup (an independent competition started in 1955 that would be renamed the UEFA Cup when later it came under the administration of Europe's governing body). Entry in '61 was by invitation and Wednesday, having finished second in the First Division to Tottenham the previous year, were offered a spot. In Europe Fantham thrived, giving a number of goalscoring displays as the Owls reached the quarter- finals.

He was, though, absent for the first round first leg away to Olympique Lyonnais in the Stade de Gerland. On a hot night in France, Lyon quickly went three ahead through Angel Rambert and two from Eugène N'Jo Léa. In the second half Wednesday recovered well, replies from Gerry Young and Keith Ellis making it 3-2. Lyon, though, having retreated into a more defensive shape to stifle the comeback, went up on the break in the last minute to get a fourth through Nestor Combin. Wednesday faced a tough home leg.

A month later at Hillsborough Fantham was back and put in a glorious performance to help send his team through. Although Lyon dominated the opening exchanges, even going ahead through Robert Salen's strike, Wednesday fought back, Fantham wandering effectively and making powerful and refreshing runs that tormented the visitors. Having already come close with two drives, he levelled the scores on the night, a looping header over the stranded Claude Hugues after Megson's free-kick. Billy Griffin then got another following a low pass from Finney before Tom McAnearney converted a penalty to make it 3-1 at half time (5-5 overall).

In the second half, Lyon's fluid play degenerated when put under pressure and Wednesday came to dominate. With 12 minutes left

Dobson held off a Raymond Gardon tackle to head the ball home from a Griffin flick (4-1 and 6-5). Three minutes later Lyon then got another back through Jean Djorkaeff. With minutes to spare, though, Fantham produced the goal of the match, a wonderful diving header from a perfect Tony Kay free kick, to send Wednesday through 7-6 on aggregate.

Next came Roma. In front of over 40,000 fans at Hillsborough, Wednesday were in control and came away with a 4-0 win. Finney terrorised the Roma defence. Fantham twice went close, then opened the scoring on six minutes, a beautiful volley past the keeper Fabio Cudicini. Next Gerry Young took over, scoring a fine hat trick. Afterwards the Roma president, Anacleto Gianni, who had spent £600,000 building his side, was said to have been shocked to learn the Wednesday team had cost less than £30,000.

Flared tempers at Hillsborough had seen a series of altercations in the second half, so the FIFA president Stanley Rous issued a 'keep it clean' appeal for the second leg. He travelled to the game at the Stadio Olympico where Wednesday fought valiantly to maintain their advantage. Though they lost 1-0, Peter Swan scoring an own goal in the last minute, the Owls still went through. As it had following the first leg, the atmosphere turned toxic afterwards, Tony Kay receiving a punch on the jaw by one of the Roma players.

In the second round Barcelona had humiliated Dynamo Zagreb 7-3 meaning Wednesday would face the previous year's losing European Cup finalists in the quarter-finals. Icy conditions in Sheffield meant that only half the expected 60,000 were at Hillsborough for the first leg where again it was Fantham who was the hero.

Barca had gone ahead through Ramon Villaverde, but Wednesday equalised after Colin Dobson, weaving along the edge of the penalty area, found Young on the left who crossed for Fantham to score. Hurtling into the box at full speed, he headed past a crowd of players and into the net for 1-1. Once more Barcelona took the lead through the Brazilian Macedo, but Wednesday came back again, Finney's drive making it all level. Then the winner. Fantham found Finney, who squared to Robin Hardy who gave it back to Fantham, racing in, to slot home. 3-2. Going to Spain the players were confident of advancing. However, in the cauldron of the Camp Nou in front of 75,000 Catalans, Wednesday were eliminated 2-0.

Wednesday had hoped to take part in the Fairs Cup again the following year. But the FA prevented them from accepting their invitation, reasoning that Sheffield United (who had finished one place above them at the end of 1961-62) should enter instead. The dispute led to only one of the original three invitees (Everton) taking part. Wednesday were back, though, in 1963-64, beating the Dutch team DOS Utrecht 8-2 on aggregate before losing 5-3 to FC Cologne in the second round. It would be almost 30 years before the club would play in Europe again.

(Those two runs in the Fairs had not been the club's only exposure to foreign opponents at that time. Under Harry Catterick Wednesday had ventured to the USSR, playing three matches against Soviet opposition. First to Moscow where they met the army side CSKA, then to Georgia and Dynamo Tblisi, before going back the 1,250 miles to Moscow to play Locomotive. Throughout the trip the squad was tracked by the KGB.)

While most of Fantham's Wednesday career was spent in the first team, 1963-64 saw him play a reduced role. Vic Buckingham, who had used him throughout his first two years in charge, now had David Layne up front, who was having a great season and had notched over 28 goals. In addition, Eddie Holliday, a former England international, and John Quinn were performing well in the inside-forward positions. It was rumoured Fantham might even be sold to another club – this not long after Harry Catterick had shown interest in taking him to Everton.

Some believed Fantham was failing to make the most of his abundant natural talent. In 1961 he had been spotted by the England selection committee and picked for a World Cup qualifier against Luxembourg at Highbury (a rare game away from Wembley for the national side). The game ended 4-1, Fantham playing the full match. However, he and the other two debutants that day, Ray Pointer and Dennis Viollet, 'from whom so much had been hoped', wrote *The Guardian*, 'were far too fitful to have any serious chances of retention'. He wasn't picked for his country again.

Had he not tried enough? Certainly, he could be absolutely electric – his talent could light up Hillsborough and he should have achieved more in the gamer. 'He was never the player to take the game by the scruff of the neck,' said one former team-mate. 'Sometimes, during a match I'd look at him and think, today's not a Johnny Fantham day.' Another, Howard Wilkinson, is of similar opinion. 'On his day John was as good as anything you'd seen. But he wasn't as driven as he might have been. I think if he'd been playing now it would have been different. In those days people might have put up with the kind of thinking that said, "well that's him". These days players who could go on to make it at the top level – like John could have done – would be made aware of their choices. They would be asked, "what do you want to do? Do you want to be one of the game's top players?"'

***

By April 1964 Wednesday appeared to have cemented their position as one of the top teams in England. Following those yo-yo-years, the early '60s had seen the stability of regular top-half finishes in the First Division. Though no longer the title challengers they had been under Harry Catterick, still they were among the best. In Ron Springett they had a top class goalkeeper. And a strong defence. Plus in Fantham, a skilful forward with the ability and quickness of feet to wonderfully link midfield and attack. Several of the Wednesday team were on the fringe of the England squad and there was strong evidence that with the correct guidance the team might again have a chance of reaching for the title. The revelations of the *Sunday People* newspaper would, however, fracture this potential

Since the previous year the paper had dripped their findings of a shameful betting syndicate that had been operating in the Football League. Led by the former Everton and Mansfield player Jimmy Gauld, the group had bet on and influenced the outcome of a number of matches. On one occasion the indebted Bristol Rovers goalkeeper Esmond Million had, it was revealed, deliberately allowed three goals past him in a Third Division match. Initially that earned him £300; then a lifetime ban from the game and prison sentence. Some time after the Million story, Gauld was revealed as the 'mastermind' of the bribes ring. He claimed players from over 20 other clubs were involved.

The *People* were now reporting that Wednesday's Peter Swan and David Layne, along with Tony Kay who was now at Everton, were also involved. The trio, the paper alleged, had each placed a £50 bet on the Owls losing their fixture at Ipswich Town the previous season. It was, read the headline, 'The Biggest Sports Scandal of the Century'.

As the police and FA conducted their inquiries, the club suspended Swan and Layne indefinitely. The FA did the same. By January '65 they, and Kay, were sentenced to four months in prison. The orchestrator Jimmy Gauld received four years. For £50, potentially returning £150, slightly more than a First Division player's monthly wage at the time, their respective careers were finished. 'I lost everything', said Kay in later years. 'They took away the game I loved and I have never really recovered from that.'

The trio's involvement in the scandal, the tentacles of which reached every division of the Football League, many matches and many players, was limited to just one game. Some said their judicial and footballing punishments were too harsh. Yet although they didn't, as it turned out, need to affect the outcome of the Ipswich game (the difficult contest was gone after an apparently genuinely conceded goal), their bets had shown an *intention* to at some point throw the result. As the great football writer Arthur Hopcraft observed, that intention threatened the whole integrity of the game. Spectators, he insisted, had to believe that the play they were paying both in time and in money to see was fairly contested, so the FA's punishment at least was somewhat justified.

The scandal rocked Wednesday, setting them on a downward spiral that would ultimately take them back to the Second Division and beyond. In Swan, the club lost a former England international (his last cap came in 1962), and in Layne, their top goalscorer. Their FA bans were overturned seven years later and both were permitted to play for Wednesday again. By now, though, the club was in the second tier, managed by Derek Dooley, and while Swan had kept himself in good fitness, making 16 appearance upon his return, Layne wasn't able to match his colleague, managing only a few games for lowly Hereford.

At the end of 1963-64 Vic Buckingham left the club, replaced by the authoritarian Alan Brown. Known as 'the strictest man in football', he had been a coach at the club in the early '50s. Like Harry Catterick, he was a fierce disciplinarian, but also 'a complete players' man,' able to foster a strong spirit and sense of togetherness within his squad. 'When you look at the qualities a strong leader requires,' said one of his former players, 'Alan had most of them. He had integrity and honesty, good ideas and was never afraid to put them into practice.' (When he managed Burnley, for instance, he kept the first team in their place by making them act as ball-boys and tea-boys for the youth team.) 'He never shirked a decision, was very protective of his players, a terrific role model, humble and caring, but didn't pay lip service to anyone – the media, the fans, anyone.'

The fall-out from the scandal hindered his efforts considerably, however – something Swan, Layne and Kay did not consider when they placed their little bets. Brown's challenge, then, was steep and not unsurprisingly league finishes under him were even more disappointing than his predecessor, 8th, 17th and 11th. The FA Cup final in '66 was a more positive sign of achievement, the club's brightest day of this period, the all white change kit they wore at Wembley giving a cleansing appearance for a club tarnished by scandal. But that was about as good as it got.

In those years Fantham continued his excellent goalscoring record, more than 60 over four seasons, as Wednesday settled into a run of mediocrity, falling behind their rivals and becoming a frustrated, almost going nowhere First Division outfit. Results painted a picture of inconsistency; a decent amount of wins coupled with a similar number of defeats. And with no compensation from the double loss of Swan and Layne to fund adequate replacements, Wednesday quickly fell behind their rivals Liverpool, Leeds, Manchester United and Tottenham. As Fantham remembered solemnly of the time, 'the club's fortunes were on the wane'.

After Brown, the appointment of his assistant, the mostly hapless Jack Marshall, then Danny Williams, did not help much. Buckingham to Brown to Marshall to Williams, each a worsening move. As for the players, Peter Eustace joined Everton, Vic Mobley went to QPR and David Ford to Newcastle. Their replacements, John Sissons from West Ham, Peter Rodrigues from Leicester and Jackie Sinclair from Newcastle, simply were not up to par, and Danny Williams struggled to recreate the good dressing room spirit he had built with his previous club Swindon. At the end of 1969-70, Wednesday were relegated, finishing as they did bottom of the table. Williams' tenure was brief – 18 months – and grossly unsuccessful.

Not long into that fateful season, Fantham was sold for £6,000 to Third Division Rotherham United. 'I was happy to stay and was sorry when Danny Williams decided to let me go', he later said. 'I felt I still had something to offer.' The previous two years he had scored 18 goals, only John Ritchie contributing more in that time. On match day he was still everywhere on the pitch, his pace still there, his finishing still sound, his passing still expert. Surely he had something to offer Wednesday as they struggled against relegation for all of that that season?

His sale ended a long and happy association with the club -11 years spent mostly in the top flight. He had performed excellently on the new stage of European competition and played in an FA Cup final. And while it cannot be said that letting individual players leave the club *causes* a decline in its fortune, as with Paolo Di Canio many years later the departure of Fantham, albeit under massively different circumstances, happened to coincide with one such decline for Wednesday.

After leaving the Owls he spent two seasons with Rotherham before moving to Macclesfield Town. It was there, in 1972, that his playing career came to an end. He later became assistant manager of non-League Hallam FC and operated a machinery business. While playing he ran several barber shops in the city, one of them on Division Street.

19

Lee Bullen

2004-08
148 appearances

In recent years, a period spent at Hillsborough has represented a stepping point on the way to, or from, somewhere better for many players. For Lee Bullen, whose varied football career took him from Scotland to Australia, Hong Kong then Greece, it was much more than that. 'I was shown around the stadium and training ground and it was bigger and better than anything else I'd been involved in before,' he says. 'I'd played around the world and seen various things, but to come to Wednesday in the twilight of my career was an exciting moment. I saw it as a great chance – play for a big club for a year and see what happened. It ended up being four years. It was the most memorable period of my career.'

In those years, 2004-2008, Bullen served the club with distinction, captaining the side to promotion to the Championship in his first season, helping them consolidate in that higher league, then taking them close to the play-offs. And while towards the end it was clear his talents were fading, his effort could never be questioned. Where before him others had treated the club and its fans with disrespect with their disinterested attitude, Bullen, a rock at the back, never weak in the tackle, always gave all he had.

At the end of 2002-03 Wednesday were relegated to the third tier of the League for only the second time. A few years before they had been a Premier League side, boasting a collection of costly continental talent. But now, heavily indebted (nearly £30 million), they were sinking like a stone. Though the cost of paying the playing staff was coming down – down to only £10 million – what it had been spent on appeared very poor value for money.

That summer, Dave Allen, owner of Napoleon's Casino and the Owlerton greyhound stadium, was appointed as chairman of the club. He had joined the board a few years before to help provide some business sense to the running of the club and had implemented ways to boost commercial revenues. As chairman he introduced a careful approach to spending that, while unpopular with some fans, was necessary to reduce the club's massive post-Premier League costs. Spending, at last, was put somewhere in line with actual earnings. He then turned his efforts to increasing income. A long-standing plan was to sell the Middlewood training ground to clear some of the deficit and provide manager Chris Turner with more funds for his playing squad so as to make Wednesday a more attractive proposition to outside investors.

However, life in the Second Division was miserable at first for the Owls. For 2003-04 Turner had had little manoeuvrability with transfers and the team fought bitterly to avoid a second consecutive drop, finishing as they did 16th. But the following year brought opportunity for change. The contracts of more expensive players were expiring and a large group were let go. Among them, Leigh Bromby, Alan Quinn and the hugely dedicated Derek Geary, were youngsters who in a better environment may have thrived, but had been relied on too heavily in their nascent careers, along with Kevin Pressman, who ended his 17 year association with the club, Mark Robins and the Beatles-haircut-flop, John Beswetherick.

In their place came a group that by the end of the season would win promotion through the play-offs. Winger Chris Brunt arrived from the fruitful Middlesbrough youth set-up (following an earlier loan spell the season before). Irish midfielder Glenn Whelan came from Manchester City. Left-back Paul Heckingbottom from Bradford City. Chris Marsden, the former Southampton midfielder. Livingston's forward John Paul McGovern. The strikers Stephen Maclean from Rangers and Lee Peacock from Bristol City. Goalkeeper David Lucas, back from Preston after a previous loan spell . . . And Lee Bullen. In all they cost just £230,000.

The new team began the season relatively brightly, putting a 3-0 home loss to Colchester behind them to win four consecutive games in league and cup. Results soon became indifferent, however. After defeat at Tranmere, followed by three draws then another defeat, Turner was sacked. While in two different spells as a player his contribution had been positive, his time as manager was not. Yet as Bullen argues in defence, Turner might have benefited from a little longer to allow his new team to settle. 'Losing 13 players and bringing in 11 was always going to make it hard for the team to bed-in,' he says. 'We were very up and down at the beginning. Chris needed a good start and unfortunately he didn't get it.'

Turner's replacement was Paul Sturrock. Despite being recently sacked by Southampton, he was still one of the better emerging managers in the League. His previous successes with Plymouth (two consecutive promotions) had got him the Southampton job, and although he found the step-up to the Premier League difficult he was a sound choice as Wednesday's next boss.

In contrast to Turner, whose post-match pattern was to reel off in monotone a list of excuses for the team's failings that week, Sturrock offered an uplifting, refreshing and matter-of-fact approach. He was impressively critical when required and upon his arrival in Sheffield declared that none of the players would be losing him his job through a lack of trying. He woke the club up. 'There wasn't particularly a change of atmosphere with Paul,' recalls Bullen, 'but he was a little more regimented in the way he wanted his football played and got us settled down. Maybe we weren't playing great football, it was more substance over finesse, but eventually we got the results.'

It was a tough introduction for Sturrock, only one win in nine – Turner was sacked for less. But after Bullen was installed as captain – a career-ending hamstring injury to Chris Marsden presenting him that opportunity – the results began to turn. 'I was gutted for Chris,' says Bullen, 'but Paul showed faith in me and gave me the chance.' Guided by their new captain, Wednesday went on a run of seven wins in ten, including a 3-0 victory at Doncaster, the striker Kenwyne Jones getting the first goal of his brief, yet high-yielding loan spell. Over Christmas a run of six more wins helped the Owls jump further up the table.

Bullen quickly became a respected and popular figurehead in the team. 'At the time all the players had to live within a 20-mile radius of Sheffield,' he says. 'Most lived in the city so there was a very good bond among the group. Everyone played a part. That bond was bigger than any signing or game that season and helped us over the line.' Captain Bullen's contribution was central to this success. 'We would all have done anything for him,' remembered the goalkeeper David Lucas.

The play-off line was crossed in April following a fantastic win at Hull City. Results in recent weeks had suffered and it was possible the top-six position Wednesday had held since January could have been lost. They had not won in eight and both Brentford and Hartlepool were threatening to displace them. It was vital they picked up at least a point in the East Riding.

Drew Talbot put Wednesday ahead in the first half, but that was negated by Stuart Elliott's penalty after an hour. Thankfully Wednesday took the win through a last minute James Quinn effort. Lee Peacock and Bullen had made contact with the ball as it bounced over the Hull keeper Boaz Myhill, but Quinn followed up on the line to score, confirming the Owls' place in the play-offs. 'We knew we had a tough game going up there,' says Bullen. 'To win 2-1 was like winning a cup. The relief was so great.'

In the first leg of the play-off semi-final at home to Brentford, Wednesday took a 1-0 win thanks to John Paul McGovern's thrashed grounded shot from the right side of the box. In the second leg at Griffin Park it was 2-1, Lee Peacock's header followed up by a deflected Chris Brunt free kick. 'I think Brentford fancied themselves in the second leg,' remembers Bullen, 'but Lee and Chris were absolutely outstanding. The game was brilliant. We defended as a unit at that compact old stadium and the travelling fans were unbelievable. They made if feel like a home game.'

Wembley was being rebuilt so Cardiff's Millennium Stadium would host Wednesday and Hartlepool United in the final. Over 40,000 from Sheffield made the journey to Wales to witness the club's best day in years, the 4-2 triumph securing their return to the second tier. 'As we arrived in Cardiff, all you could see was a sea of blue and white', says Bullen. 'People hanging out of the windows. It was absolute bedlam.' As Sturrock led out his men, the noise was thundering. Lucas. Bruce. Wood. Heckingbottom. McGovern. Whelan. Rocastle. Brunt. Peacock. Quinn. And Bullen.

On a difficult, heavy pitch Wednesday dominated the early play in midfield, but it proved hard keeping possession. Bullen, the oldest player on the pitch, made several strong important headers and early efforts from Brunt and Whelan went astray. Shortly before half time they took the lead, Rocastle playing a tidy one-two with Peacock before surging into the area to hit a low cross along to the far post which McGovern met.

Hartlepool recovered, however. Eifion Williams equalised before Jon Daly, heading in a free-kick, put them ahead. With less than ten minutes to go many Wednesday supporters were beginning to think the club's big day would end in disappointment and defeat. Heads were in hands (or rested on bars) as the minutes went by – but a lifeline came. Drew Talbot, on as a substitute, turned Chris Westwood who then pushed the young striker in the back. Though innocuous, the incident earned the Hartlepool defender a red card and Wednesday a penalty. Steve Maclean, also on from the bench having being injured since March (it had been close whether or not he played at all) stepped up confidently and scored. 2-2. Heads out of hands.

In extra-time Wednesday took over. A long high ball out of defence from Bullen was dealt with poorly by Hartlepool allowing Glenn Whelan to nudge the ball into his possession and hit a fine left-footed shot from the edge of the area. 3-2. Bedlam in the stands of the Millennium Stadium. Then came another. After winning a heading contest with Darren Craddock in the centre circle, Talbot ran forward unopposed, rounded the keeper before placing it into the net. Bullen remembers the moment of that fourth goal vividly. 'It was surreal when Drew went through. The whole place went quiet. The people of the stand had been sitting down and you could see in your peripheral vision everyone slowly rise up. The stadium seemed to lift about two feet. He took it round the goalie and that was it. 4-2. Game over.'

After two relegations in four years, Wednesday, and the fans, had their day to remember. 'At the final whistle I deliberately stood back,' says Bullen. 'I let the boys celebrate as I tried to take it all in. I knew I wasn't ever going to be in a situation like that again. Those memories are brilliant. Absolutely it was the best moment in my career.'

***

Bullen's career had begun in 1988 playing as a striker with Dunfermline Athletic. When they released him he moved around several Scottish clubs, periods spent at Meadowbank Thistle, Stenhousemuir and Whitburn Athletic while working for a building society. 'At that point I thought my opportunity in football was gone,' he says. 'But then I got the chance play in Australia. I wasn't enjoying my job and wanted a change so I thought I'd go and travel for a year, picking up a game while I was there.' In Australia he played part-time for CYC Stanmore in the suburbs of Sydney, before moving to Wollonwong Wolves in the Australian National Soccer League. Then came another offer from Hong Kong. 'Out of the blue an agent approached me offering me a move to a club called Kui-Tan. At the time Hong Kong was still British owned so you didn't need any work visas. "What the hell", I thought, it was full-time football.'

Things went well with Kui-Tan, prompting a move to their rivals Golden. Later he joined South China FC, the biggest club on the island. The league there was a curious mix of domestic talent and foreign imports. As Bullen explains, 'A player there once said to me, "Hong Kong is a place of has beens and never have beens." I was in the second bracket. I'd never played at any sort of level and there were a lot of pros coming over who were at the end of their careers.' When England toured the region before Euro '96 Bullen played against them for a League XI side. He missed a great chance one-on-one with David Seaman. 'I got past Tony Adams and by the time I regained my feet David Seaman was out, super-fast', Bullen later said. 'He went down early and I just tried to lift it over his shins . . . it came off the end of my toe and against his legs. I have still got it on video and I rewind it and watch in slow motion and try to lift it a little bit, though it still doesn't go in.'

At the end of 1997 a Greek businessman, who had seen Bullen's performance against England, persuaded him to move to back to Europe and his club Kalamata. 'I'd had a good life in Hong Kong,' he says, 'it had given back my confidence in my game. Nobody had known who I was over there and didn't have any pre-conceived opinions of me. I got to rebuild my career and went to Greece a better player.' Three years after that came a move back to Scotland and Dunfermline. The club which had released him as a youngster was now playing in the Premier League. This time around he was playing in defence, his experiences of being a striker converted to defender helping him adapt to the manager's requirements. 'Having played up front I certainly had an idea of what I was up against, what would I do in this situation as a striker, and I'd try to cancel that out,' he says. Indeed, it helped when Wednesday brought him down to Sheffield to play in their defence.

After the delight of Cardiff, 2005-06 was a season of consolidation for the Owls. They hovered around the relegation places all season but Paul Sturrock managed to achieve his sole objective of the season; survival. Resources were still limited but he was able to bring in several good new signings to supplement the promotion-winning squad. Defenders Frankie Simek, Graham Coughlan and John Hills each arrived on free transfers, as did the midfielders Burton O'Brien and Ritchie Partridge. The only fee that summer went to Wigan, £250,000 for the striker David Graham. Later, as the campaign drew on, chairman Dave Allen helped out from his own pocket, funding the loan of Liverpool's excellent young goalkeeper Scott Carson and the Manchester City defender Mikkel Bischoff, along with the permanent signing of Rotherham's experienced centre-forward Deon Burton.

Bullen spent much of the early part of the season on the bench, coming into the side after Coughlan picked up an injury in training. By the end of the season, though, he would have played in every position on the pitch. Away to Millwall he even played in goal for 70 minutes. 'It was a big game that we had to try and win,' Bullen recalls. 'So Paul decided to go with an extra striker on the bench instead of a goalkeeper. Sods law, David Lucas got injured and I went in goal. If you could choose a place to do that it wouldn't be Millwall, with that hostile crowd behind you. But in the second half I had the Wednesday fans behind me and they were absolutely fantastic. So were the four defenders in front of me – Richard Wood and Drissa Diallo in the middle won every header that came their way. Then Frankie Simek went up the other end and scored.' In recognition of his versatility Bullen received an award from the Football League. Through 2006-07 Wednesday continued their upward climb, taking them as close as they had come to a return to the Premier League since relegation six years before. But only after Paul Sturrock was sacked, replaced by Scunthorpe's Brian Laws.

Though Sturrock had strengthened his squad with the signing of

Crewe's Kenny Lunt and the erratic, yet talented Madjid Bougherra, his team did not enjoy the best of starts to the season. It took four games to register a win, another eight until the next, and after a 4-0 midweek defeat at Colchester Dave Allen terminated his contract. Sturrock had been a popular figure whom many believed should have been given time to turn it around. But while Allen had risked increasing his unpopularity with certain elements of the support for the sacking, his choice of successor, Brian Laws, a former Nottingham Forest right-back, proved a relative success, bringing adventurous play and almost a play-off spot.

While the Laws deal was worked out, the academy boss Sean McAuley was put in charge in the interim. His record was impressive, three wins against Queens Park Rangers, Leicester and Crystal Palace and a draw against Wolves, and there were calls from some fans to keep him on. After Laws eventually did take charge, Wednesday first settled into a mid-table position, then embarked on a fantastic end-of-season run of one defeat in 14 that had fans believing a leap into the play-offs might be a possibility.

They won 3-2 at Leeds, Chris Brunt scoring wonderfully from around the halfway line, then later took consecutive 2-1 wins away from Crystal Palace and Cardiff. Going to West Brom Wednesday knew a win would propel them closer to the top-six. At the Hawthorns Bullen and Richard Wood were outstanding in defence, preventing the home side's advances all game. Then, in the 59th minute the away end went mad as Deon Burton met a Brunt cross to hit home the close-range winner. The Owls were tenth.

Ultimately that late surge proved fractionally too late. They went on to beat Coventry but needed something from their trip to Birmingham. By now they were hamstrung by the departures of the loanees Steve Watson and Iain Turner, who had returned to West Brom and Everton respectively, and lost 2-0 at St. Andrews, ending those play-off hopes. 'If Kenny Lunt had scored instead of hitting the underside of the cross bar we'd have gone on and won that game,' says Bullen. 'We had the momentum, we were flying, but Cameron Jerome scored then they got another one later on. That was the dream over.'

Sadly, with Wednesday still massively indebted (£35 million) they could not afford to build and sustain a team capable of a proper promotion challenge. Strength in depth was an unaffordable dream; the better first team players had to be sold. Majid Bougherra joined Charlton for £2.5 million in January 2007. Chris Brunt went to West Brom for £3 million in August and Glenn Whelan to Stoke for £500,000 in January '08 (a fee reduced because his contract was due to expire that summer when he could have left for free). 'Chris and Glenn were big assets,' says Bullen, 'and there was always the chance we might have lost them eventually for nothing if the club hadn't cashed in. They needed a platform to go and show themselves, which Wednesday gave them. But they were fantastic servants for us in the short spell they were with the club and probably deserved their moves.'

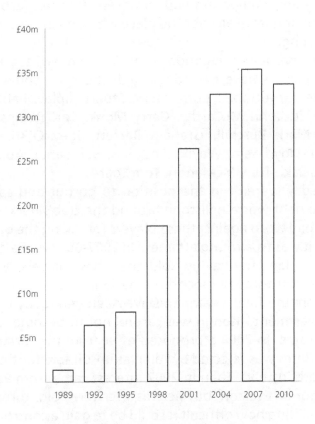

Sheffield Wednesday Debt: 1989-2010

Most of the money from these sales went towards servicing and reducing the deficit, with only a small amount freed up to make loan signings (which along with free transfers was about as much as the club could manage at the time). When used sparingly, the loan system had in recent years enhanced a settled Wednesday side. Kenwyne Jones' goals had proved invaluable in the promotion of 2004-05, while the goalkeeper Scott Carson helped massively in the return year. Yet at times of real trouble, temporary signings can have the reverse effect. As Bullen explains, 'In our promotion year the two or three loan signings we had made a massive difference. But when you start looking at five or six you lose that team bond. I'm not a major fan of the loan signing policy other than taking maybe one or two at a time. If you start going above that it can be detrimental, destabilising and hampering your progress. By then [around 2007] lads were coming from all over the place which meant the team spirit wasn't as strong.'

Since Wednesday's relegation from the Premier League in 2000, many loan players have passed through the club. Some a success, others quite forgettable. Con Blatsis. Stuart Ripley. Pablo Bonvin. Bojan Djordjic. John McCarthy. Garry Monk. Carl Robinson. Adam Chambers. Mark Burchill. Graham Barrett. Joey O'Brien. Gabriel Agbonlahor. Lloyd Sam. Wayne Andrews. Ben Sahar. Adam Bolder. Bartosz Slusarski. Tony McMahon. Tom Soares . . .

'Wednesday weren't in the position to go out and spend,' says Bullen. 'The debt was a millstone around the club's neck. You could never say a bad word against these players for taking the opportunity to play, but it was frustrating at times.' In 2007-08, a year after coming close to the play-offs, having sold their best players, Wednesday finished 16th, just three points off relegation.

Away from the field, chairman Dave Allen was ready to entertain offers of investment, though was careful not to become too excited when they came. In 2004 a proposed offer from the former Chelsea owner Ken Bates was rejected by Allen as unsuitable for the club – he went to Leeds instead. Then in 2007 interest came from Paul Gregg, an ex-director of Everton, but he was, we were told, turned off the club after realising how difficult it could be to gain a controlling stake. The Owls Trust supporters group (later renamed Wednesdayite) were, it was claimed, unlikely to give up their 10.07% shareholding, and

Gregg apparently believed their continuing influence might prevent him from running the club how he wished. The fact that 9.6% of that shareholding had been gifted to the group by Allen, Geoff Hulley and Keith Addy when they acquired Charterhouse's 37% stake in 2000 became the cause of contention between Allen and the group. In the Gregg case it appeared to have prevented a takeover and rescue of the club and Allen was notably aggrieved. First, because the Trust initially had appeared to have sided with Ken Bates. And second, for the Gregg complications. Allen was vocal in his disdain for the group whose influence had after all had in part been gifted by him.

The search for investment appeared unending. Allen's thrifty, and necessary, spend-what-you-earn policy was not popular with many, even though the alternative would have been to go further in to the red, and after gifting several million pounds to the club without much thanks, he left in November 2007. It was some while before a new chairman was found, through which time the club, directionless, flirted with yet another interested party, the 'businessman' Geoff Sheard.

It was regularly reported that Sheard had significant money to invest in the club. But none ever materialised. Later it emerged that a letter produced by him as proof the funds he potentially could bring had been produced by a convicted fraudster, and that the Dominican Republic bank from which it originated was non-operational. That he was even entertained by the club is astonishing.

Meanwhile, Bullen's time at the club had been winding down and he left in the summer of 2008. 'Brian [Laws] came to me in the January and said my contract wouldn't be renewed at the end of the season,' he says. 'That gave me six months to try and find another club. I'll always respect him for that. I could have left straight away, a couple of clubs wanted me on loan with a view to a permanent deal, but the club were struggling at the bottom of the league and I felt as club captain I still had a part to play, whether that was in the changing room or on the park.'

In early '09 the telecoms entrepreneur Lee Strafford became the club's next chairman. He arrived with grand claims of attracting investment and revolutionising the way the club was run, introducing a new ticketing price structure, inviting past players on to the pitch, and having a big flag made for the Kop – 'Forward Together' it read inspiringly. He also gave away shirt sponsorship to the city's Children's Hospital and between his arrival and departure increased the player wage bill by £2.6 million. The message from him was this: Wednesday, the caring club, is on the up. Who wouldn't want to invest?

As Allen had found before him, though, it wasn't so easy. Interest came from an Indian-American consortium and the Chicago-based Club 9 Sports, but each, for various reasons, came to nothing. Meanwhile, for a variety of reasons, Strafford's plans were not working out. Costs had risen significantly, the higher wages and £300,000 to change kit manufacturer, for example. But even though revenue was generally on the increase, it hadn't risen enough to offset the increased costs. Later, Strafford also claimed, legitimately it appears, that a £1.5 million gap in the budget was discovered, all but derailling his work. By May 2010 the debt still sat at over £30 million and, a few days after the club had been relegated to League One, following a 2-2 draw with Crystal Palace at Hillsborough, Strafford resigned.

His successor as chairman was Howard Wilkinson. More than two decades after leaving for Leeds in 1988, he had been brought on board by Strafford to help find a buyer for the Owls. When Strafford left, Wilkinson stepped in. 'I had no clue as to the impending predicament of the club,' Wilkinson remembers. After a further £3 million gap in the budget had emerged after relegation, after Wednesday had stopped paying their PAYE and VAT bills, Wilkinson worked against a backdrop of several HM Revenue and Customs winding up orders to find a buyer. Two notable contenders emerged. A Middle-Eastern/Scandinavian consortium fronted by Chris Turner and Milan Mandaric, the former owner of Leicester City and Portsmouth. The club's salvation would rest with the latter individual.

Having sold Leicester to a Taiwanese consortium in February for a reported £40 million, Mandaric was on the search for a new club. Importantly for Wednesday, where all others before him had promised but failed to deliver, he had the cash to make the deal happen. In late 2010 he took control, settling the £23 million of Co-op Bank loans for only £7 million, while agreeing to pay back an undisclosed fraction of the loans provided by the club's directors. Dave Allen waived the interest on his loans and received only a portion of what was owed to him (believed to be £750,000 plus another £750,000 should the club make it back to the Premier League). After so many years Wednesday's financial troubles were finally resolved. 'I know what this club can achieve,' stated Mandaric upon his arrival, 'and it is an honour to be given the chance to take one of the oldest names in the game and work to make it great again.'

After leaving Sheffield, Bullen had moved back north to Falkirk. He played on for two seasons before beginning a coaching career with the club. After being released in 2011 he returned to the city, becoming a partner in an estate agency. He also began helping out at the Wednesday academy. By now, thanks to the backing of Mandaric and the guidance of manager Gary Megson (and later, Dave Jones), Wednesday were rising, the dramatic promotion to the Championship in 2011-12 suggesting that their recent troubles were seemingly behind them. 'I'm enjoying it here now,' he says, 'learning the trade at a good club.'

20

Roland Nilsson

1989-1994
186 appearances

12 games into 1989-90 Wednesday sat bottom of the First Division, just two goals and a single victory having quelled much of the promise built by Ron Atkinson at the end of the previous season. As autumn turned to winter, three new signings galvanised the squad and gave hope of survival: John Sheridan, Phil King and a Swedish international and UEFA Cup winner, the 'immaculate' right-back Roland Nilsson.

Nilsson and the club quickly became friends as he consistently gave excellent performances through the late 1980s and early '90s. He was a superb defender able to calmly assess oncoming threats before gliding into the appropriate position before executing a perfectly- timed interception. He had the technique and assurance on the ball to match and could carry the ball out of defence, moving it along safely and accurately to a team mate. He was, along with Sheridan, the perfect representation of the Ron Atkinson-Wednesday style, grounded rather than lofted play. One of the finest sights ever in a Wednesday shirt, Nilsson, said one astute observer, was 'almost perfect'.

Atkinson had been looking for a new left-back. His search had taken him to Roger Nilsen and Stefan Schwarz, though in the end he bought Phil King from Swindon. A friend, though, had recommended to him another Swede, Roland Nilsson. After the departure of Mel Sterland to Glasgow Rangers in March '89, Atkinson still needed a new face at right-back as well. Several players had been tried there but no-one had fit. Alan Harper and Jon Newsome were not up to standard and it wasn't the natural position of Nigel Worthington or Nigel Pearson. Having seen Nilsson play twice for his country, and aware he could get him for a knockdown price, Atkinson then offered him a trial. He spent a week in Sheffield, impressing in two reserve games before he was offered a move. His club IFK Gothenburg, who received £375,000 in the deal, were among the best in Sweden, but the chance of games in the English First Division was too good to reject. 'Ron said to me, "We're missing a full-back at the moment,"' says Nilsson, 'and explained how he'd already tried a few others there but couldn't get it to work. He sold me the club and said if I came over we'd turn the league situation around. So I did. I spent a week there and that was it really.'

Manchester United were also interested. 'That's what I'd heard anyway,' he says. 'But when I asked the agent, United said they could only offer a few months contract. Wednesday offered me a proper one and at that stage if I was going to be moving over from Sweden I wanted to know it would be for a long period – not a short, wait and see period.' So he signed for the Owls.

As 1989-90 drew on, Wednesday, thanks in no small part to the contributions of Nilsson, Sheridan and King, recovered. A run of just two defeats in the 12 after Boxing Day took them out of the relegation places and up the table to 13th. It had taken a little time for the new man at right-back to adjust, but he eventually became accustomed to the quicker pace and greater physicality of the English game. 'It was a big step up,' he says. 'The tempo was high. I had 25 caps or so for Sweden before and had played against good players, but the speed in England was very different. Each game started straightaway with the high tempo and kept on until maybe the 75th or 80th minute. Only then did it start to die down a bit.

'The games were very competitive, lots of physical tackles and so on, but there was some good play, too. The players were good. You met strong sides every week and you had to perform. I had to get used to passing the ball quicker and doing the right things better. If you didn't work hard or weren't alert and focused on what you were doing you had no chance.'

Following that good mid-season run, relegation on the last day came as a massive surprise to the club. A five-game spell at the end, similar to the run at the beginning of the season where four were lost and only one was won, meant Wednesday dropped out of the division. While other results had gone against them on that final day, namely Luton's 3-2 win at Derby meaning that the Hatters stayed up, Atkinson's side should have been good enough to survive. 'When I came over we were at the bottom,' remembers Nilsson. 'We managed to win some games and get up over the relegation zone. With five games left we thought we had a very good chance of staying up. We played well in those games but couldn't score [just three goals, all of them from David Hirst]. That was frustrating. At the end we thought we'd made it but the results didn't go our way. That was very hard.'

The picture widely presented of the Wednesday players at that moment was a group that had the utmost devotion to the club's cause, all pledging to stay and help return them to the First Division. Yet Nilsson, along with Sheridan, had a clause in his contract which would have allowed him to leave. It was then only after assurances were made by the board that the squad would be kept intact that he and others pledged their immediate futures to the Owls. 'After a relegation you never know how it's going to be,' explains Nilsson, 'whether they will keep the players on or want to sell them. I spoke with Ron and said I wanted to know what was going to happen. He said he had spoken to the chairman and they were going to try and keep all the players and go for promotion. We knew we had a good side and had been a bit unlucky to be relegated, so once they had said that I was happy to stay. You could say there is an obligation for players to stay, but if the club says they need to start selling people; that they're not going to keep the players and have the best team, then it's a different story.'

In 1990-91, down in the Second Division, Wednesday were strong. They had a great defence, one of the best in the division, which thanks to Nilsson on the right and Phil King on the left was regularly able to support the midfield, joining in with the team's constant wave of attacks. Often these advances ended in a goal for the forward pairing of David Hirst and Paul Williams. In the games Nilsson played – sadly a cruciate injury picked up at Millwall reduced him to only 22 appearances – his role in both of these aspects, defence and attack, was notable.

Famously in the Wembley League Cup final against Manchester United, the Swede combined brilliantly with John Harkes, playing in front of him on the right of midfield, quelling the threat of United's exciting left-winger Lee Sharpe. Harkes and Nilsson had had a plan to contain one of the brightest prospects in English football at the time. 'I had played against Sharpe before,' recalls Nilsson, 'so I knew he'd be a handful. I spoke to John about what we could do to stop him having an influence, how he could help me and I could help him.' They had practised what to do in training, using squad player Steve McCall as a stand-in, rehearsing what side Sharpe should be shown and so on. 'And it worked.'

Their efforts paid off and were vital to Wednesday's success that day (in impairing Sharpe they thereby restricted the service to Mark Hughes up front). Nilsson and Harkes harassed Sharpe all game, their tackling, said the *Yorkshire Post*, proving 'too firm and quick' for the 'withered' teenager. Eventually Sharpe's colleagues all but gave up passing to him. After going 1-0 up in the first half thanks to John Sheridan's long strike, the Owls held on and won. 'A very good day,' says Nilsson.

But thanks to an injury it had been close whether Nilsson was even going to play at all that day, especially after Harkes and Viv Anderson each had so ably deputised earlier in the season. (Anderson, though, would have been cup-tied after already playing for Manchester United, the opponents that day, in the tournament.) Nilsson worked to at least get back and give himself a chance of playing. 'I knew it was going to take a long time to get back,' he said. 'But I trained as well as I could. Luckily for me I had good people around me and I could see that everything was working in the right way. I had no setbacks so when I started to train it was just a case of having no worries and being glad to be back training with the guys again. It went well and I got the chance to play in the final.'

In the league that year Nilsson's attacking performances were equally as adept as his defensive ones. Most often he looked for the grounded pass, in line with the style dictated by Ron Atkinson, giving the receiver greater chance of controlling the ball and making use of it. Nilsson had the technique to make the space for this, turning attackers by feigning one way to send his presser another, allowing him the time to see the pass and execute. With the ball he could move up the pitch effortlessly, into more dangerous areas from where he could deliver the crosses or cutting passes to the other forwards. In the games he did play during that promotion season he managed to get forward very regularly, galloping elegantly up the wing to have a hand in many of the 80 goals Wednesday scored that year. It helped them secure promotion from the Second Division from third place.

In 1991-92 Nilsson and Wednesday easily adjusted to life back in the First. The team continued to play the impressive style that had brought them promotion and Nilsson, once again, was delivering excellent performances from the back. After addressing the frailties shown against Aston Villa in the opening game of the season, where a 2-0 lead was turned in to a defeat, the defence did shore up, the Swede playing his part. As he had done previously, he continued to get involved with the forward play, too, feeding the midfield as carefully as he had done before. He even scored a goal – a rarity for him – against Norwich at Hillsborough, a superb long- range strike with the outside of his foot.

***

Today Nilsson is a successful manager. In 2011 he took over at regular Danish champions FC Copenhagen (unfortunately lasting only a few months, even though his team sat top of the league). Before then he was at Malmo FF, five miles away over the Øresund road and rail bridge that links Denmark and Sweden. In his third season in charge there he won the Allsvenskan, his team playing a cultured passing game in line with the spirit of their manager in his playing days.

As a manager he is his own man but acknowledges that the traits of those he has worked under have influenced his style. 'I am the person that I am,' he says. 'I don't change because I know Big Ron was like this, or that another manager was like that. That's how they are. But I will take the bits and pieces that I feel fit within my style of thinking and doing things. Some things you go, "yes I can take that in," other parts, "no that's not for me." For me, management is not all about having good players but making players gel together so they can do things together, better.

'That's something Ron brought to my way of thinking. He was the best man-manager I've seen. He could pick up the players. He'd say to John Sheridan, "today you have the key role, you will have a lot of the ball and you need to be on your toes". He would go through maybe two or three players like that and was hardly ever wrong. And because of that he made those players feel important and so that player would lift themselves a bit. The coach who took me to Gothenburg, Gunder Bengtsson, also showed me that you need to repeat things so that the players will gel together and know exactly what to do, knowing the effect they will have on each other.'

Before Malmo was GAIS, the Gothenburg based club at which he spent four years, winning a promotion to the Swedish top flight. GAIS had been the proper beginning to his managerial career, a modestly-sized club in his home country; a role that was a better fit than his first job, player-manager at Coventry City.

After leaving the Owls in 1994 Nilsson spent a few seasons back in Sweden before making a surprise return to England and Coventry (managed by Ron Atkinson). Atkinson, as he had been those years before at Wednesday, was once again in need of an able right-back and Nilsson, still in great physical condition, was an ideal choice. 'Ron phoned me offering me the move', he recalls. 'If it hadn't been for him I wouldn't have gone back to England. David Pleat had asked me earlier to come back to Sheffield, but he wasn't sure of my abilities. I thought at that stage if he didn't know what type of player I am then it may have been that I wouldn't have played in the first team. So I turned it down.'

When Atkinson was moved up to the position of Director of Football in late 1996 Nilsson, who by now was back in Sweden playing for Helsingborgs, came back to be assistant to Gordon Strachan. A good first step to a coaching career. 'I signed a three-year contract and thought that it would be great. Work with Gordon, develop and get the coaching courses.' When Strachan was sacked Coventry turned to Nilsson as his replacement. He made a good start, losing only once in his first 14 games in the First Division, but form fell away and before the season had ended he was released. A harsh introduction to the job, one which he acknowledges came too early for him. 'I was thrown into it and wasn't actually prepared,' he admits. 'I said I'd do the best that I can but at the same time I felt like that I needed more time to understand the coaching side. Going from a player to a coach or a manager is totally different. It helps being a former player, but there are some things you need before you can do a good job as a coach.' The experience left him low and it took him a while to regain much enthusiasm for the job. Though after returning to Sweden again to give a few more years playing time to the club GAIS, the wanting did return. Second time round, it brought better rewards.

***

By the time of the FA Cup Final replay against Arsenal at the end of 1992-93, their fourth visit to Wembley that season, Wednesday had already completed 64 fixtures. There was little left in the Owls' tank, or for that matter, Arsenal's. As the replay approached both sides prepared for one last, laboured push for success. For Nilsson the game would prove a particularly big test of endurance. Preceding his 45th game for Wednesday that season was Sweden's World Cup qualifier against Austria in Stockholm. He was required to help his country reach USA '94 and, determined to keep his place in Tommy Svensson's side, knew he must play.

(Nilsson is Sweden's third leading ever appearance-maker, 116 caps; two World Cups and one European Championship. A notable highlight was the 2-1 victory over England in Malmo in the 1992 Euros against a team containing the Wednesday players Chris Woods and Carlton Palmer. Another was World Cup 1994. A draw with Cameroon in Los Angeles, a win over Russia, then a draw with Brazil in Detroit had set-up Saudi Arabia in the second round. The Saudi's were overcome 3-1 meaning a meeting with Romania in the quarters. That finished 2-2 after normal time. In the shootout Dan Petrescu, soon to be an Owl, missed. Then Nilsson scored his. When Dumitrescu missed in sudden death, Sweden were through to the semis to again face Brazil. In Los Angeles the eventual tournament winners were too good for Nilsson and his team- mates, winning 1-0, but Sweden would go on to secure third place with a 4-0 victory over Stoichkov's Bulgaria. 'In '94 nobody said that we were going to come third,' says Nilsson, 'but we set the goal before and because of that and our work weren't surprised when we were there.')

Before flying to Stockholm for the Austria qualifier in '93, Nilsson said to *The Guardian* (in reference to the timing of the replay), 'It's the worse possible thing that could have happened'. 'I spoke to Svensson,' he remembers now, 'and he said if we do well you might not play the full 90 minutes. We'll just have to wait and see how the game goes . . .' Sweden won 1-0. 'I played 80 minutes.'

Drained, he then made his way back to England and on to Wembley. 'When we [Sweden] played the game my focus was on trying to win. Afterwards, as quickly as I could, I started to refocus on the replay. I began to take in the carbs, bananas and so on. I did everything I could to get the energy back in to my body. I had a private flight that took me back to London. I arrived back at the hotel, I think, at 12am, got a bit of sleep, got up, had some breakfast, then joined the rest of the team.'

Remarkably he had a good game – 'I felt OK, that I still had energy left' – and lasted until just before the end of extra time, 118 gruelling minutes. 'Then I could start to feel my legs going. I got cramp and could start to feel my body giving up. So I had to go off. At that moment I thought it was best to have a fresh player on the field who could do a better job than I could. I could have played on but might have made a mistake going full out in a run, a player could have got in and scored.' He wasn't on the pitch when Andy Linighan headed the winner to end Wednesday's season trophy-less.

Having played for his country, then, a day later, his club, Nilsson had shown enormous spirit – possibly lunacy – at Wembley. But that's the player he was. 'I was sick for a week after that, though,' he adds. 'My body was totally burnt out. I wouldn't recommend that anyone does that. But at that stage of the season I thought it was OK.'

In the winter of 1993 he asked to leave the club. His family wished to return home to Sweden, yet unsurprisingly, with time still left on his star right-back's contract, the manager Trevor Francis was reluctant to let him go. He wanted him at least to see through the rest of the 1993-94 campaign. A brief, potentially unpleasant tussle ensued – Nilsson indicating the West Ham game in December would be his last for the club – before an agreement was eventually reached. He would, it was decided, stay in Sheffield and finish the season then join Helsingborgs, his hometown club where his career had begun, on a free transfer (even though he was rated at around £2 million at the time). Seemingly Francis had warmed from his earlier days in management where once, when in charge of Queens Park Rangers, he fined Martin Allen for attending the birth of his child instead of making himself available for a game. No such penalty for Nilsson.

He played almost every game that last season, as consistent and dedicated as his first game in late 1989. If Nilsson's mind was back in Sweden, his performances never showed it and he was given a happy send-off by the crowd after his last game against Manchester City at Hillsborough. The Wednesday fans have strong, fond memories of him and, looking back, he of them, too. 'I had a fantastic four years there,' he says. 'The fans were absolutely marvellous. Sometimes when we had played a lot of games you felt you had no energy. Before the game you thought it was going to be a tough day. But then you came out in the warm-up and the crowd started to cheer. Suddenly you didn't feel that bad. Many times, especially at Hillsborough, you lifted yourself because of that support.'

Since his time no such perfection has been seen on the Hillsborough pitch, at least not in a Wednesday strip.

***

Through its long past a great number of players have passed through the books of Sheffield Wednesday Football Club. Each has helped provide many memorable seasons, matches and moments (and some less so). Some of these players made a more lasting impression than others. David Hirst and Derek Dooley – will Wednesday find another striker as potent as those two? Dedicated club men like Kevin Pressman and Redfern Froggatt. Hardworking and earnest professionals like Jimmy Mullen and Lee Bullen. The leaping Ron Springett. John Sheridan – midfield excellence. And the masterful Albert Quixall and Chris Waddle. Not to forget the managers, Howard Wilkinson, Harry Catterick, Jack Charlton.

But it is Roland Nilsson, who throughout his career was called 'Legend' by his team mates, who most distinctly endures, giving always as he did an immaculacy of performance that the Wednesday support deserves. Right-back is among the least glamorous of positions, but for four-and-a-half years in Sheffield he shone so brightly from there. 'Well,' he says, 'I always tried to do my best . . .'

Bibliography

Books

Anderson, Viv, *First Among Unequals: The Autobiography* (Fullback Media, 2010)

Arlott, John, *Concerning Soccer* (Longmans, Green and Co, 1952)

Arlott, John (ed.), *Soccer: The Great Ones* (Penham Books, 1968)

Armitage, Simon, *Dead Sea Poems* (Faber & Faber, 2001)

Ashurst, Len, *Left Back in Time: The Autobiography* (Know the Score Books, 2009)

Atkinson, Ron, *Big Ron: A Different Ball Game* (Andre Deutsch, 1998)

Auclair, Philippe, *Cantona: The Rebel Who Would be King* (Macmillan, 2009)

Ball, Alan with Mossop, James, *Playing Extra Time* (Sidgwick and Johnson, 2004)

Banks, Gordon, *Banksy: My Autobiography* (Michael Joseph, 2002)

Bar-On, Tamir, *Where Have All the Fascists Gone?* (Ashgate Publishing, 2007)

The Big Book of Football Champions (L.T.A. Robinson, 1955)

Burns, Jimmy, *Barca: A People's Passion* (Bloomsbury, 1999)

Carter, Neil, *The Football Manager: A History* (Routledge, 2006)

Cascarino, Tony with Kimmage, Paul, *Full Time: The Secret Life of Tony Cascarino* (Simon & Schuster, 2000)

Chapman, Lee, *More Than a Match: A Player's Story* (Stanley Paul, 1992)

Chapman, Peter, *The Goalkeeper's History of Britain* (Fourth Estate, 1999)

Charlton, Bobby, *The Autobiography: My Manchester United Years* (Headline, 2007)

Charlton, Jack, *Jack Charlton: The Autobiography* (Partridge Press, 1996)

Conn, David, *The Beautiful Game? Searching for the Soul of Football* (Yellow Jersey Press, 2005)

Conn, David, *The Football Business: Fair Game in the '90s?* (Mainstream, 1997)

Cooper, Andrew, *Eric Taylor: A Biography* (A. Cooper Publications, 2011)

Corbett, James, *Everton: The School of Science* (Macmillan, 2003)

Coupland, Douglas, *Generation X* (Abacus, 1992)

Davies, Pete, *All Played Out: The Full Story of Italia '90* (William Heinemann, 1990)

De Bilde, Gilles and Raes, Frank, *Gilles: Mijn Verhall* [*My Story*] (Van Halewyck, 2004)

Delaney, Miguel, *Stuttgart to Saipan: The Player's Stories* (Mentor Books, 2010)

Dewhurst, Keith, *When You Put on a Red Shirt: The Dreamers and their Dreams* (Yellow Jersey, 2009)

Di Canio, Paolo with Marcotti, Gabriele, *Paolo Di Canio: The Autobiography* (Collins Willow, 2000)

Dickinson, Jason, *One Hundred Years at Hillsborough: 1899-1999* (Hallamshire Press, 1999)

Dickinson, Jason and Brodie, John, *The Wednesday Boys: A Definitive Who's Who of Sheffield Wednesday Football Club, 1800-2005* (Pickard Communications, 2005)

Dickinson, Jason and Brodie, John, *Sheffield Wednesday: The Complete Record* (Derby Books, 2011)

Dixon, Keith, *Jackie Sewell* (The Derby Books Publishing Company, 2010)

Doherty, John, *The Insider's Guide to Manchester United: Candid Profiles of Every Red Devil Since 1945* (Empire Publications, 2005)

Dooley, Derek and Farnsworth, Keith, *Dooley* (Hallamshire Press, 2000)

Doyle, Roddy, *The Van* (Martin Secker & Warburg, 1991)

Dunphy, Eamon, *A Strange Kind of Glory: Sir Matt Busby & Manchester United* (William Heinemann, 1991)

Ellis, Arthur, *Refereeing Round the World* (The Sportsmans Book Club, 1956)

The FA Book for Boys: Number 13 (William Heinemann, 1960)

The FA Book for Boys: Number 15 (William Heinemann, 1962)

Fagan, Andrew and Platt, Mark, *Joe Fagan: Reluctant Champion: The Authorised Biography* (Aurum Press, 2011)

Farnsworth, Keith, *Sheffield Football: A History, Volume I, 1857-1961* (Hallamshire Press, 1995)

Farnsworth, Keith, *Sheffield Football: A History, Volume II, 1961-1995* (Hallamshire Press, 1995)

Farnsworth, Keith, *Wednesday Every Day of the Week* (Breedon Books Publishing, 1998)

Farnsworth, Keith, *Wednesday!: The History of Sheffield's Oldest Professional Football Club* (Sheffield City Library, 1982)

Ferguson, Alex, *Managing My Life: The Autobiography* (Coronet, 2000)

Ferris, Ken, *The Double: The Inside Story of Spur's Triumphant 1960-61 Season* (Mainstream, 1999)

Finn, Ralph, *Champions Again: Manchester United 1957 and 1965* (Robert Hale, 1965)

Firth, John, *I Hate Football: A Fan's Memoir* (Peak Publish, 2009)

Foot, John, *Calcio: A History of Italian Football* (Fourth Estate, 2006)

Foulkes, Bill, *Bill Foulkes: United in Triumph and Tragedy* (Know the Score Books, 2008)

Giles, Edward, *Billy Walker: Once, Twice, Three Times a Winner* (Desert Island Books, 2008)

Giller, Norman, *The Footballing Fifties* (JR Books, 2007)

Gladwell, Malcolm, *The Tipping Point: How Little Things Can Make a Big Difference* (Little, Brown and Company, 2000)

Glanville Brian, *The Story of the World Cup* (Faber and Faber, 2010)

Gordon, Daniel, *A Quarter of Wednesday: A New History of Sheffield Wednesday, 1970-1995* (Wednesday Publishing, 1995)

Gordon, Daniel, *Blue and White Wizards: The Sheffield Wednesday Dream Team* (Mainstream, 2002)

Graham, George and Giller, Norman, *George Graham: The Glory and the Grief* (Andre Deutsch, 1995)

Haddrell, Ian and Michael Jay, *A Season to Remember: Bristol Rovers' Promotion Season 1973-74* (The History Press Ltd, 2010)

Hall, David, *Manchester's Finest: How the Munich Air Disaster Broke the Heart of a Great City* (Bantam, 1997)

Hare, Geoff, *Football in France: A Cultural History* (Berg, 2003)

Harkes, John, *Captain for Life: And Other Temporary Assignments* (Gale Cengage, 1999)

Hattersley, Roy, *A Yorkshire Boyhood* (Chatto & Windus, 1983)

Hattersley, Roy, *Goodbye to Yorkshire* (Littlehampton Books Services, 1976)

Harman, Ruth and Minnis, John, *Pevsner Architectural Guides: Sheffield* (Yale University Press, 2004)

Harvey, Colin, *Colin Harvey's Everton Secrets* (Trinity Mirror Sport Media, 2005)

Hayes, Dean, *The Hillsborough Encyclopedia: The A-Z of Sheffield Wednesday FC* (Mainstream, 1997)

Hodge, Steve, *The Man with Maradona's Shirt* (Orion, 2010)

Hopcraft, Arthur, *The Football Man* (Collins, 1968)

Hornby, Nick (ed.), *My Favourite Year: A Collection of Football Writing* (H.F. & G. Witherly, 1993)

Hughes, Charles, *The Winning Formula* (Collins, 1990)

Imlach, Gary, *My Father and Other Working-Class Heroes* (Yellow Jersey Press, 2005)

Inglis, Simon, *Engineering Archie: Archibald Leitch: Football Ground Designer* (English Heritage, 2005)

Inglis, Simon, *Football Grounds of Britain, Third Edition* (Collins Willow, 1996)

Inglis, Simon, *Soccer in the Dock: A History of British Football Scandals, 1900 to 1965* (Willow, 1985)

Keane, Roy with Dunphy, Eamon, *Keane: The Autobiography* (Michael Joseph, 2002)

Kendall, Ray, *An Away Game Every Week: Memories of Bristol Rovers* (Breedon Books Publishing, 2001)

Kuper, Simon, *The Football Men: Up Close with the Giants of the Modern Game* (Simon & Schuster, 2011)

Kuper, Simon and Szymanski, Stefan, *Why England Lose: And other Curious Football Phenomenon Explained* (Harper Collins, 2009)

Lansdown, Harry and Spillius, Alex (eds.), *Saturday's Boys: The Football Experience* (Willow Books, 1990)

Liversidge, Michael and Mackender, Gary, *Sheffield Wednesday: Illustrating the Greats* (Pickard Communication, 2005)

Luscombe, William (ed.), *The Park Drive Book of Football 1968-69* (Pelham Books, 1969)

The Park Drive Book of Football 1969-70 (Pelham Books Ltd., 1970)

Mallalieu, JPW, *Sporting Days* (Phoenix Sports Books, 1955)

Marwood, Brian with Woolnough, Brian, *The Life of Brian: The Brian Marwood Story* (Mainstream, 1990)

McArdle, David, *Football, Society and the Law* (Routledge-Cavendish, 2000)

McGuiness, Wilf with Ponting, Ivan, *Manchester United: Man and Babe* (Know the Score Books, 2008)

McIntosh Ian, *Football Fables: True Stories of Triumph and Despair from Footballs Mavericks* (A&C Black, 2008)

McKinstry, Leo, *Jack and Bobby* (Collins Willow, 2002)

McKinstry, Leo, *Sir Alf: A Major Reappraisal of the Life and Times of England's Greatest Football Manager* (HarperSport, 2006)

Meek, David, *Manchester United 100 Greatest Players* (Manchester United Books, 2004)

Nicholson, Bill, *Glory Glory: My Life with Spurs* (McMillan, 1984)

Okwonga, Musa, *Will You Manage: The Necessary Skills to be a Great Gaffer* (Serpents Tail, 2010)

Papin, Jean-Pierre, *Franc Jeu [Fair Play]* (Éditions Ramsay, 1998)

Phillips, Steven, *Rochdale AFC, The Official History 1907-2001* (Yore Publications, 2001)

Phillips, Steven, *The Survivors: The Story Of Rochdale Association Football Club* (Sport and Leisure Press, 1990)

Robinson, Peter, Cheeseman, Doug, Pearson, Harry and Cornwall, Philip, *1966 Uncovered: The Unseen Story of the World Cup in England* (Mitchell Beazley, 2006)

Ruhn, Christov (ed.), *Le Foot: The Legends of French Football,* (Abacus, 2000)

Scovell, Brian, *Bill Nicholson: Football's Perfectionist* (John Blake Publishing, 2010)

Seed, Jimmy, *The Jimmy Seed Story* (The Sportsmans Book Club, 1958)

Shankly, Bill, *Shankly* (Arthur Baker, 1976)

Sillitoe, Alan, *Saturday Night and Sunday Morning* (W.H. Allen & Co., 1958)

Somerton, Gerry, *The Definitive Rotherham United* (Pendragon Books, 2003)

Sparling, Richard A., *The Romance of the Wednesday: 1867-1926* (Desert Island Books, 1997)

Stein, Mel, *Chris Waddle: The Authorised Biography* (Simon and Schuster, 1997)

Sterland, Mel with Johnson, Nick, *Boozing, Betting & Brawling: The Autobiography of Mel Sterland* (Green Umbrella, 2008)

Swan, Peter with Johnson, Nick, *Setting the Record Straight* (Tempus Publishing, 2006)

Szymanski, Stefan, *Football Economics and Policy: 1* (Pelgrave Macmillan, 2010)

Tallentire, Becky, *Talking Blue* (Breedon Books, 2000)

Tallentire, Becky, *Still Talking Blue* (Mainstream, 2002)

Taylor, Daniel, *Deep into the Forest* (The Parrs Wood Press, 2005)

Taylor, Graham with Shaw, Dennis, *When England Called* (Pipkin Press, 1991)

Tomkins, Paul, Riley, Graeme and Fulcher, Gary, *Pay As You Play: The True Price of Success in the Premier League Era* (GPRF Publishing, 2010)

Troilett, Alan and Brodie, Eric, *The Jackie Robinson Story* (Pickard Communications, 2004)

Walker, Billy, *Soccer in the Blood* (The Soccer Book Club, 1960)

Ward, Andrew and Williams, John, *Football Nation: Sixty Years of the Beautiful Game* (Bloomsbury, 2009)

Warman, C. R., *Sheffield: Emerging City* (The City Engineer and Surveyor and Town Planning Officer, Sheffield, 1969)

Watson, Don, *Dancing in the Streets: Tales from World Cup City* (Victor Gollancz, 1994)

Wheeler, Kenneth (ed.), *Soccer: The British Way* (Nicholas Kaye, 1963)

Wilkinson, Howard with Walker, David, *Managing to Succeed: My Life in Football Management* (Mainstream, 1992)

Wilson, Jonathan, *Brian Clough: Nobody Ever Says Thank You* (Orion, 2011)

Wilson, Jonathan, *Inverting the Pyramid: The History of Football Tactics* (Orion, 2008)

Wilson, Jonathan, *The Anatomy of England: A History in Ten Matches* (Orion, 2010)

Winner, David, *Brilliant Orange: The Neurotic Genius of Dutch Football* (Bloomsbury, 2000)

Winner, David, *Those Feet: An Intimate History of English Football* (Bloomsbury, 2005)

Wolstenholme, Kenneth, *Kenneth Wolstenholme's Book of World Soccer* (World Distributors, 1967)

Yorath, Terry, *Hard Man, Hard Knocks* (Celluloid, 2004)

Young, Percy M., *Football in Sheffield* (Stanley Paul, 1962)

Journals and Reports

The Hillsborough Stadium Disaster: Inquiry by Lord Justice Taylor: Interim Report (HMSO, 1989)

Husband, H. C., Holmshaw, T. and English, H. C, 'A Cantilever Stand for The Sheffield Wednesday Football Club Ltd.', *The Structural Engineer*, 40 (11), 351-359, 1962

Husband, H. C., Holmshaw, T. and English, H. C, 'Discussion Paper', 41 (8), 258-260, 1963

Reep, Charles and Bernard, Benjamin, 'Skill and Chance in Association Football', *Journal of the Royal Statistical Society*, Series A, 131 (4), 581-585, 1968

Newspapers and Magazines

90 Minutes

Charles Buchan's Football Monthly

The Daily Mirror

Financial Times

FourFourTwo

Goal

Green 'Un

The Guardian

The Independent

L'Equipe (France)

The New York Times

The Observer

The Scotsman

Sheffield Morning Telegraph

Sheffield Star

Sheffield Telegraph

Sunday People

The Sunday Times

The Times

When Saturday Comes

Yorkshire Post

Websites

adrianbullock.com (The Sheffield Wednesday Archive)

englandstats.com

rsssf.com (The Rec.Sport.Soccer Statistics Foundation)

soccerbase.com

statto.com

swfc.co.uk

tonykempster.co.uk (Results and league tables)

Other

Various club programmes, publications and company accounts